THE UNLEASHED SCANDAL

The End of Control in the Digital Age

BERNHARD POERKSEN
AND HANNE DETEL

Translated by
Alison Rosemary Koeck and Wolfram Karl Koeck

imprint-academic.com

Copyright © Bernhard Poerksen and Hanne Detel, 2014

The moral rights of the author have been asserted.
No part of this publication may be reproduced in any form
without permission, except for the quotation of brief passages
in criticism and discussion.

Published in the UK by
Imprint Academic, PO Box 200, Exeter EX5 5YX, UK

Distributed in the USA by
Ingram Book Company,
One Ingram Blvd., La Vergne, TN 37086, USA

The German original was first published under the title *Der entfesselte Skandal. Das Ende der Kontrolle im digitalen Zeitalter*, Herbert von Halem Verlag, Köln, 2012.

English translation by
Alison Rosemary Koeck and Wolfram Karl Koeck.
The translation of this work was funded by Geisteswissenschaften International — Translation Funding for Humanities and Social Sciences from Germany, a joint initiative of the Fritz Thyssen Foundation, the German Federal Foreign Office, the collecting society VG Wort and the Börsenverein des Deutschen Buchhandels (German Publishers & Booksellers Association).

Cover illustration: Claudia Ott/ Grafischer Entwurf, Düsseldorf.

ISBN 9781845407193

A CIP catalogue record for this book is available from the
British Library and US Library of Congress

Contents

I. The Unleashed Scandal: An Introduction ... 1

II. The New Disclosers & the Old Media ... 32
    1. Matt Drudge & the experiment with the truth ... 33
    2. Jessica Cutler & the illusion of intimacy ... 47
    3. *WikiLeaks* & the uncontrollability of the data ... 59
    4. Karl-Theodor zu Guttenberg & the power of a swarm ... 82

III. The New Victims & the Power of the Public ... 99
    1. The hounding of Gao Qianhui & the emergence of a cybermob ... 101
    2. The fate of the student Wang Qianyuan & the clash of cultures ... 109
    3. The humiliated husband & the divorce battle of Trishia Walsh-Smith ... 119
    4. The pillory website for Amir & the joys of defamation ... 128

IV. The New Technologies & the Opportunities of Ruthless Documentation ... 137
    1. The photographs of Abu Ghraib & modern eyewitness testimony ... 139
    2. The camera phone film from Hong Kong & the mobile phone as an all-purpose weapon ... 161
    3. The calamitous e-mail & the easiness of misfortune ... 175
    4. The tell-tale SMS & the economy of morality ... 180
    5. The embarrassing *Twitter* message & the nature of sexuality ... 189
    6. The social media campaign of Greenpeace & the vulnerability of power ... 198

V. The End of Control in the Digital Age: A Programmatic Résumé ... 210

Index ... 223

I
The Unleashed Scandal: An Introduction

The omnipresence of media

It is a moment of innocence and play. The story unfolds in Corfu in front of a restaurant and a holiday centre. Three boys tear across the road together with a small Greek stray dog. Two of the boys know each other from Berlin. They have come with their mothers. The youngest boy is from another city, he is seven years old. He is with his parents. The boys have all just met. One of the boys—twelve years of age—has a mobile phone. This will remain unknown until later in the evening. The three boys and the dog eventually disappear between the houses. "Really nice and funny somehow" the two new boys were, the youngest boy will tell his parents later that evening. They shot a little film—of him and the dog and their games. The dog had jumped up on him, had clasped his leg with his front paws and had rubbed itself against him repeatedly. Then he wanted to know what "shagging" meant. For they had used this very title for the film: "Dog shags boy." What did it all mean? And when leaving one of the boys had called to him that he would publish it all on the Internet. Would it function as simply as all that and what did it mean?

This is a good question but difficult to answer. What would have happened if the boy had not said anything and the video of the two chance acquaintances had indeed landed on the World Wide Web? Perhaps nothing at all. Which is, by the way, most likely. The clip might simply have been swallowed up like millions of snippets of reality before and after on all the different platforms and would simply have faded away. But possibly not.

And in the extreme case the seven-year-old, like many before him, might have achieved *Net-fame against his will*.[1] Gary Brolsma celebrated such a success in 2004 with a 97-second clip, which he had created just for fun and for the entertainment of his friends. In it he grimaces and gesticulates to the sounds of a Romanian pop song and sings: "Miya-hee, miya-hoo, miya-ho, miya-haha." Today everyone in the world knows him as the *Numa Numa-Guy* who is trying hard to cash in on his accidentally gained celebrity status. By November 2006, his video, according to the estimate of the British marketing firm *The Viral Factory*, had been accessed 700 million times.

The pudgy Canadian boy who acquired dubious fame as *Star Wars Kid* deserves to be mentioned here, too. In November 2002 he shot a short video, in which he imitated the swinging of the lightsabers in *Star Wars* with a golf ball retriever — again one of those absent-minded moments in a clumsy, inept game, which haunts him to the present day. He had accidentally left the video at his school where it was discovered by four of his classmates. In 2003, they began to distribute the clip through file sharing networks on the Internet thus making him into a first-rate Internet celebrity. Around one thousand million requests of the many video-versions circulating on the Net have allegedly been registered — with disastrous consequences for the ad-hoc imitator and his desire for privacy. He had to leave his school because he could no longer bear the constant teasing, was given private tuition, underwent psychiatric treatment, and finally, with the help of his parents, started legal proceedings against the pupils who had kick-started everything and had thus subjected him to such excessive attention. There was always someone who shouted "Star Wars Kid, Star Wars Kid". "It was simply unbearable, totally", he explains in an interview, still

---

[1] On the following case histories see: Lischka, Konrad (2007) Verglühte Netzsternchen [Burnt-out Net starlets]. In: *Spiegel Online*, 24 July 2007, www.spiegel.de/netzwelt/web/0,1518,496118,00.html (Retrieved 24 September 2013).

overcome with consternation. Even today only a few mouse clicks are needed to stumble on the diverse videos, hundreds of articles, and a *Wikipedia* entry on this hard-hit youngster.

In contrast, Matt Harding, the dancing globetrotter with his feel-good videos, met with a happier fate. He quit his job as a designer of computer games one day and went on a tour of the world. Somebody somewhere must have given him the idea to dance in front of the various sights and in the most unlikely situations (in the corridors of a Russian train, on the peak of Kilimanjaro, on a road in India) — filming everything at the same time. The resulting film that was just meant to entertain his friends and relatives, his collage of clips showing him at diverse places on earth, have by now become a sort of livelihood for him and turned his funky chicken dance for a world audience into a sort of business. Today Harding travels the world, sponsored by a bubble gum firm, supported by his girlfriend, and performs his own strange, funny, and somehow even touching dances, encouraging others to join in. He gives numerous interviews, appears at the conferences of the Bohemian digital community, has published a book in 2009 with the title *Where the Hell is Matt? Dancing badly around the world* — and quite obviously enjoys the good sides of a weird and completely unplanned kind of celebrity. Everything started with the publication of his video on his website and the adding of a link by a distant acquaintance of his and a few bloggers. Matt Harding: "Much to my surprise, they loved it. The bad dancing seemed to disarm the most jaded of viewers and the stream of far-off locales stirred in them a sense of possibility. The overriding sentiment from the forum of commenters was a sudden desire to stop letting life pass them by. People were actually inspired."[2]

Considering these cases, and taking into account the strange and scarcely estimable butterfly effects governing the attention economy of the Internet, the question arises what the con-

---

[2] Harding, Matt (2009) *Where the Hell is Matt? Dancing badly around the world*, New York: Skyhorse Publishing, p. 30.

sequences might have been for the seven-year-old boy whom his friends on Corfu instigated to play with the dog in front of their mobile phone's camera. The answer can only be: there is no way of knowing. The omnipresence of digital media has created a kind of media ubiquity that nobody can escape, a novel kind of universe of visibility in which individuals are losing control of their self-constructs and their public images. *Big Brother*, the television show, has thus become the guiding metaphor of the media culture of our age — an expression of the fact that everybody may be observed everywhere and at all times and that it has become practically impossible to disappear from the monitors under the given medial conditions. The modern self is squatting in a container everywhere, as it were, and permanently exposed to the watchful eyes of other people. "Nobody can be sure nowadays not to be seen", Markus Brauck, Isabell Hülsen, and Martin U. Müller describe the state of mind of this *container-self*. "They may be observed drunk at the *Oktoberfest* and snapped by a camera phone, caught picking their noses on an underground train by bloggers, or run into the lenses of professional reality-TV: sheer presence has become the universal standard."[3]

Once again: there is no telling. But a drooling and context-blind Net community might very well have scandalised the behaviour of the boy on Corfu and an amused mob would have become flustered by his apparently shameless playing with a humping dog: "Just look how this stupid little creature is carrying on!" And this moment of innocence and playfulness could have developed into a new type of scandal. *For the simple reason that anyone can become the target of undesired, potentially worldwide attention — quite independently of their social status.*[4] The unleashed scandal is no longer governed by relevance and hierarchies or

---

[3] Brauck, Markus/Isabell Hülsen/Martin U. Müller (2010) Das Container-Ich [The container-self]. In: *Der Spiegel*, 04 January 2010, no. 1, p. 65.
[4] See also: Bergmann, Jens/Bernhard Poerksen (eds.) (2009) *Skandal! Die Macht öffentlicher Empörung* [*Scandal! The power of public outrage*], Cologne: Herbert von Halem Verlag, p. 15.

exclusively by the wrongdoings of elites and groups of power; it has to do with the alleged or assumed norm violations of everyone. These self-fabricated curiosities and norm violations may be spectacularly unimportant and may appear to possess public significance only in the eyes of the Net voyeurs. The directly involved participants may have been totally unaware of these antics. They actually mask the actual norm violation, i.e. the unauthorised publication — with no reference to its history and development, without any context enabling the recipient audiences proper assessment, and without any attempt at a proper placement of events in appropriate contextual frameworks.

The dilemma of presentation

It is one of those days of normal university business. A student on a bachelor course appears in order to discuss final arrangements for a course presentation on the topic of "privacy in the digital age". The student seems to have prepared his subject matter well, has independently researched a case history, and has already submitted a PowerPoint presentation. The initial impression is a fairly good one. Opening the presentation, however, arouses irritation in an academic context. The reason is the very first image: a photograph of Uta Friesing, a girl whose identity the student has tried to protect rather clumsily by covering her eyes with a black bar.[5] "Car bonnet Uta" is the title chosen by the student for his presentation. The actual presentation makes clear that the student has fallen prey to the fascination of his case story: his handling of the story is an exemplary illustration of the destruction of the very privacy that he was originally expected to analyse. The student lacks the distance required for an analysis of his topic — an instructive result with regard to the subject matter of the present book — i.e. he lacks the right *mixture of proximity and distance* for proper analysis. Uta Friesing, he reports, attended an all-you-can-drink party on

---

[5] All names have of course been changed.

New Year's Eve, 31 December 2005, somewhere in the south of Germany, where she met the 19-year-old Jens Altmann. The case history that the student wanted to present in the consultation meeting and later in the seminar consisted basically in four images, i.e. these four images made up the bulk of his presentation. In the first image one can recognise, at considerable distance, a girl engaging in sexual intercourse with a boy on a car bonnet, the boy's trousers down to his knees. The following mobile phone pictures zoom closer and show details. The student's documentation of the case makes clear that the photographs of this drunken night of love soon afterwards circulate at the youngsters' school and in their town because they have been relayed to other mobile phones immediately and sent via e-mail the following day. Then they are spotted on the Net. Jens Altmann gets hold of them and boasts about them at his sports club among his sports comrades and among his other friends. Word goes round in the small town that he is proud of his "conquest"—and that he is delighted with the precise documentation of his performance and potency. Uta Friesing, however, is berated as a "floozy" and a "slut". As soon as she realises that she is the cause of the general suggestive whispering and laughing at school and is shown the images of the anonymous lay paparazzo, she escapes to what she expects to be the protective enclosure of her family home—and has herself signed off sick. However, the mobile phone images finally reach the girl's father and also the university student introduced earlier who has been hunting for a form of direct empirical research. And in the course of this process the nickname is created, which will from now on remain in circulation without having been invented by the student himself: "car bonnet Uta."

These events—despite their irrelevance and their lack of any disruptive social power—pinpoint something typical of the unleashed scandal: the *loss of informational security and confidence* on the part of an individual who is turned into a powerless object by nightmarish coincidences. It is difficult and sometimes impossible to know exactly what people know about a person and how they have acquired that knowledge, what digital trails and traces they are pursuing, what photographs they have found by pure accident—and what they intend to do with them, to whom they will pass them on, how they will change and scatter them. In the extreme case, the most intimate pictures of individuals may become public—without the victim's slightest awareness of such things happening behind their backs and without any possibility of influencing the currently circulating public image.[6] The lawyer Daniel J. Solove has formulated this problem of context-free information and scandalisation most precisely in his brilliant book *The Future of Reputation*: "But now someone reading an online report about some faraway stranger rarely knows the whole story—the reader has only fragments of information, and when little is invested in a personal relationship, even information that is incomplete and of dubious veracity might be enough to precipitate ridicule, shunning, and reproach."[7] And by the way: the pre-history of the seminar presentation that did not take place after all or, to put it differently, that was stopped in good time, demonstrates an analytical dilemma, which must worry all those who are occupied with factual or alleged scandals—and this is why the presentation in question can claim a sort of secondary interest despite the irrelevance of its content. *The analysis of an alleged norm violation inevitably reproduces this norm violation; it furthermore creates the danger of repeating the abuse if only under the cloak of information, enlightenment, and analysis.*

Variants of voyeurism

There are evidently two basic variants of voyeurism. The first form of voyeurism is naked; it seems to lack foundation, appears without accompanying justification, and is therefore honest in an obscure way. In this case, people with no feelings

---

[6] Spärck Jones, Karen (2003) Privacy: What's different now? In: *Interdisciplinary Science Reviews*, vol. 28, pp. 287–292.

[7] Solove, Daniel J. (2007) *The Future of Reputation: Gossip, rumor, and privacy on the Internet*, New Haven/London: Yale University Press, p. 37.

of shame enjoy observing the successes or misfortunes of other people, their fates and tragedies. Pornography of this kind is in no need of any additional elements. The second form of voyeurism could be called a sort of *voyeurism of the second order*. Here pornography is shown with something akin to critical-reflective subtitles, when for instance supplying strange, bizarre, and repulsive acts under the auspices of an interest in enlightenment. In this way, its spectators are positively conditioned for its relaxed reception and enjoyment without remorse or twinges of conscience. The allegation of voyeurism is inherent to this manner of presentation and thus seems neutralised by the overall conception of the project and its context (an academic presentation, a book about Internet scandals and the loss of reputation in the digital age, etc.). The distinction between different variants of voyeurism signals a challenge in its own right. Dealing with an unleashed scandal, a scandal that may hit each and every one of us, is a constant balancing act between proximity and distance, between enlightenment and voyeurism, between analysis and gossip. How can the story of the then 15-year-old participant of a New Year's Eve party be dealt with without damaging her further while generating still more obviously undesired publicity by incorporating her case as an example in the literature of media studies? How does one report the case of the German holidaymaker in Brazil who is clandestinely filmed in a brothel and then in desperation tries to stop the epidemic spreading of the Net video on numerous sex sites with the aid of a professional Internet service provider? Is such a case admissible at all? How can one tell the story of the producer of pop songs and television programmes, who becomes a victim of stalking because one hate-driven person defames him with all the available means and all the refined cleverness of *negative campaigning*? How can one proceed if the topic of analysis and criticism deals with the *cult of irrelevance,* which is dependent on a form of dense description together with a considerable number of potentially quite explosive case histories so that the content—declared irrelevant—is unavoidably presented and thus spread again?

In view of this presentation dilemma, there is certainly one *pragmatic* and quite practical answer: some of the case histories in this book were consistently anonymised (names, place names, dates were changed) in order to make targeted research at least more difficult. Other stories were simply left out because their presentation appeared to be too risky for the persons concerned. Still other cases were reported because their essential elements and basic structures have already become known or because they are directed against powerful and famous people or consist in the legitimate scandalisation of reprehensible behaviour. There is, however, a *general* response to the temptation of a voyeurism of the higher order. It simply requires the clear and open presentation of the dilemma of this kind of research and analysis from the very outset, the readiness to admit the possibility of failure, the exhortation of the readers not to detach the stories from their delineated contexts and, finally, a thorough check of whether the authors have properly adhered to the standards they have formulated for themselves. Is it possible to write about the unleashed scandal in a manner that does not succumb to the now ever-present inclination towards scandalisation?

Features of the typical scandal

Scandals are everywhere as can easily be shown.[8] And it has become tremendously simple to feel indignation—even without the informational thunderstorms of the ubiquitous digital media. It is enough to pick up a newspaper, at best the papers with big block capital headlines. It is enough to switch on the evening newscasts, preferably of the commercial stations. It is enough to connect oneself in some way or other with the excitation machines of the modern media society. And there it is,

---

[8] The following draws on previous publications by Bernhard Poerksen. See: Poerksen, Bernhard (2010) Skandal! [Scandal!]. In: *Chrismon.de*, 28 May 2010, http://chrismon.evangelisch.de/artikel/2010/bernhard-poerksen-skandal-4318 (Retrieved 24 September 2013).

irrepressible, meddlesome, and noisy: the scandal. It gnaws at us if only briefly; it demands sacrifices that we quickly forget; it forces us to do public penance, which we enjoy. The scandal is omnipresent — and it has become a sort of *medium of media*: a pattern for the organisation of knowledge and attention, a possibility of classifying and ordering remote unknown spheres of reality with lightning speed and to evaluate them without major intellectual or other expenditure.[9] And not a single day passes which does not supply society with new suggestions to get worked up about and outraged. There are scandals in the world of finance, scandals of corruption, sex, and abuse, scandals of the *feuilleton* as well as the intellectual debate, political scandals, scandals in the churches and the unions, the enterprises, the banks and the media, in sport, in the theatre and in the world of literature. Entering the word "scandal" in *Google*, i.e. conducting the modern form of a proof of existence and relevance, lands 142 million hits. "Day by day", the philosopher Peter Sloterdijk notes, "journalists try very hard to introduce new infectious agents into the arena, and they observe whether the scandal which they want to release starts to blossom. One must not forget that 20 to 30 suggestions for indignation are launched every day in every modern nation most of which naturally do not lead to the desired result. Modern society may be a form of life that enjoys scandalisation but it does not take up every suggestion of scandalisation. Most of the suggestions to get worked up about are rejected or only studied with moderate interest."[10]

An analysis of the paths of distribution of such suggestions for indignation and a reconstruction of the different phases of

---

[9] Smoltczyk, Alexander (1999) Skandal! Die nackte Wahrheit [Scandal! The naked truth]. In: *Spiegel Reporter*, no. 12, pp. 16–29.

[10] Sloterdijk, Peter (2007) Am Medienhimmel. Ein Gespräch mit [In the media sky: A conversation with] Jana Kühle and Sugárka Sielaff. In: Jens Bergmann/Bernhard Poerksen (eds.) *Medienmenschen. Wie man Wirklichkeit inszeniert* [*Media People: How to stage reality*], Münster: Solibro, p. 273.

scandalisation show that the typical scandal embedded in the logic of the mass media has differing features. At the beginning, there must inevitably be some kind of misbehaviour, the violation of a norm. Then comes the revelation engineered by journalists, then — if the topic has taken hold — the outcry, the collective outrage of the public, and finally the ritual of reprocessing and public accusation with all the variants of such a reaction. Some of the accused justify their behaviour or reject everything. They apologise in public and confess to their guilt. More or less defiantly, they declare themselves to be victims and insist that the real injustice and the real scandal is the fact that they have been attacked at all. There is the final step. "Both groups of participants, the scandalisers and the scandalised", we can read in a book by the sociologist Karl Otto Hondrich, "must execute it themselves in some sort of subversive collaboration. But they do this under compulsion: the collective feelings, whipped up to enormous heights, demand satisfaction. Violated values must be restored, imprecise rules must be sharpened, careerist high-climbers must be toppled, individuals must be sacrificed — on the altar of the most widely shared moral emotions."[11] And after all that the great process of forgetting sets in, not for the actors, not for the victims, but certainly for the majority of the readers and listeners and spectators. What remains is at best shreds of memory, opinions, sensed truths. The public loses interest and, usually after about six to eight weeks, turns to new topics because general indignation has a very short half-life. Every exciting event carries a close best-before date. Nevertheless — despite all its volatility — the actual moment of collective outrage is particularly enlightening. In it, the general public re-enacts the great moral dialogue and explains to itself what values are in force or should be. With the scream for scandal, individuals or even whole nations reveal

---

[11] Hondrich, Karl Otto (2002) *Enthüllung und Entrüstung. Eine Phänomenologie des politischen Skandals* [*Disclosure and Outrage: A phenomenology of the political scandal*], Frankfurt on the Main: Suhrkamp, p. 16.

their understanding of normality and assure themselves of the values they believe in: the more homogeneous the outrage, the more stable and accepted the system of values that is under attack. An open and pluralistic society that no longer feels bound by particular positive values, a society that disintegrates into quite different worlds and realities, fakes agreement and collective morality by distancing itself with commonly shared anger from all that which it has recognised as bad and evil. Even the confrontation with the outlandish, the immoral and scandalous, allows a society to reinforce moral norms and to make limits visible again by their very transgression, as already pointed out by Emile Durkheim, one of the co-founders of modern sociology. This is the morality of immorality.

This general lust for scandal, however, this modern form of the debate about values, does not usually get a good press. It is taken notice of but with some disgust. In the struggle for attention and a share of the market, journalists are seen to practise a brutal form of manhunting. The scandal is perceived as an extremely pernicious form of communication. Truth may still be recognised, therefore, affirms the communication researcher Hans Mathias Kepplinger, but it no longer stands a chance of winning the day. The scandalisers, in his opinion, are artists rather than analysts, anyway, because they creatively fabricate the scandal from the mass of observable social grievances and nuisances.[12] This means: even the typical form of a scandal, launched and spread by the mass media, is in fact an instrument of enlightenment—and of counter-enlightenment. It enforces, often with extreme brutality and efficiency, responsibility and possibly vital new beginnings—certainly a positive feature—but frequently stimulates only rather thoughtless schadenfreude, voyeuristic pastimes, the collective amusement caused by the dramatic downfall of a once celebrated hero. It determines agenda and makes the moral debate appear urgent, it intimi-

---

[12] Kepplinger, Hans Mathias (2012) *Die Mechanismen der Skandalisierung* [*The Mechanisms of Scandalisation*], Munich: Olzog, pp. 22, 196.

dates the powerful and destroys hierarchies of domination, and it sometimes even gains the power of an ur-democratic election that topples dangerous charismatic leaders and despots. Even the typical scandal has two faces. Often banalities are simply blown up to sensations. And the number of victims is high, the reason being that a scandal often damages innocent or scarcely guilty people and deprives them of their honour.

Characteristics of the unleashed scandal

However, in the shadow of the now pervasive inclination to outrage—the central thesis of this book—a new scandal schema is emerging. It is caused by the fact that the scandal has cut its ties with the linear and largely interaction-free logic of the traditional mass media and has entered a new evolutionary phase. It even emancipates itself from restrictions imposed by physical, spatial, or temporal constraints and, furthermore, separates itself from traditional themes and the societally relevant norm violations. It expands its spectrum of contents— in particular through the aggressive activities of those who once formed a mass media public that was formerly condemned to be a passive mass of recipients. Now the many individuals can assemble to form a superpower in mass communication. The key features of the unleashed scandal will be presented in the following summary, which does not, however, claim to be more than a first introductory survey:

- The *initiators and revealers* of processes of scandalisation are no longer just the journalists, as is still hinted at by the finely honed rhetoric of Peter Sloterdijk's attack, no longer necessarily the professional gatekeepers who may in their hearts still cultivate particular interests in questions of public relevance. Now there are also all the bloggers, the saboteurs banding together in swarms and mob formations on the social web, or even individuals who seize the right moment to present their most personal issue to a receptive global public. Everybody can scandalise effectively today as long as they manage to attract sufficient attention.

- Recording media like mobile phones, digital cameras, high-performance computers, distribution media on the social web like network and multimedia platforms such as *Facebook*, *Twitter*, or *YouTube*, blogs, personal websites and wikis are the *novel instruments of such processes of scandalisation*. They are potentially available to everyone now.

- There are *new victims* — because now even totally helpless and completely innocent persons and, what is more, people who were previously completely unknown may become the object of collective outrage and undesired excesses of attention. Status, celebrity, and power are no longer prerequisites for effective scandalisation. Still in evidence are, naturally, the "old", traditional forms of the public clearing and settling of accounts directed against the members of a social elite. But the social drop height is no longer a key criterion.

- The typical *spectrum of topics*, pre-structured by the mass media, has been stretched to the limits of its admissible extremes, to put it mildly. Relevant information and private narration, genuine deficiencies and abstruse claims, bizarre and nauseating material, significant disclosures as well as expectorated banalities may be encountered in equal measure and are used in novel mixtures, provoking their own peculiar forms of the treatment of, and the collective play with, such kinds of content. The question of societal significance is no longer of prime importance. *Human interest dominates relevance.*

- The outrage of a *public* oscillating between extremes, whether a small enraged community or a global mass, blazes its own trail in a more or less unfiltered manner — in contrast, for example, to the more or less thoroughly adapted letters to the editor of a traditional newspaper. The public now acts, in a previously unknown measure, as the time-beating band leader of the processes of scandalisation; it turns into an active performer.

- In the twilight of monitors and data streams, *new forms of uncertainty* emerge. None of the involved individuals can ever be sure to know what others know about them, on what grounds their own selves are reconstructed in the forms of their digital images. And the recipients must constantly question the correctness of it all, i.e. assess the kind of truth status that may or must be granted, for whatever reasons, to the free-floating sets of information and the so easily retouchable images. In case of doubt, the authority and credibility of the source will take priority over a document that is all too easily modifiable and thus forever doubtful. The source is, consequently, the decisive kind of meta-information in times of growing uncertainty.

- The already fairly restricted *possibilities of the control, the direction, and management of scandals* decrease dramatically under these circumstances. The broad distribution of the data, their simple accessibility, their potentially global circulation, the permanence of their presence, their quick researchability and easy recombinability, the difficult identification of originators and releasers—all these features render the usual forms of scandal management (attempts at censorship and intimidation by aggressive media attorneys, counterclaims, corrections, etc.) appear comparatively weak; individuals simply have no leverage to focus attention and to establish their versions of reality.

The consequence is: the newly emerging forms of disclosure and the public articulation of outrage are increasingly experienced as a fundamental loss of control both by those who are involved and by those who are targeted. The digitalisation of information technology has become the central precondition for this change. What does this mean? Analogue materials are inert; they are place-bound, corporeal. It is comparatively laborious to copy them and make them accessible to a broad mass of recipients. It needs time and patience. The specific features of this kind of materiality block quick transfer, easy reproduction, and speedy accessibility. The process of digitalisation, in a first step, transforms the multiplicity of analogue materials into a stream of bits and bytes so that the physical-material constraints of images and sounds, books, texts, and films disappear. Everything coded in this way may be processed by computers, may be reproduced in arbitrary numbers—and may be sent round the world at lightning speed. "With digitalisation an ever-increasing number of things previously tied to particular non-interchangeable materials changes into a new aggregate state", the philosopher and poet of the data universe Peter Glaser writes. "Cultural things in the widest possible sense—drawing boards, sound studios, television sets, books, you name it—become data. This kind of digital substance exhibits an essentially new kind of lightness. Such digital things may be moved with incredibly greater ease than before, may be spread, received, transformed, copied, shared, remixed—worldwide. The phenomenon of remixing, in particular, indicates the unstable state in which the whole development finds itself now. What is in fact mixed are fragments, pieces of film, snippets of sound, shreds of other cultural objects, reconstituted in the new forms."[13]

Remixing and resampling are thus the cultural technologies of the moment. In an arbitrarily expandable space of possibilities, conceptions of realities may now be rearranged, combined, transformed by using ever new approaches and taking into account an ever changing, ever new public. "Music, texts, images, but also modular software or encyclopaedic knowledge find themselves in a state of latent dissolution in the digital world", Peter Glaser continues in his essay *Cultural atomic power*. "The time-honoured cultural molecular combinations—the complex forms they have assumed across the centuries—are now all being cracked open or are breaking down into their basic constituents. The transition into the digital aggregate first creates a kind of primal soup consisting of fragments and

---

[13] Glaser, Peter (2009) Kulturelle Atomkraft [Cultural atomic power]. In: *Berliner Zeitung*, 25 August 2009, http://www.berliner-zeitung.de/archiv/die-digitalisierung-zersetzt-alte-medienformen---ihre-atome-suchen-hitzig-nach-neuer-synthese-kulturelle-atomkraft,10810590, 10661634.html (Retrieved 24 September 2013).

atomised cultural goods, which is highly reactive, however. It resembles free radicals in chemistry, which seek to attach themselves in an aggressive manner."[14] Once again: *digitalisation permits total transformation.* In the digital age, being means changeability — but on a global scale and without any unconditionally legitimate barriers to access. Even that which was once volatile and place-bound now becomes stable and possibly available worldwide. It may be searched very rapidly, it may be copied practically without expenditure and context-free, it may be recombined over and over and transferred to new contexts at the speed of light. Due to the very fact that the digitalised data possess this particular kind of lightness, this possibility of total transformation and global presence, particular shreds of texts, accessible fragments of images, pictures, temporary recordings may be turned into collectively effective stimuli of outrage — quite independent of their original utility — that can, in extreme cases, circulate worldwide and reach a barely identifiable and certainly in no way calculable public. The unleashed scandal is inconceivable without these new aggregate states and the *collapse of context.*[15]

The blogger and the net of effects

The relationship between laypersons and professional journalists is also becoming unstable, is being transformed in the process of the present development of the media. At the centre of the trends, as they unmistakably unfold, is an ongoing *radical democratisation of the media-based practice of revelation and scandalisation.* This is the decisive initial consideration in the attempt to

---

[14] Glaser, Peter (2009) Kulturelle Atomkraft [Cultural atomic power]. In: *Berliner Zeitung,* 25 August 2009, http://www.berliner-zeitung.de/archiv/die-digitalisierung-zersetzt-alte-medienformen---ihre-atome-suchen-hitzig-nach-neuer-synthese-kulturelle-atomkraft,10810590, 10661634.html (Retrieved 24 September 2013).

[15] We owe this formulation to: Wesch, Michael (2009) YouTube and you: Experiences of self-awareness in the context collapse of the recording webcam. In: *Explorations in Media Ecology,* vol. 8, no. 2, pp. 19–34.

explore the rearrangement of the scandal schema: to utilise the traditional mass-media concept of the scandal as a contrasting foil and background as well as an instrument of interpretation. Processes of revelation and outrage are becoming a field of action for masses. Moreover, the unleashed scandal may hit anyone. It can influence the lives of the powerful and determine the fate of the powerless, nor does it leave the analysts and inhabitants of the ivory tower unaffected. It may even turn against the scandalisers themselves. In brief: *the unleashed scandal is no longer a distant event; it is always embedded in personal spheres of life and part of direct practical experience.*

Everybody has a tale to tell about individual experiences and adventures. Here now, by way of illustration, is a case history from our own familiar academic world. On 2 June 2010, the German newspaper *Münchner Merkur* wrote about the possible reasons for the resignation of the Federal President of Germany: "Student causes Köhler's downfall. The Internet makes it possible: a student has seriously engineered the resignation of Horst Köhler." Further: "Jonas Schaible is probably guilty of the whole kerfuffle—he and a few of his colleagues of the Internet. Schaible is 20, a student of political science in Tübingen, and had begun to wonder a few days before—why nothing was happening. Schaible had read Köhler's statements on the mission of the *Bundeswehr* in Afghanistan and had felt irritated—particularly by the fact that the newscasters were not reporting anything at all. So he simply sat down and sent e-mails to some of the national media. In addition, he used the short message service *Twitter*. And suddenly the story gained momentum. Its outcome is very well known. Nobody could have foreseen it—not even the studiosus Schaible." The previous day, Federal President Horst Köhler had resigned from his office, to everyone's surprise. His public appearance—pale in the face, the eyes wide with anxiety and tension, and his wife at his side—is disturbing. It seems to be a sort of publicly celebrated attack of weakness, the disruption of a customary stage ritual, stripping down the respectable status of the presidential office and the requirements of a tightly corseted form of representation.

Figure 1: **In the presence of his wife, Federal President Horst Köhler announces his resignation in Bellevue Palace in Berlin.**

The public reactions to Köhler's unexpected departure are devastating ("desertion", "mindless", "act of desperation"). Köhler himself berates the media in his short speech. He thinks that what he said in the interview about assignments of the Federal Army abroad has been intentionally misunderstood and abusively misinterpreted as a justification of economic warfare in violation of the German constitution. In the ensuing vacuum of interpretation, the hectic search for causes and explanations, the sights are directed at that Tübingen student as the perpetrator of a kind of "regicide".[16] In all the messages that suddenly flare up, he is the person accused of bringing about

---

[16] The following presentation relies heavily on the careful analysis performed by Marcel Wagner. See: Wagner, Marcel (2010) *Auch du, Brutus? Wer waren die Königsmörder?* [*Et tu, Brute? Who were the regicides?*], unpublished manuscript, pp. 1–9.

the downfall of Federal President Horst Köhler with the help of a few e-mails, some *Twitter* messages, and a media-critical blog. The story shows a kind of archetypal topicality and is narrated in a strictly monocausal manner: blogger topples Federal President, David slays Goliath. In the German ZDF-TV news programme *heute-journal* the anchorman, Claus Kleber, presents the case as a "story of the power of the Internet" and adds that it will one day "be part of the history books". One of the student's professors at Tübingen University — one of the authors of these lines — puts in a somewhat unfortunate appearance in that news programme, speaking of a kind of "scandalisation from below". His insistently repeated statements in the actual interview that network effects cannot be personalised because this would contradict the logic of the whole sequence of events fall victim to the simplification constraints of the medium. Nevertheless, the story remains most enlightening even without its hostile dramatisation because it demonstrates something else: the unleashed scandal does not function according to linear cause and effect arrows (A generates B and B generates C) but violates our traditional idea of causality. There is little point in leading the established mass media into battle against digital media because they both need each other. In the blogosphere the suggestion of outrage is launched, tested, checked, and varied, it is then supplied with the necessary aggressive force by newspapers and journals, Net media, and television. The mails, the *Twitter* messages, *and* the reactions of journalists create a sort of mesh of effects. In such a mesh of effects, apparently quite insignificant incidents may suddenly generate massive unexpected consequences.

The mobilising power of suspicion

Straight to the point and in detail now. First there is an interview whose potentially explosive quality remains practically unnoticed. Returning from Mazar-i-Sharif in Afghanistan in the night of 21 May 2010, Horst Köhler formulates the following sentences — amongst others — in the presence of the *Deutschlandradio* reporter Christopher Ricke: "In my view, we are all in all on a good track to reach a broad understanding in our society that a country of the size of ours, with its dependence on external trade activity, must realise that in cases of doubt and emergency even military action is necessary to protect our interests — for instance, free trade routes, for instance, to prevent instabilities affecting whole regions that would quite definitely have negative repercussions on our chances of securing jobs and incomes in our own country. All this must be discussed — and I think we are not on such a bad course." This interview was broadcast on *Deutschlandradio Kultur Berlin* and on *Deutschlandfunk Cologne*. The passage that was to become the bone of contention later on could only be heard in the broadcast by *Deutschlandradio Kultur* and is also quoted in its newscast. The version on the Internet, however, had been stripped of the decisive passages. Pure coincidence, a case of negligence, the radio editors declare in later comments. In this *latency phase of the scandal* the statements disappear on the Net more or less without trace; they are, however, eventually picked up by the blogger Stefan Graunke, who discovers that the passage that was to become so crucial later can be traced in audio documents but is missing in the word and text versions retrievable online.[17] The bloggers now suspect censorship and manipulation, bombard the editors with e-mails, transcribe the significant text passages. Conspiracy theories blossom. Stefan Graunke launches diverse queries: why were the decisive passages of the interview that possibly point to an anti-constitutional position of the Federal President eliminated? A lively discussion begins. Interested circles, the assumption is, wanted to suppress the interview. For this reason, security back-up copies are made.

This supposition of an attempt at control provokes opposition, and the suspicion of censorship turns the topic into an

---

[17] The phase model used here as a grid for analysis and presentation can also be found in a slightly modified form in: Burkhardt, Steffen (2006) *Medienskandale. Zur moralischen Sprengkraft öffentlicher Diskurse* [*Media Scandals: On the explosive moral force of public discourses*], Cologne: Herbert von Halem Verlag, see especially p. 181 and p. 204.

infectious agent for the blogger scene, mobilises an ur-angst of manipulation, and feeds the great suspicions of the mainstream media. Gradually the relevant utterances undergo a metamorphosis of context and function. A text originally used for the purposes of critical media analysis ("censorship at *Deutschlandradio*") becomes a document directed against the political elite and is interpreted accordingly ("military expeditions for securing national wealth"); the contents have by themselves become topics of discussion, not just their alleged manipulative treatment. The Tübingen student Jonas Schaible sends e-mails to the online offices of the great national newspapers (*Süddeutsche Zeitung, Frankfurter Allgemeine Zeitung, Die Zeit, tageszeitung, Frankfurter Rundschau, Die Welt*, etc.) and to big news agencies, with the query as to why they did not report the case—simultaneously supplying the scandalised interview passages as evidence for a possible scandal. He formulates the following questions for the journalists: "I would be interested to know why you did not pursue this? Do you not think that the quotation merits discussion? [...] Why was the topic not included in the newspaper/the online presentation? And finally: May I quote your eventual reply in my blog?" He then intensifies his blogging about the case and continues to ask the editorial offices for information via *Twitter*. The scandal now slowly enters the *phase of growth*. *Zeit Online* expresses gratitude for the suggestion. A section editor of *Frankfurter Rundschau* announces reports and comments in the paper, admits however to Jonas Schaible that the interview and its explosive contents had simply been overlooked. Some of the other editorial offices react —for no lesser reason than that they have been made aware of the case by other readers. *Spiegel Online*, the most influential German agenda-setter in the online universe, publishes an article under the title "Bundeswehr in Afghanistan—Köhler sparks new war debate", together with critical statements of the opposition parties. *Frankfurter Rundschau* joins in shortly afterwards: "Anger about Köhler pronouncements—the ominous word of economic war." Further reports appear, fuelled by comments of opposition parties ("Cannon boat politics"), accompanied by a single and rather incompetent attempt at scandal management. The Federal President's Office issues a statement to the effect that there is a misunderstanding: Horst Köhler did not intend to refer directly to the mission in Afghanistan with his utterances, he was in fact commenting on the ongoing mission of the Bundeswehr against piracy at sea. This attempt at clarification is torn apart in a flash, i.e. by the straightforward presentation of the original sound version and the increasing number of critical voices of the political opponents. *Süddeutsche Zeitung* ("Speechifying in Bellevue Palace") and the Monday edition of *Der Spiegel*, which was already available on the preceding Saturday and therefore all over the government's quarters, attack Horst Köhler with unprecedented harshness as "Horst Lübke" — an allusion to the former Federal President Heinrich Lübke. Lübke did not find fame as a master of the spoken word and is supposed to have repeatedly made a fool of himself. Once, when on a state visit in West Africa, he allegedly addressed an assembly with the words: "Dear ladies and gentlemen, dear negroes…"

Finally, the *decision phase* arrives, and the climax of the blitz resignation. Now a kind of team-play resulting in a highly nervous kind of communication manifests itself. It is governed by the properties of enormous speed and unsurpassable advantageous information as well as instruments of ad-hoc verification. Hastily individualised e-mails and *Twitter* messages can be sent without great expenditure at any time, day and night, to all the influential opinion leaders; the data files and original documents — decisive pieces of evidence — can easily be integrated into personal packages of information and offers of outrage. Moreover, this very interplay of technical possibilities and sudden outrage on the part of a media public with growing power creates a new mesh of effects. The original interview passage whose explosive quality was simply overlooked has become a new topic via the detour of a differently grounded suspicion ("censorship", "manipulation"). There follows a second agenda-setting by means of e-mails, *Twitter* messages, and journalistic reflexes of the blogger scene: "The explosive power", Jonas Schaible states, for instance, in his blog, "contained in this quotation is gigantic". And further: "The fact that the German Federal President advocates military missions in such a blatant manner, that he breaks with the traditional, at least the official, reason of state, and that he quite unashamedly suggests to safeguard national economic interests by means of armed force, is a downright scandal."

The broken arrow of time and the eternal present

The example shows, furthermore: the traditional guiding mass media, the established online media, the bloggers, and an aggressively operating opposition *actually* cooperate despite all kinds of *fundamental,* mutually cultivated animosities. Obviously, there are massive prejudices on all sides. Journalists plainly know why politicians of the opposition keep dramatising their theses about political opponents, why they keep offering the media particular suggestions for topics and interviews, why they provide quotable formulas in acts of strategic self-subjugation. Journalists understand very well what motives concerning the personal and political gain of power inform and feed the driving forces behind these actions of politicians, and what constitutes the basic lines of their inveigling advances. In addition, if asked backstage in a quiet moment, politicians will readily confess that they have a low opinion of bloggers and their so self-assuredly flaunted performances. The bloggers themselves enjoy observing all the aberrations of the established media and continue watching them with their own peculiar mixture of fascination and condescension; they happily celebrate the mistakes of the professionals as though they were evidence for their own competence and proof of their own exceptional kind of superiority. Nevertheless, all these differences in content — and this is the important point here — are not necessarily of communicative relevance. In the particular situation during the summer of 2010, they all contribute to the collective firing-up of the debate, generating a climate that seems to lead to the panic reaction of a resignation that is still not fully explained.

The typical, the normal pattern in the causality of a scandal — first the violation of a norm, then the medial revelation of this norm violation, and finally the collective outrage of the public — is obviously rearranged here and partially suspended. Public outrage throws new light on what has already been published and only sloppily spread and makes it now suddenly appear incendiary and potentially scandalous. Sections of the public itself step forward in the roles of researchers, activists, and informants, as suppliers of evidence and as journalism-inspired accusers. The established mass media react to the still uncoordinated indicators of outrage and provide them with the necessary supplementary force and also elements of additional legitimation. They channel the attention. They focus the budding readiness for enragement — right up to the moment of decision in which the Federal President, still filled with bewilderment, offers his resignation. The case shows, furthermore, quite independently of how the actual events and the factual explosiveness of this presidential interview are appraised, that *the unleashed scandal is characterised by its very own temporal form, the form of the potentially eternal present*. The linear arrow of time pointing from past to present and then to the future seems broken. Thus, even things of the past become retrievable, and naturally all the stuff that has since been sent out and has thankfully remained unnoticed — a thoughtless remark, an idiotically failed performance, and an off-putting moment of blackout. In case of need it may all regain a renewable present and, what is more, remain forever in the background as a threatening poisonous brew for future exploitation. *Even marginal failures remain publicly retrievable and thus potentially present worldwide.* Digital memory is by no means absolute, it is not at all total; but the forgetting and obliterating of traces occurs in ways and manners that are difficult to control. One can never know what is still left despite the fact that all comments may have been removed, the servers may have been switched off, and the links may have become useless.

The tendencies of a tool

One may bemoan or criticise this potentially eternal present, one may claim the label of a neutral analysis for one's own position, or one may welcome the emerging developments euphorically as the realisation of a vision of total transparency that could generate the foundations of a new kind of ethos. The simple motto might be: as everybody knows (practically) everything, anyway, it is no longer worth trying to conceal whatever is objectionable. So why not behave correctly from the start in order to escape the unavoidable unmasking? To some, the story of the little boy playing with the dog and the experiences of the party girl from the south of Germany will certainly appear insignificant or of no greater significance than phenomena of transition. It could be objected, for instance, that they must be interpreted as the expression of still insufficiently sensitised minds that are unaware of the possibility of becoming objects of attention everywhere and at all times. Other interpretations are possible, however. Even a cultural pessimist might raise his voice at this point and bewail the generally spreading deterioration and the loss of privacy, i.e. fit the case histories into his schema of decline and prophesied scenarios of degeneration. These very indications of such a potential multiplicity of interpretations of the presented case histories make one thing very clear: *scandal is a matter of opinion.*[18] Sometimes things that one person considers scandalous appear to be mere trifles to another, or even as evidence for a particular form of morality. "Therefore, the concept of scandal does *not* refer to the violation of a socially valid norm", writes the sociologist Ronald Hitzler, "but rather to the accepted *labelling* of an event or a state of affairs that do not conform to a norm. In brief: a state of affairs

---

[18] Hitzler, Ronald (1989) Skandal ist Ansichtssache. Zur Inszenierungslogik ritueller Spektakel in der Politik [Scandal is a matter of opinion: On the logic of staging ritual spectacles in politics]. In: Rolf Ebbighausen/ Sighard Neckel (eds.) *Anatomie des politischen Skandals* [*Anatomy of the Political Scandal*], Frankfurt on the Main: Suhrkamp, pp. 334–354.

turns into a scandal because it is published and successfully *defined* as a scandal."[19] If these pronouncements are to be taken seriously, they entail the challenge for all observers to make their positions and perspectives explicit and transparent and to specify exactly their attitude and approach. For it is eminently evident that all the interpretations of the pieces of evidence and the histories presented in this book inevitably boil down to one thing: a matter of opinion. This book is the result of a more or less successful, more or less convincing, attempt at interpretation whose plausibility must be judged by those for whom all this has been written down, its readers.

However, despite all fundamental scepticism, one thing may be stated with certainty: it is far too early to undertake a final assessment, to make a definitive judgement or take a decision with reference to all the extant extreme views and interpretations. Such a fundamental all-or-none decision will most probably be quite impossible, anyway, because relevant evidence can be adduced for all the positions in question. *The telos of digital tools and the by now ubiquitous media does not point in one unique and clearly identifiable direction, but there exists a prevalent tendency.* The utilisation of digital tools is open but it is not totally arbitrary. The tools set a frame for communication, they stake it out, they create certain possibilities and block others, and they shape their users. Once again: digital tools open up new forms of debate and participation, they force a hitherto unknown pace of dissemination and distribution, a novel dimension of combinatorial variety and rapid accessibility. They allow for different and hitherto unknown stages of evolution and escalation in the process of scandalisation. But they cannot determine actual events and given contents in an infallibly cal-

---

[19] Hitzler, Ronald (1989) Skandal ist Ansichtssache. Zur Inszenierungslogik ritueller Spektakel in der Politik [Scandal is a matter of opinion: On the logic of staging ritual spectacles in politics]. In: Rolf Ebbighausen/ Sighard Neckel (eds.) *Anatomie des politischen Skandals* [*Anatomy of the Political Scandal*], Frankfurt on the Main: Suhrkamp, p. 334 [author's emphasis].

culable way and manner; behind the tool and the medium there will always be individuals, i.e. ultimately responsible human beings, with all their good and bad intentions, goals, longings, and desires. What follows? It is time to make the current mantra of media theory more precise. *The medium is not the message, but traces of the medium and the properties of the tool become manifest in the message.*[20] The instruments of communication and the media of the digital age are not totally neutral apparatuses of mediation, which function according to the principles of postal delivery, but instances with their own inherent effectiveness, trailblazers. Media researchers have to decipher these trails and to make them legible for themselves and for others, to work out, with the help of individual cases and exemplary phenomena, the general pattern and the fundamental principles of effective functioning. In the ideal case, such procedures will help to apprehend and experience the particular logic of the Net medium and to make its stage management methods transparent—and to contribute to the self-enlightenment of a media society.

The form of the essay

There is a fundamental multiplicity of goals involved in the use of media; the choice amongst goals, however, is strictly a matter of individual responsibility. Consequently, a simplificatory mono-perspective is no longer helpful or productive. Optimism and pessimism—elevated to principles and dogmas—are equally dim-witted and but expressions of a sort of obsessive thinking that tends to react to different phenomena with essentially identical approaches. The fixation on extremes necessarily leads to identical assessments, i.e. euphoria or disgust, utopian sentiments or wholesale horror. In contrast, the point must be made that the digital age has its own beauties as well as its own

---

[20] Krämer, Sybille (2008) *Medium, Bote, Übertragung. Kleine Metaphysik der Medialität* [*Medium, Messenger, Transmission: A brief metaphysics of mediality*], Frankfurt on the Main: Suhrkamp, pp. 11ff.

amazements. It possesses its own special kind of radiance as well as its particular brand of brutality. It is *polymorphic*, comparable to those strange figures and hybrids that vary their appearance according to the perspective of onlookers and the interests of observers. They always appear different, always new. Ludwig Wittgenstein, in his *Philosophical Investigations*, analyses a figure that may be perceived—from varying angles of vision—as a hare or as a duck, and he calls it the H-D-head. Now it is one of the variants, and then the other one, on one occasion we see the hare, on another one the dominant image is the duck. Whoever wants to determine the meaning of this figure once and for all wants ultimate non-ambiguity or even a final moral judgement on the peculiar properties and the essence of the figure, fails to capture the phenomenon, misses its point. For its essence consists precisely in the very absence of an identifiable core essence; and this is the reason why its forms of appearance can be seen and interpreted in multiple ways. "Polymorphs", an essay formulates, "point to a world beyond polarities. We Europeans tend to see things from two perspectives only, shadowy or bright, a grey uniform future or a variegated, herbaceous sunny one. Beyond such antinomies things have many different shapes and forms."[21]

It will not strike the readers of this book as a surprise that in its context the unleashed scandal is part of the group of polymorphic communication events. From a moral perspective, these events appear to oscillate and can all too quickly provoke a harsh verdict. However, an over-hasty and unnecessarily rigid judgement can only hamper its proper understanding and restrain an observer's analytical flexibility. What is needed primarily is close scrutiny, the reconstruction and documentation of cases and experiences with as much precision as possible in order to show that some scandalisations are justified, that others, conversely, are nothing but cruel spectacles to destroy

---

[21] Poerksen, Uwe (1989) *Polymorphe. Ein mexikanisches Tagebuch* [*Polymorphs: A Mexican diary*], Stuttgart: Klett-Cotta, p. 31.

the personal way of life of innocent and defenceless people. However, these examples and stories are not intended to be just plain contributions to a theoretical discussion of media and scandals or mere scholastic finger exercises. They are carefully selected case studies aiming, on the one hand, at meticulous and detailed case reconstructions, and on the other, at the identification of general patterns and commonalities in the material data. The great common denominator in all these cases and case histories is that they reveal in graphic detail the forms of the loss of control as well as the democratisation of the revelatory practices of the digital age, all of which the traditional investigation of scandals is inevitably fated to overlook, fixated as it has remained on the mass media and the once so powerful and dominant journalistic gatekeeper. Whoever is interested or willing may today launch a scandal report. They do not need editorial offices as business partners or the support of media enterprises. All they need is Net access and a minimum of technological competence. The different cases are definitely not comparable in content, on the contrary, they stem from highly dissimilar countries and lifeworlds. The following chapters will deal with political and sex scandals, business and environmental scandals, genuine globally debated scandals, invented scandals, and suspected norm violations. Extreme cases deal with torture and murder (Abu Ghraib), or with very private acts of totally unknown people, which are of no relevance at all for the public but have been grabbed and attacked by a mob lusting for outrage. It may be a passenger throwing a tantrum on a night bus in Hong Kong recorded by a mobile phone that raises a collective outcry; it may be the negligent spreading of a *Twitter* message that leads to the implosion of a political career. Some of these stories of scandalisation are of extraordinary triviality — as far as their content is concerned — i.e. they do not even reveal some real scandalous misbehaviour. However, they bring to light, indirectly as it were, the peculiar features of the medium and the novel dynamics of outrage.

How did we proceed? First, we built up a wide-ranging database of case histories, from which we then selected a number of characteristic and particularly instructive cases and subjected these to careful in-depth examination. The collected and analysed material consisted of newspaper articles and, as far as available, topically relevant professional publications; furthermore, of a large number of sources accessible online or reconstructible from caches (buffer stores) and Internet archives. Whenever possible and advisable, we interviewed involved individuals, consulted with action groups for victims as well as media lawyers, exchanged letters with initiators of campaigns, and discussed our results with qualified partners. Finally, we took the decision to break open and relax the corset of customary scholarly presentation, to demonstrate as graphically as possible styles of staging and disruptions in stage management processes, and to relate the scandal stories from a close angle and without the distancing formulae of traditional academic treatises. The effort to formulate our presentations and reflections in the style of an essay may be deplored by some and welcomed by others. It is, however, part of our personal understanding of a university existence that cultural and social science studies, too, should have the courage to formulate, support, and defend a thesis or two. This is possibly of particular importance in an age where one race for some academic evaluation cup follows the next, in which intellectually rather undemanding competitive contests between universities threaten to paralyse creative activity because they address different and alien genres and forms of expression and, despite claims to the contrary, do not really reward public interventions. It is one of our academic dreams that what we have written will in the final reckoning lose the character of a more or less sterile monologue, that it will prove a source of stimulation both for others and the authors themselves, in order to improve their theses and ideas by means of dialogue and disputation.

II

The New Disclosers & the Old Media

Once upon a time, journalists wielded the power of *gatekeepers* styling the worldview of a public condemned to passivity. They determined what was important and what was not. They laid down what was to be viewed as a scandal — and what not. "What we know about our own society, even about the world in which we live, we know through the mass media", the German sociologist Niklas Luhmann stated some time ago in a since famous book.[1] In the present age of digitalisation, the power of the mass media has certainly not vanished but it seems to have had its wings clipped. This in no way implies that television and radio stations, newspapers and magazines, have been rendered superfluous. However, the number of sources of information about the world in which we live has simply expanded explosively. Today every human being is — at least potentially — a broadcaster. All we know about our society we also derive from those who exploit the new means of communication, who recommend links, pass comments, tweet, blog, broadcast.

The consequence is: the traditional media are no longer the essential primary triggers and central agenda-setters of scandalous events, no longer the all-determining agents with the power to implement clear, authoritative orders of relevance. Naturally, they still function as media of disclosure but they have inevit-

---

[1] Luhmann, Niklas (1996) *Die Realität der Massenmedien* [*The Reality of the Mass Media*], 2nd enlarged ed., Opladen: Westdeutscher Verlag, p. 9.

ably also become *chroniclers, analysts,* and *re-enforcers* of scandals that may very well have been initiated by others. They provide evaluative classification, orientation, and background. They penetrate events, research them exhaustively. They generate widely recognised attention and furnish scandal-prone topics together with bids for outrage with public legitimacy. However, their undoubtedly persisting relevance cannot camouflage the crucial change: the new power of individuals, the new strength of irritable amateurs, of enraged laypersons, who have entered the spheres of activity of journalists and publicists. Individuals have practically become gatekeepers in their own right, assuming widely differing roles, sometimes rapidly jumping from one role to another. They may act as informants and scandalisers, as publicists and media entrepreneurs, or as intermediaries trading explosive information. These gatekeepers in their own right, whenever necessary, root out and select their own channels and platforms. They utilise new media and, with the support of an interested public, establish their own topics and publish independently, paying no attention to the standards of the journalist establishment, often at breakneck speed, sometimes with worldwide effect.

1. Matt Drudge and the experiment with the truth

The ideology of a headline

Late in the evening of 17 January 1998 Matt Drudge, who had long been ridiculed as a mere journalist impersonator and the "abomination of the Internet" (*Baltimore Sun*), publishes a piece of news on his website. This piece will transform him, finally, into an iconic figure of dubious disclosure and the pace setter of the first global Net scandal. It reads: "At the last minute, at 6 p.m. on Saturday evening, Newsweek magazine killed a story that was destined to shake official Washington to its foundation: A White House intern carried on a sexual affair with the President of the United States! The Drudge Report has learned that reporter Michael Isikoff developed the story of his career, only to have it spiked by top Newsweek suits hours before publication. A young woman, 23, sexually involved with the love of her life, the President of the United States, since she was a 21-year-old intern at the White House." Only eight hours later, Drudge's computer has received 15,000 e-mails with comments. Innumerable visitors to his website have devoured the story. His account of the affair begins to seep through the digital universe for days before it finally explodes in the first world of the established mass media. Drudge himself recorded a detailed protocol of the hours and minutes before he sent the story online — a story that is by now considered to represent a caesura in the history of the media and of scandals. It can now be found reprinted in his book *Drudge Manifesto* — a hotchpotch of precise chronological description, gossip and rumour, e-mails from fans, and home-baked poems on the state and the future of journalism, displayed in an eccentric layout.[2]

Figure 2: **The man with the modem: Matt Drudge's manifesto.**

---

[2] On the process of "research" and, particularly, the different stages in the production of a front-page story, see: Drudge, Matt (2000) *Drudge Manifesto*, New York: New American Library, pp. 55ff.

If Drudge's own account can be accepted as truthful then he had been given somewhat diffuse tip-offs that the *Newsweek* reporter Michael Isikoff, after months of research, was going to publish a big story on the sex affair of the President with a White House intern, including the possible instigation to perjury. He wants to publish an exclusive first notice relating to this story on his website, which he had begun as a simple e-mail newsletter in the mid-eighties, and therefore tries to contact Isikoff by telephone in the early evening, is however fobbed off by his wife. Now he feels unsure about whether he should actually publish the shocking lead story that he has already formulated and prepared for publication and frantically begins to search for further corroboration. His title was: "Newsweek bombshell: tapes reveal intern in white house sex shocker." Here a most revealing pattern manifests itself: *the headline he intends to publish is to hand before he has concluded his research; the research itself is merely meant to serve the speediest verification of a sensation, which is already being traded as a certainty.* Having first attempted to speak to Michael Isikoff on the telephone and having been stalled by the presence of mind of Isikoff's alert wife, Matt Drudge now contacts another informant. Her name is Lucianne Goldberg. She works as a literary agent in New York, has connections with the social environment of Monica Lewinsky, and describes herself as a person who passionately hates Bill Clinton. She can unquestionably not be classified as an independent or neutral source but tells him that the editors at *Newsweek* have stopped the story for reasons that are unknown to her, and that she feels totally depressed and completely shattered by all this. Only one thing is certain at this stage: Isikoff's story will not (yet) be published. Matt Drudge is unable to glean any further information but, on the basis of what he has and what he has learned through the telephone conversation with Lucianne Goldberg, he formulates a new headline that runs as follows: "Newsweek kills story on white house intern. Blockbuster report: 23-year-old, former white house intern, sex relationship with president!!!" However, this makes him feel queasy again; he hesitates and asks himself whether this story would destroy him if it turned out to be false. He contacts his lady informant again, who now supplies a number of biographical details on Monica Lewinsky. He thinks that this will suffice. He therefore produces the final version of the lead story, adding that he found it impossible to query Isikoff and *Newsweek* via the telephone. According to his own reconstruction—a truly crazy document of self-unmasking—he then moves the computer mouse into position, presses the enter key—and thus catapults the story of the White House intern and the President into the world. *This kind of extremely hasty and scrappy research exemplifies the characteristic disproportion between the energy expended by the researcher and the potential consequences of a publication for other affected parties – possibly innocent and uninvolved – who were not contacted directly let alone interviewed. The originator of the Drudge Report thus fashioned an asymmetric kind of journalism unrestrained by established professional standards.* One might say that Matt Drudge is experimenting with true and false hypotheses in the realm of public life. He seeks to test possible versions of events by simply publishing them and delegates the work concerning the final verification of assertions to the mainstream media, which he despises but still cannot live without.

Publicity as a news factor

The style of the interaction with the informant Lucianne Goldberg is chummy, as can be gathered from the records of his conversations; his information base is narrow, and there is no comprehensive double-checking whatsoever. If one is prepared to believe his own accounts, then he has expended only a few hours to do the initial research on the sole basis of a single central source for a story whose publication rocked the world. The first reaction is from the *Washington Post* of 21 January 1998. The thematic peg for the story four days after its Net appearance: Bill Clinton has urged his ex-playmate to lie. Then *Newsweek* publishes the "Diary of a Scandal" on its own website with quotes by Monica Lewinsky, analyses details and backgrounds, and tries hard, by means of special ad-hoc information, to stake out its claims to a coup that was originally its very own but was regrettably launched by somebody else. Slowly the reporting begins to gather noticeable momentum.[3] Numerous media enter the communicative match and orchestrate global media reverberations. Meanwhile, Matt Drudge—world-exclusive once more—supplies the next sensation by reporting online that Monica Lewinsky still has her as yet unlaundered black cocktail dress with the President's semen on it.[4] And thus Matt Drudge transmutes into the sought-after expert in news programmes of national television stations—an expert, however, who can produce no evidence for his story at this stage but who is nevertheless still welcomed as a most opportune witness. He had heard of the semen dress, is all he can say in reply to submitted questions. The result is a phase of detailed underwear reporting even in the quality press. *Newsweek* and *Time* in their subsequent issues report that Lewinsky supposedly said that she would never ever wash the said dress again. The principle of thematic legitimation governing this situation may be condensed into the following formula—independently of the very concrete question of truth content and the actual existence of this dress: *the very fact of the publication on the Net leads to the publication of the assumed facts in the mainstream media. Bare publicity – detached from the trustworthiness of the sources – becomes a complementary news factor, an additional supplementary criterion, and an opportunity for reporting.* The danger is possibly that, in the extreme case, the reference to the reports by others will replace the proper search for evidence and the effort to perform adequate independent investigations.

---

[3] On the quantity of reporting see: Williams, Bruce A./Michael X. Delli Carpini (2004) Monica and Bill all the time and everywhere: The collapse of gatekeeping and agenda setting in the new media environment. In: *American Behavioral Scientist*, vol. 47/9, pp. 1208–1230.

[4] On the role of Matt Drudge in the public debate of Monica Lewinsky's dress see: Cohen, Adam (1998) The press and the dress. In: *Time on Politics*, 16 February 1998, http://www.cnn.com/ALLPOLITICS/1998/02/09/time/cohen.html (Retrieved 24 September 2013).

Paradoxes of journalism

It may be worthwhile in this connection to illuminate the backgrounds of the scandal — not least in order to gain some understanding of the hesitation on the part of the professional gatekeepers in the editorial centre of the magazine *Newsweek* by contrasting it with the role of the investigative reporter Michael Isikoff.[5] We must remember, first of all, that the affairs of the American President, at the time, appear so explosive because Bill Clinton was variously under investigation anyway and for manifold reasons. His private life, in particular, was a prime target in order to topple him. On the one hand, there had been repeated attempts from 1994 onwards in connection with the so-called Whitewater affair (controversial real estate transactions of the Clinton couple). On the other hand, Paula Jones, a state employee from Arkansas, had already filed a lawsuit against Bill Clinton, accusing him of sexual harassment in a hotel room in Little Rock. Her lawyers were combing the social environment of the President in order to discover further potential victims and to establish some characteristic behavioural pattern that might be of use in court — and so they hit upon Monica Lewinsky. Furthermore, Kenneth Starr, the federal judge appointed special investigator by Congress, had shown particular interest in this young woman, the former White House intern, because he was not only investigating — according to his original brief — the Clintons' controversial real estate deals but also eagerly seeking to uncover other cases of presidential misconduct. He eventually manages to acquire decisive evidence. In the court proceedings of Paula Jones, Monica Lewinsky declares under oath that she has never had a sexual relationship with Bill Clinton. However, in a telephone conversation with a

---

[5] An extensive reconstruction may be found in the following document: Hummel, Hartwig (1999) *Monicagate. Die Clinton-Lewinsky-Affäre und das politische System der USA* [*Monicagate: The Clinton-Lewinsky affair and the political system of the USA*], Lecture at the University of Trier, 07 January 1999, www.phil-fak.uni-duesseldorf.de/politik/Mitarbeiter/Hummel/monicagate.pdf (Retrieved 24 September 2013).

friend of hers she talks in detail about just such an intimate relationship. She also reveals that there was a mutual agreement to deny any such affair. What she does not realise is that her friend, Linda Tripp, records a good 20 hours of these telephone conversations—and informs the special investigator Kenneth Starr about this explosive material. Starr then expands his investigations against the hated President and arranges several meetings between Tripp and Monica Lewinsky, which are all tapped with a bugging system.[6] The two friends again speak about the affair and the "Big Creep"—referring to Clinton—this time overheard directly by agents of the FBI. Finally, the agents appear at a meeting in a hotel bar, force a desperate Monica Lewinsky into a room, and threaten her by confronting her with photographs and tapes and informing her about the transcripts of her wiretapped conversations, which they have acquired from Linda Tripp. The charge against the President now is: instigation to perjury.

The journalist Michael Isikoff, a reporter renowned for his independence and his investigative pluck, is aware of these transcripts of the tapped conversations and their explosive content. Moreover, all the relevant participants in these goings-on, which extend right up to the President of the USA, have known for some time that Isikoff knows something.[7] In the end, he is offered a deal from the entourage of Kenneth Starr. He is requested to wait a little longer with the publication of his materials on the current investigations in connection with the Lewinsky case. Furthermore, should he be willing to reveal the

---

[6] On the details of these events see also: Anon. (1998) Im Theater des Absurden [In the theatre of the absurd]. In: *Der Spiegel*, 02 February 1998, pp. 128–133.

[7] Isikoff reflects on his role in his own book on the topic. See: Isikoff, Michael (1999) *Uncovering Clinton: A reporter's story*, New York: Crown Publishers. There is extensive coverage of his approach and his tackling of the diverse attempts to instrumentalise him in the *New York Times*. See: Goldstein, Tom (1999) All the president's women. In: *New York Times*, 04 April 1999, http://www.nytimes.com/1999/04/04/books/all-the-president-s-women.html?src=pm (Retrieved 24 September 2013).

results of his own investigations he would be rewarded with an exclusive story at some later date. Isikoff rejects the offer and now tries very hard to keep his movements unobtrusive in this minefield of influences and dependencies that has, of course, already changed by virtue of his mere presence. He keeps in contact with the bugging specialist and self-appointed friend of Monica Lewinsky's but refuses to listen to the tapes while the bugging of the nightly confessions by telephone still continues. This would have violated his ethics as a journalist, he will later state. He says that he would have changed from researcher and reporter into an agent, and that he did not at all want to be instrumentalised by a woman informant whose only too conspicuous single goal was to bring the President down. The journalist's dilemma of the difficult balance between maximal proximity and maximal distance, as it manifests itself here, is a fundamental one. Maintaining too much distance may result in missing sufficient background information; immersing oneself too deeply in the milieu under consideration may endanger independence, turn observers into agents in the world of the events to be described and assessed. To maintain one's independence and still acquire relevant information thus means to recalibrate responsibly the relationship between proximity and distance, participation and neutral observation, in every new situation. During the "hot" bugging phase, Michael Isikoff therefore first of all bides his time and maintains his distance to his key informant Linda Tripp. At some stage, however, he too gains possession of a 90-minute conversational sequence. He finally decides, after a whole year of work and research, to expand his investigations and to place the scandal story with the news magazine *Newsweek*, whose employee he had become in 1994. In the editorial centre all the available tapes are played and assessed together. The chief editor, Richard M. Smith, still harbours doubts. He asks questions, voices reservations, and finally declines publication. In February 1998, the magazine publishes the following statement: "So why didn't Newsweek print the story? The magazine was fully prepared to disregard any objections from the prosecutors and publish. But two aspects of the story troubled editor-in-chief Richard M. Smith amongst other editors. Contrary to expectations, the 90-minute tape the magazine heard neither confirmed nor disproved the most explosive legal allegation—obstruction of justice. Apart from Tripp's accusations, the magazine had no independent confirmation of the basis for Starr's inquiry on that subject. Second, the editors were concerned that while the magazine had heard a great deal about Monica Lewinsky from Tripp, its reporters had never seen her, talked with her or done enough independent reporting to assess the young woman's credibility. Before putting her name in print for the first time and publishing a story that would inevitably change her life forever, the editors felt they needed to know more about her and the motives of the other players. In the end, time ran out. After a long discussion in which the editors raised their concerns and Isikoff argued calmly and forcefully to print, Smith decided to hold off writing the story and to continue the reporting."[8] The reasons advanced here (doubts as to the credibility of the central informant, remaining obscurities, lack of time, the protection of a young woman, the production schedules of a magazine) again highlight a central conflict of goals, a fundamental paradox of trustworthy, research-intensive journalism. On the one hand, one may not have done sufficient adequate research; on the other, one clearly wants to see one's own story in print to secure its presumed effect. On the one hand, one may cause a stir by publishing quickly thereby beating the competitors; on the other, a premature publication that proves to be faulty may damage one's credibility and the image of the medium for which one works.[9]

---

[8] The complete statement may be found here: Anon. (1998) Newsweek's decision. In: *Newsweek*, 01 February 1998, http://www.newsweek.com/1998/02/02/newsweek-s-decision.html (Retrieved 24 September 2013).

[9] On such aporias, paradoxes, and dilemmas of journalism see: Krainer, Larissa (2001) *Medien und Ethik. Zur Organisation medienethischer*

The neo-form of the rumour

For Matt Drudge, the conflict between the goals of speed and exactitude as described above exists only in an extremely rudimentary form, if at all. He acts as an agenda-setter with no obligation to credibility, who exploits the Net for his own experiments with facts and fictions — and this does not only apply to the scandals surrounding the American President. An older study published in the media magazine *Brill's Content* is based on the analysis of 51 Drudge reports between January and September 1998, which Matt Drudge had advertised as exclusive to his readers.[10] The study shows that only 31 stories could actually claim to be exclusive news messages. Ten of these were false or had never even taken place. Eleven stories proved to be correct. The correctness of the remaining publications was doubtful or could not be verified definitively. In other words: the truth content of Drudge's publications is more than fragile. Some things written by Matt Drudge are accurate, others are not; some of the things he spreads are banal, others show a certain degree of relevance. Occasionally he draws attention to distant publications, thus serving as a "driver of traffic" who is even roped in by some journalists for their own stories, journalists who therefore tip him off in advance of publication with anonymous mails.[11] The analysis of some of the contributions reveals motives of an extremely conservative publicist with a right-wing political orientation. He appears as a person with a keen interest in campaigning, in test runs for rumours — which flies in the face of the temporal order of proper traditional

---

Entscheidungsprozesse [*Media and Ethics: On the organisation of media-ethical decision processes*], Munich: KoPaed.

[10] McClintick, David (1998) Town crier for the new age. In: *Brill's Content*, November 1998, http://web.archive.org/web/20000819015036/http://www.brillscontent.com/features/cryer_1198.html (Retrieved 24 September 2013).

[11] Sappell, Joel (2007) Hot links served up daily. In: *Los Angeles Times*, 04 August 2007, http://www.latimes.com/business/la-fi-drudge4aug04,0,4136919,full.story?coll=la-home-center (Retrieved 24 September 2013).

research, even tending to reverse it. *What cannot be verified quickly and definitively is not patiently and scrupulously researched to the end but instead published at lightning speed.* The publication is *not* the natural culmination and conclusion of a successful process of the verification of initially still diffuse and obscure suggestions and presuppositions. It much rather occurs — in contrast to serious methodical journalism — close to the starting point of a debate, it may in the extreme case even figure as its kick-off. Sometimes Matt Drudge's peculiar ways of experimentally testing hypotheses and trickeries of his informants in the public sphere are immediately followed by retractions. It is rather rare that injured parties try to defend themselves with the help of lawyers and demands for high damages. Lawsuits also tend to be avoided to prevent a story from gaining momentum. Occasionally, Matt Drudge offers an apology and officially withdraws his exclusive but unfortunately false report together with a few lines of regret. Something will inevitably stick, however, because a rumour has been launched, a topic, a perspective, a possible turn of thought has been presented and continues to exist in the world.

A few examples may now demonstrate the forms and consequences of such rumour reporting. Drudge attacked an adviser of President Bill Clinton, the political journalist Sidney Blumenthal, on the eve of taking office in August 1997 in a massive way. Referring to information from an "influential Republican", who — naturally — preferred to remain anonymous, he spread the message that Blumenthal had become conspicuous by violence in his marriage and that the case was now on record. He was, however, unable to supply trial minutes or other documentary evidence. And the appalled journalist did not learn of the publication through a query or a request for an opinion from the *Drudge Report* but through pure coincidence: as a visitor of the website on the eve of his taking office.[12]

---

[12] On the details of this case see: McClintick, David (1998) Town crier for the new age. In: *Brill's Content*, November 1998, http://web.archive.

Moreover, in February 2004, Matt Drudge falsely claimed that the Democrat and presidential candidate John Kerry had been involved in a long-standing affair with journalist Alexandra Polier. He wrote that the woman had since been taken abroad — purportedly at Kerry's request. A former rival in the fight for the presidential candidacy, Wesley Clark, was quoted with the words: "Kerry will implode over an intern issue." When the publication was proved false, Drudge apologised to Polier. With other stories, however, not a single word of regret was offered. For instance in the case of Michael Ware, a CNN journalist and war reporter. Claiming the support of an anonymous witness, Matt Drudge smeared the American war reporter who was unpopular in right-wing circles. The accusation: at a press conference, Michael Ware had supposedly treated the Republican presidential candidate John McCain with absolute disrespect, interrupted him, mocked him, and laughed at him. But the video clips of that very event did not show a trace of relevant evidence. Michael Ware pointed out, furthermore, that he had not posed a single question and that the story was totally without foundation. Still, the message was out and about. One last example: in the year 2008, an older snapshot in the pages of the *Drudge Report* showing the presidential candidate Barack Obama on a visit in Kenya created a bit of a stir. Obama was wearing a turban and traditional African clothing.[13] The message of the image, which — according to Drudge — had been sent by supporters of the then rival candidate Hillary Clinton, seemed unambiguous: an alien is trying to grab the office of American President, a man with a turban on his head, not a true American.

---

org/web/20000819015036/http://www.brillscontent.com/features/cryer_1198.html (Retrieved 24 September 2013).

[13] On the debate about the origin and the effect of this image see: Allen, Mike (2008) Obama slams smear photo. In: *Politico*, 25 February 2008, http://www.politico.com/news/stories/0208/8667.html (Retrieved 24 September 2013).

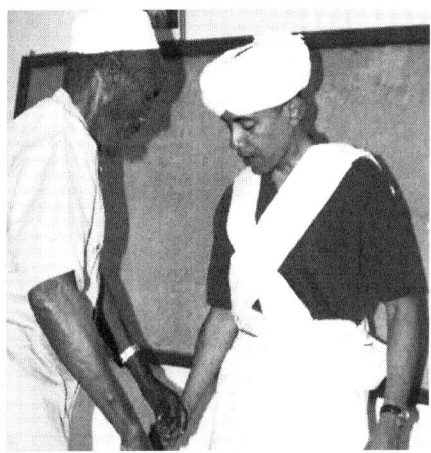

Figure 3: **A photograph of the American presidential candidate Barack Obama with a turban on his head in the pages of the *Drudge Report*.**

All these examples show that the power to defame people who are different or different-minded ultimately results simply from the accumulated attention on the part of the public and the massive attention churned up by the established mass media. The different media wind each other up, link headlines, propagate exclusive stories about presumed affairs — and make the contents of the *Drudge Report* appear ever more significant.[14] *Attention — whether positive or negative — is the central capital of the website; once attention has been created it will, in a cyclical process of self-reproduction, generate ever new waves of attention.*[15] The enormous impact of Matt Drudge's topic-setting can certainly, on the one hand, be attributed to the anxious-nervous political

---

[14] Structure and presentation style of the *Drudge Report* are described in the following article: McClintick, David (1998) Town crier for the new age. In: *Brill's Content*, November 1998, http://web.archive.org/web/20000819015036/http://www.brillscontent.com/features/cryer_1198.html (Retrieved 24 September 2013).

[15] Franck, Georg (1998) *Ökonomie der Aufmerksamkeit. Ein Entwurf* [*The Economy of Attention: An outline*], Munich/Vienna: Carl Hanser Verlag.

Washington scene, which—especially in times of election campaigning—diligently follows his *Report* and fears nothing more than an uninhibited smear campaign from the other camp.[16] Drudge owes his influence, on the other hand, to the television and radio stations that invite him, thus styling him as an expert and a greatly feared opponent of the Establishment and thus raising him to the status of a serious commentator. And he, finally, owes it to all the readers and bloggers who link him, the newspapers that quote him, and the critics whom he provokes and disgusts. Up to 900 million page views per month hit his extremely artless *Drudge Report* (consisting of a few lines and hyperlinks in black and red ink, some photographs, a collection of standard links), according to the agency responsible for acquiring his advertisements. 2 million visitors on average are counted every weekday. Matt Drudge, whom *Time Magazine* already in 2006 (significantly enough in the category "artists and entertainers") had reckoned to be one of the 100 most influential people in the world, has long been established as a most susceptible *gatekeeper of the second order*, operating according to very personal and occasionally extremely subjective standards. He refers to existing and already reported information very effectively and sometimes exclusively, and rearranges already given arrangements (i.e. information and content presented by the media) for other audiences. He acts as a human aggregator—and sometimes also, rarely enough, as a more or less serious

---

[16] "Drudge's chief influence derives from the links he chooses to highlight on his site", write the political journalists Mark Halperin and John F. Harris, "although his own exclusives (however inaccurate they may be at times) certainly stir up conversation. If a political item is prominently displayed on the *Drudge Report*, it is guaranteed that the topic will be talked about by people who matter in modern campaigns. It will colour the perceptions of journalists and campaign strategists and even candidates. It will prompt questions at news conferences and White House briefings. And some of this trickles down to the voters, many of whom habitually read the *Drudge Report* themselves." Halperin, Mark/John F. Harris (2006) *The Way to Win: Taking the White House in 2008*, New York: Random House, p. 53.

discloser of exclusive items of news that are actually results of his own research. Whatever he writes, according to the magazine of the *New York Times*, can trigger a "tsunami of public mentions", although the traded stories and mini-tales may seem to be utterly irrelevant from the perspective of traditional newscaster journalism.[17] "Now with a modem", Matt Drudge writes in one of his rare programmatic statements, "anyone can follow the world and report on the world. No intermediary, no big brother. And I guess this changes everything."[18] The fundamental principle illustrated by the man with the modem, the protagonist of a feverish-aggressive sensationalism operating with ever new approaches and garish headlines, can be condensed into the formula: *mass beats content; the simple overkill by the attention of the big audience marginalises the question of relevance.* What is made to appear important becomes important.

2. Jessica Cutler and the illusion of intimacy

Mechanisms of self-revelation

Jessica Cutler was never really aiming at a big audience. Her blog from Washington was intended for the eyes of a few friends only — De Luca from San Diego, Rachel Robertson from New York, and one or two other girlfriends whose names remain unknown. Her blog, she felt certain, was just an insignificant and hardly recoverable needle in the haystack of digital data.[19] No stranger would ever discover what she had written;

---

[17] Weiss, Philip (2007) Watching Matt Drudge. In: *Nymag.com*, 24 August 2007, http://nymag.com/news/media/36617/index5.html (Retrieved 24 September 2013).

[18] See: Matt Drudge at the National Press Club on 02 June 1998, www.youtube.com/watch?v=tkk7VUMSUlo&NR=1 (Retrieved 24 September 2013).

[19] This chapter is based on newspaper articles, published books, and personal interviews with Jessica Cutler conducted via e-mail. On the reconstruction of the case see, in particular: Witt, April (2004) Blog interrupted: When Jessica Cutler put her dirty secrets on the web, she lost her job, signed a book deal, posed for Playboy — and raised a ton of

no (possibly unauthorised) browser would show even the slightest interest. A password for the defined audience consisting in a personal circle of friends would, therefore, be unnecessary, Jessica Cutler felt with certainty. Her own little life, the stories about occasional alcohol excesses and parties, sex and expensive clothes, and the unutterably boring job of sorting and distributing the mail in the office of the Republican senator Mike DeWine in Washington would be nothing but tedious and uninteresting for outsiders. She really did not want to force her friends to type in a password every time. Despite her relaxed attitude to the newly created spheres of publicity she nevertheless decided, when creating her online diary, that her blog should not be accessible via *Google*. She tested her arrangement repeatedly and beyond that made sure that a certain measure of anonymity was guaranteed for all the participants—a minimum of privacy in the public sphere that she deemed sufficient. She called herself *Washingtonienne* and coded the names of her friends and ex-friends, her workmates and sex partners, by using the initial letters of their first and second names. She went online with her blog on 5 May 2004 for only 13 days. On 18 May 2004, she frantically tried to delete all her postings and to wrest what she had written from the rapidly emerging big audience, to reverse the process of an unexpectedly expanding self-revelation and to restore a sphere of intimacy for herself and her sex partners. Without success. *Her case demonstrates the mechanisms of self-exposure on the grounds of insufficient media competence.*

In a first posting on 5 May 2004 at 17.48h Jessica Cutler, alias *Washingtonienne*, presented herself to a micro-public with a few sentences of precisely targeted information. "I have a 'glamour job' on the hill", she wrote. "That is, I could not care less about gov or politics, but working for a Senator looks good on my

---

questions about where America is headed. In: *Washington Post Magazine*, 15 August 2004, p. 12; Solove, Daniel J. (2007) *The Future of Reputation: Gossip, rumor, and privacy on the Internet*, New Haven/London: Yale University Press, pp. 50ff.

résumé. And these marble hallways are such great places for meeting boys and showing off my outfits." In the days that follow, she writes about parties, American television series, her difficulties of living off a small office salary. She notes in passing with whom she had lunch, how long they were kept waiting to gain entrance to an in-venue, and what the usual gossip was in the office. The principal topics of her diary entries, which she always composes at the desk of her senatorial office, are the sex escapades with different men. Among them are married men and some "generous older gentlemen" who give her presents and sometimes even pay her—a fact that worries her and even makes her feel guilty. She therefore takes great care to make the money handover as casual as possible. There are friends and ex-friends who visit her for a few hours and for erotic adventures. At some stage, one of the female readers of her blog loses her orientation in the maze of different initials and sex stories—and demands an explanation, i.e. a sort of comprehensive table. On 11 May 2004, Jessica Cutler obliges and writes: "By popular demand, I have finally created a key to keeping my sex life straight. In alpha order: AJ=The intern in my office whom I want to fuck. F=Married man who pays me for sex. Chief of Staff at one of the gov agencies, appointed by Bush. J=Lost my virginity to him and fell in love. Dude who has been driving me crazy since 1999. Lives in Springfield, IL. Flies halfway across the country to fuck me, then I don't hear from him for weeks. MD=Dude from the Senate office I interned in Jan. thru Feb. Hired me as an intern. Broke up my relationship w/QV (see below). MK=Serious, long-term boyfriend whom I lived with since 2001. Disastrous break up in March, but still seeing each other. R=AKA 'Threesome Dude.' Somebody I would rather forget about. RS=My new office bf with whom I am embroiled in an office sex scandal. The current favourite. W=A sugar daddy who wants nothing but anal. Keep trying to end it with him, but the money is too good. Shit. I'm fucking six guys."

Front region and back region

Her special favourite is a man in the senator's office whom she refers to with the initials "RS" — his actual initials. Their relationship — his bad luck — starts right in the decisive blogging phase. Jessica Cutler meets him on 6 May, thinks she is falling in love with him, begins to consider marrying him, but develops a bad conscience because she has already given away some intimate details to her colleagues in the office. Eventually she presents "RS" in ever greater detail, creates an informational mosaic that facilitates identification and step by step demolishes the private sphere of the unsuspecting man. The man is Jewish and has a twin brother. He is a co-worker and lives in the Northwest of Washington. She goes on to divulge that he enjoys beating or being beaten during sex, that he has problems with condoms and that there are handcuffs in his house which he would like to use on her. She also records conversations about an Aids test, the number of ejaculations, and the causes of erectile dysfunction. Then again, she writes: "But last night was fun. He's very up-front about sex. He likes talking dirty and stuff, and he told me that he likes submissive women. Good, now I can take it easy in bed. Just lay back and watch him do freaky shit." The idea of a marriage along these lines, Jessica Cutler notes, might seem somewhat bizarre, however. After all, they would not practise sex like man and woman but rather something ugly and crude. In brief: *this blogger utilises the hybrid Internet medium under the illusion that she can determine the desired mode of communication according to her own free will, as if her intentions and a few scanty precautions to protect anonymity were sufficient.*

At this point, a key concept of sociologist Erving Goffman comes in handy to advance the analysis. It is the distinction between "front region" and "back region" or "backstage" introduced in his book *The Presentation of Self in Everyday Life*.[20] The back region, according to Goffman's theoretical conceptions,

---

[20] Goffman, Erving (1959) *The Presentation of Self in Everyday Life*, New York: Doubleday, pp. 106ff.

comprises communicative situations and interactions that are invisible to outside observers. Consider, for instance, the kitchen of a restaurant — a classic example. A waiter is a person that continually crosses the threshold between backstage and the front region. The waiter's behaviour must adapt to the situation in the restaurant as soon as he enters this region. The waiter must assume the correct posture, speak the right kind of language, and must conform to the generally prescribed conventions of restaurant service. Facing the guests, waiters may possibly appear servile. In the secluded back region, however, they may bitch, mock, whinge. In the back region, things may happen that must not be seen in the front region. People say things there which are not intended for a wider public. However, the backstage is not a physically-materially tangible place (although Erving Goffman's kitchen and restaurant example might erroneously suggest something like that). It represents a sphere that is characterised by the exclusion of a particular segment of the public and is not necessarily tied to a specific place or locality. It is a different and peculiar world of information and communication inhabited and sustained by a defined number of people.[21] The guests of a restaurant have no place in the kitchen, they are located in the front region, where things are done and shown in a way that can and ought to be perceived. It is the sphere of socially acceptable presentation and action. In the front region, norms and conventions are in force. Here role concepts may turn into corsets, which must be endured if one wants to be part of things. Moreover, here one shows indignation if backstage communication or some more or less hidden behaviour suddenly becomes manifest. These considerations

---

[21] On this understanding of "place" and a media-analytically oriented new conception of the sociology of interaction and situation by Erving Goffman see: Meyrowitz, Joshua (1990) Redefining the situation: Extending dramaturgy into a theory of social change and media effects. In: Stephen Harold Riggins (ed.) *Beyond Goffman: Studies on communication, institution, and social interaction*, Berlin/New York: Mouton de Gruyter, in particular pp. 87ff.

and distinctions help to provide a more precise analysis and understanding of Jessica Cutler's communicative drama — a drama permanently enacted in the digital age because the backstage regions of our lives have become threatened spheres, and because apparently stable barriers of communication and perception have turned out to be extremely tenuous. The analysis of this case with the help of the guiding distinctions introduced by the sociologist Erving Goffman makes clear: *Jessica Cutler practises backstage communication without any front region awareness, without any sensibility for the possibility of quick audience change and the rapid transformation of the backstage into a dazzlingly illuminated front region.*

Unmasking in real time

On 18 May 2004, her birthday, Jessica Cutler meets the married man whom she refers to as "F" — and then returns to her office in the afternoon.[22] "I just took a long lunch with F and made a quick $400", she notes at 14.10h. "When I returned to the office, I heard that my boss was asking about my whereabouts. Loser." A little later she finds two messages on her computer. The first one is: "Oh my God, you're famous." The second one provides a sort of explanation: "Your blog is on Wonkette." The reference is to a website of Ana Marie Cox, much read in Washington, a mixture of gossip, satire, and political news, combined with sex stories. One of Jessica Cutler's friends had almost certainly given the decisive tip to gossip journalist Cox by sending a link. Thus, *Wonkette* attracted one and a half million visitors in May 2004 alone, and Washington was presented with a nationally commented sex scandal. *This very link unveiled the backstage region of the communicative events that had up to now been taking*

---

[22] The following quotations are from *Wonkette*, from the later indictment by an ex-lover of Jessica Cutler's, and from diverse extensively documented versions of her blog that have survived and are still circulating on the Web. We cannot present evidence in detail here; it would overload bibliographies and source references. We recommend again the precise reconstruction of the case by Daniel J. Solove and April Witt.

place within a private universe of friends; it quasi-blasted it open. The present case shows that the range of operations of a personal public sphere, originally intended to encompass but a narrowly bounded and clearly defined target group, cannot be safeguarded effectively. Apparently, audiences can no longer be scaled properly.[23] *A single mouse click makes it possible to fuse previously separate spheres of communication and enclaves of meaning and to make intimate information public.* In the early afternoon of 18 May, *Wonkette* offers the following text: "A girl after our own heart (She's so getting a book deal out of this). We realize that some of you who follow this link will never come back: Compared to our humble blog, Washingtonienne has half the politics and twice the ass-fucking. And she apparently gets paid for it. The ass-fucking, we mean. (Wish we'd thought of that.) But how could we not introduce you to her? She's like a Hill-based Belle de Jour and is full of, uhm, good advice."

During the hours that follow a bizarre battle begins between the two women, which may be seen as a confrontation of two principles. On one side is a comparatively powerless Jessica Cutler who initially tries desperately to defend her private sphere but soon resigns and seeks to turn the public attention achieved into personal advantage. On the other side is Ana Marie Cox, who reacts with a mixture of playful amusement and brutality. She acts as a protagonist of aggressive investigation work, who in effect determines the dramaturgy of what happens and the timing of events. Jessica Cutler first attempts to cover her tracks, logs onto *blogger.com*, hurriedly deletes her own blog and tests the link on *Wonkette*, which yields the desired result: "Page not found." However, her online diary has already become a central topic of conversation by now. First printouts are available, the news travels at lightning speed, and

---

[23] On the inadequate scalability of the public and other features of personal public spheres see: Schmidt, Jan (2009) *Das neue Netz. Merkmale, Praktiken und Folgen des Web 2.0* [*The New Net: Features, practices and consequences of Web 2.0*], Konstanz: UVK Verlagsgesellschaft, pp. 107f.

the decisive link jumps from computer to computer. Lover "RS" —a printout in his hand—appears in her office to announce the end of their relationship. A female colleague whom she had characterised as a "pimp" screams at her. Jessica Cutler leaves her place of work in shock. Immediately after the deletion of *Washingtonienne* a message combined with a search request appears on *Wonkette*: "The Washingtonienne blog appears to be busted/pulled down/a figment of my imagination. Let me know if you can confirm its continued existence." At 16.07h she is practically being hunted with a search warrant. "We're starting to feel a little bad about Washingtonienne", a message with feigned sympathy runs. "In any case, we hope Washingtonienne isn't gone for good. And we hope she still has a job. A real one. Not the ass-fucking one. (That's really more of a profitable hobby.) If you did get your walking papers today, sweetie, drop us a line. We'll see what we can do. (And, uhm, if anyone else has heard about some sudden dismissal of a female staffer this afternoon... We'll think of something to trade.)"

A good hour later the news breaks that *Washingtonienne* has been fired. Moreover, already at 18.32h the blog that has just been deleted can be read again. Obviously, a careful reader had saved it for reasons of precaution, and then sent it to Ana Marie Cox, who immediately made it accessible online again. Now the story jumps onto the traditional mass media. Jessica Cutler is transformed into a media celebrity who is rewarded with attention in exchange for her scandal production. She becomes a topic not only in the political scene of Washington but also in numerous national newspapers, television stations, magazines. Articles appear in the *Washington Post*, the *New York Times*, the *Manchester Guardian* and the *National Enquirer*, in the *Scotsman*, the *Star*, and the *New York Post*. Even the *Times of India* joins in and labels Jessica Cutler as "New-insky", alluding to Monica Lewinsky and the sex scandal with Bill Clinton. *Washingtonienne* has by now been identified as Jessica Cutler. Gutter journalists of the *National Enquirer* offer her 10,000 dollars for names as it seems possible that some influential and powerful politicians in Washington may have been among her sex partners.

Search game for informers

The Net abounds with fervid speculation about the identity of her different lovers, and thus begins a sort of mischievous search operation run by a diffuse collective that is bent on unmasking anonymous people and on enjoying the very action of ripping masks from faces. Ana Marie Cox also fuels this search. *The classic quest of a single individual is here replaced by unmasking operations performed collectively in public – another common pattern – a diffuse public participates by combining fragments of information in a happy-go-lucky way.*[24] In the case at hand, the following happens: Cox places the photographs of such potential suspects online as match the descriptions in the blog in some way or other; no clear explanation of the actual matching operation is given. On 20 May 2004, the following text is published (together with 13 photographs of purported suspects and the headline "Would you sell sex to this man?"): "We've put together a lineup of all the pictures of male chiefs of staff that we could find. The only thing left to do is to figure out which one of these guys looks like he has to pay for sex." However, the search game for informers does not yield defensible findings and results which could be reported on *Wonkette*. The call for a collective manhunt and the publicist experiment based on nebulous suspicions prove unsuccessful. Nevertheless all this is instructive because it reveals the popular enthusiasm for shared puzzle work geared towards assembling fragments of information to construct a genuine, real-life identity – with all the consequences and side effects for those who are accidentally caught in the sights of the self-appointed search battalions. For a short time one Frank Jimenez, concealed behind "F", is, for instance, suspected to belong to the circle of Jessica Cutler's lovers.

---

[24] There is an analogous case that has been intensively debated in Germany: the rapid unmasking of purported paedo-criminal men who were shown in an RTL2 programme *Tatort Internet* [*Crime Scene Internet*] in a poorly anonymised form and could eventually be identified – some even during the airing of the show – by Net searches carried out by inventive spectators.

Friends of his anxiously enquire, when the false accusation emerges, whether his career is now over. He is put under massive pressure. But he is saved because the adduced fragments of information do not really fit the bill: Jimenez is single; the lover in question is married. He is publicly exonerated by Ana Marie Cox, and she also publishes a cautious-anxious letter he had sent her in order to dispel the very last traces of doubt. Jimenez states that he had never in his life felt so happy living his life as a single person. In addition, he had never paid for sex and the favours of a woman. He succinctly comments the brief threat of losing his reputation in the *New York Times*: "I would hope that bloggers would be more circumspect about what they post on the Web: it's no different than old-fashioned gossip spread by word of mouth, but modern technology has magnified its impact a millionfold, and it's potentially more harmful because of its permanence."[25]

The capitalisation of attention

One reason for the failure of the amateur sleuths is that Jessica Cutler refuses to give names and to verify suppositions. However, she starts giving interviews and makes — together with Ana Marie Cox — a television appearance that is still retrievable from the Web. She changes her strategy, intuitively, it might seem. Her effort to protect her secrets turns into an attempt to cash in on the oppressive excess of attention that she has been subjected to. Her approach could be termed *scandal surfing* (in analogy to *agenda surfing*, the attempt to profit personally from an unanticipated topic career); she seeks to exploit the public outrage following her behaviour and turn it to her own benefit by capitalising on the attention achieved, i.e. to transform the

---

[25] Rosen, Jeffrey (2004) Your blog or mine? In: *New York Times*, 19 December 2004, http://www.nytimes.com/2004/12/19/magazine/19PHENOM.html (Retrieved 26 September 2013).

disadvantage of public scandalisation into material advantage and profit.[26]

> **Scandal surfing**
>
> Scandal surfing is a special strategy of topic management. Whenever the reporting of certain news items cannot be stopped, suppressed, or controlled directly, people may try to derive profit from the attention that has been created. In the minority of cases, the scandalised persons attempt off their own bat and with their own methods to make some kind of capital out of the negative attention directed at them — here Jessica Cutler would serve as a prime example. More frequently, however, comparatively uninvolved commentators raise their voices, order the sequence of events, and exploit the waves of outrage for their own interests, their own political parties and camps, etc. The scandal is merely a vehicle to launch their own ideas and stories in the media.

Jessica Cutler's chosen kind of role play is staged skilfully and with a sound sense for effective provocation. She celebrates her new status as a scandal blogger, her good looks, her sangfroid, and she performs without any visible sign of remorse. "I'm not naming names", she states in an interview. "I'm not ashamed of anything I wrote in the blog. And people are sad if they're interested in such a low level sex scandal. I wrote the blog not to ruin people's lives. It was just for the amusement of me and my friends." She undresses for *Playboy*. She pockets a $300,000 advance payment for a book contract and submits to her agent's order not to give any interviews before the book is published. A year after the scandal she publishes a hastily formulated *roman à clef* with the title *The Washingtonienne* — a scantily camouflaged reconstruction of her office and sex experiences. The book

---

[26] On the different strategies of topic management (agenda setting, agenda cutting, agenda surfing) see Brettschneider, Frank (2002) Die Medienwahl 2002. Themenmanagement und Berichterstattung [Media choice 2002: Topic management and news reporting]. In: *Aus Politik und Zeitgeschichte*, 09 December 2001, issues 49–50, p. 38.

kindles some interest in the American film industry.[27] (The pilot film produced by Sarah Jessica Parker in the same mould as *Sex in the City* turns out to be a flop, however.) Even American intellectuals and culture theorists are noticeably fascinated by this young woman and her private normative parallel universe. Jessica Cutler impresses them as an icon of a post-feminist generation, living an ironic-aggressive individualism and a radical sexuality devoid of any traces of sacredness.[28]

Jessica Cutler's ad-hoc celebrity does not last, however, and the attempt to present her as an exemplary character is not really successful. *The scandal involving her person loses its potential to excite and fascinate paradoxically through the very act of publication and its massive dramatisation. More generally: scandals produce and cannibalise outrage; they arouse it and thus simultaneously generate the conditions of its gradual fading out.* This peculiar logic of scandalisation forces the core events into a universally human cycle of attention and consideration that consists of different phases and a clearly definable point of culmination. Nobody can be permanently outraged by one and the same story for weeks and months. If it proves impossible to discover a new angle or a new drama from time to time, the consequence is that stories quickly begin to lose their medial attractiveness; this too is demonstrated by the Jessica Cutler case. When "RS" sues her for the sum of 20 million dollars and later even starts legal proceedings against her publisher, the media only occasionally report on the court case that drags on for several years and finally forces Jessica Cutler to file for bankruptcy. In the text of the indictment "RS", later employed as a lawyer by a university, states: "No reasonable person would want the intimate physical, verbal, emotional, and psychological details of his or her sexual life and romantic relationships exposed against his or her will on the

---

[27] Cutler, Jessica (2005) *The Washingtonienne*, New York: Hyperion.
[28] Witt, April (2004) Blog interrupted: When Jessica Cutler put her dirty secrets on the Web, she lost her job, signed a book deal, posed for Playboy — and raised a ton of questions about where America is headed. In: *Washington Post Magazine*, 15 August 2004, p. 12.

Internet for the entire world to read. It is one thing to be manipulated and used by a lover, it is another thing to be cruelly exposed to the world."

The confrontation in a court of law is, however, not really suitable for creating a sensation because it does not add anything essential to the known events. The reporting is therefore gradually reduced. When Jessica Cutler marries a young lawyer from New York in October 2008, there is hardly a newspaper that wants to cover it. The *New York Times* rejects articles by a freelancer. Only the website of *The Daily Beast* publishes an extensive account that again assembles all the relevant links four years after the scandal happened and, furthermore, supplies answers to the question how "The D.C. sex blogger [...] went from slut to housewife". There is the name and the profession of the new man and a sort of relationship practice protocol that does not exclude even the most insignificant detail: the first meeting in a bar in New York, the first night together, and the day of the wedding. In addition, there is an image of the newlyweds. The style of the article is reminiscent of a blog. The author seems more than well informed, even close. It is Jessica Cutler.

3. *WikiLeaks* and the uncontrollability of the data

Document of a manhunt

As far as one can be certain, Bradley[29] Manning, the 22-year-old American soldier, is not fully aware of the explosive content of the video recording that he is about to send to *WikiLeaks*.[30] He is

---

[29] On 22 August 2013, Bradley Manning made the announcement that he would like to live as a woman, and wants to be called Chelsea. However, in the following chapter the name Bradley is used because Manning became known to the public with that name during the *WikiLeaks* scandal.

[30] This chapter is based on a large number of sources, among them the self-presentations by *WikiLeaks*, chat transcripts, films, Net debates. Here is the alphabetical list of the most important books and articles: Domscheit-

in no way sure, at first, he will later put on record, how to categorise and interpret what was happening. What were the shots for, why laughter, why dead people? Why was there a minivan and why were children injured? Is the recording just showing the dirty and bloody reality of war — or a criminal act? It is a 40-minute recording made through the camera of an Apache helicopter. Under the title *Collateral Murder,* it will trigger a scandal and cause worldwide outrage. It will make *WikiLeaks* a global brand and the Australian Julian Assange, the man behind *WikiLeaks*, a media star, and an information activist of a new type. Bradley Manning, in a US prison since the early summer 2010, has been facing trial by military court. Years in prison await him. The video recording is quite clearly not showing the normality of war. What Bradley Manning makes known to the world public, with the aid of the whistleblowing platform *WikiLeaks*, appears to be far more probably the document of a manhunt. At first, we get the bird's eye view of the helicopter camera and the marksman and see a dozen people walking along the street, one of them talking on a mobile phone, another

---

Berg, Daniel (2011) *Inside WikiLeaks: My time with Julian Assange at the world's most dangerous website*, New York: Crown Publishers; Flade, Florian (2010) US-Soldaten töten Reuters-Journalisten in Irak [US soldiers kill Reuters journalist in Iraq]. In: *Welt Online*, 06 April 2010, http://www.welt.de/politik/ausland/article7069862/US-Soldaten-toeten-Reuters-Journalisten-in-Irak.html (Retrieved 23 September 2013); Görig, Carsten/Kathrin Nord (2011) *Julian Assange. Der Mann, der die Welt verändert* [*The man who changes the world*], Berlin/Munich: Scorpio; Khatchadourian, Raffi (2010) A reporter at large: No secrets. Julian Assange's mission for total transparency. In: *New Yorker*, 07 June 2010, http://www.newyorker.com/reporting/2010/06/07/100607fa_fact_kh atchadourian#ixzz1HRLail8k (Retrieved 23 September 2013); Knobbe, Martin (2010) Dieses Milchgesicht blamiert die USA [This milksop disgraces the USA]. In: *Stern*, 02 December 2010, pp. 30–42; Rosenbach, Marcel/Holger Stark (2011) *Staatsfeind WikiLeaks. Wie eine Gruppe von Netzaktivisten die mächtigsten Nationen der Welt herausfordert* [*Enemy of the State WikiLeaks: How a group of Net activists challenges the most powerful states of the world*], Munich: Deutsche Verlags-Anstalt; Sifry, Micah L. (2011) *WikiLeaks and the Age of Transparency*, New Haven/London: Yale University Press.

one carrying a camera. Not all of them can be identified. But today we know that the man carrying the camera was the Reuters journalist Namir Noor-Elden, and the man talking on the mobile phone was his Iraqi driver Said Chmagh.

One can hear the ritualised radio communication of American soldiers followed immediately afterwards by hammering shots. One of the soldiers reports that he recognised about six persons, armed with an assault rifle and an anti-tank missile. He claims to have heard shots—a further disastrous message, fatal for the people on the ground.[31] Some of the audible fragments of sentences are "All right, firing.—Let me know when you've got them.—Let's shoot.—Light 'em all up.—Come on, fire!—Keep shoot'n, keep shoot'n, keep shoot'n.—[…] —All right, we just engaged all eight individuals.—Yeah, we see two birds and we're still firing.—Roger, I got 'em.—[…]—Oh, yeah, look at those dead bastards.—Nice.—[…]—Good shoot'n. —Thank you." The driver of the Reuters journalist, four-times father Said Chmagh, has survived the first attack. Bleeding, he crawls across the ground seeking shelter behind a house wall. High above in the circulating helicopter the soldiers debate whether to finish the man off and how to justify the final shot. "All you gotta do", one of the soldiers says jokingly, "is pick up a weapon." Then a minivan rushes on the scene, two men jump out and try to pick the man up and carry him into the van. These are civilians driving a boy and a girl to school. What now happens is reminiscent of the sequences of a videogame—only with real casualties and genuine dead human beings. The helicopter targets the civilian helpers and their van and shoots with armour-piercing ammunition. "Oh yeah, look at that", one of the soldiers calls, "Right through the windshield!" American ground troops eventually hit upon the injured and the dead individuals strewn about the area. The heavily injured children

---

[31] It is apposite to emphasise that the assessment of what happened has been controversially debated among journalists. There is no reliable verification.

are still alive and taken to an Iraqi hospital. The father of the children is dead.

Figure 4: **Stills from the** *WikiLeaks* **video** *Collateral Murder*, **showing how American soldiers kill human civilians in the East of Baghdad.**

Again, a voice can be heard from the helicopter, saying that one of the vehicles has probably driven over a corpse, and that that was not really tragic at all because the people down there were dead anyway. And the children? "Well, it's their fault", one of them says, "for bringing their kids into a battle." "That's right", another one affirms. The soldiers then fly — as the video shows in its complete unedited version — to another place of action. They shoot at a building where armed insurgents are supposed to hide; it belongs to an English teacher, according to investigations by *WikiLeaks*, who claims that his wife and daughter were killed in this attack. Here again the criminal aggression of the soldiers flying across the city becomes strikingly obvious for the observer. *The images shot by the camera, which eventually travel round the world, are inexorable in their documentary power. They render the suspicion entertained by the individual observer a proof of guilt for the wider public.* In the complete version of the video recording, one can observe a casual passer-by who saunters past the entrance to the building shortly before the bombardment begins — an unarmed man, without any recognisable connection to the presumed or actual enemies inside. It would have taken him two or three minutes to leave the danger zone but the soldiers in the Apache helicopter had no intention of waiting that long. He is blown up and killed without the slightest hesitation, without even a minimum of reflection or a single moment of doubt.

Technical competence and social needs

Bradley Manning discovered this document of a manhunt at the end of the year 2009 in the data stock of an army lawyer, which he is entitled to access like many other American civil servants and soldiers. It cannot be ascertained with total certainty and in detail how and under what circumstances this happened; the essential clues come from an extensive chat transcript involving Bradley Manning and the well-known American ex-hacker Adrian Lamo published by the technology magazine *Wired*.[32] As far as one can be certain, Bradley Manning was looking for a like-minded person, contacted Lamo (probably alerted by a

---

[32] The transcripts may be consulted at the following Net address: http://www.wired.com/threatlevel/2010/06/wikileaks-chat/ (Retrieved 23 September 2013).
    There is a detailed analysis as well as a concise translation of some of the passages in the following book: Rosenbach, Marcel/Holger Stark (2011) *Staatsfeind WikiLeaks. Wie eine Gruppe von Netzaktivisten die mächtigsten Nationen der Welt herausfordert* [*Enemy of the State WikiLeaks: How a group of Net activists challenges the most powerful states of the world*], Munich: Deutsche Verlags-Anstalt.

Wired portrait of the hacker published on 20 May 2010), started chatting with him hour after hour—and finally gave away the background of his spectacular action of disclosure. Manning and Lamo chat on for several days, often for many hours, and in this dialogue the soldier and betrayer of secrets tries to understand what he has done, how his scoop should be assessed, as the effects of such actions can never be predicted with ultimate certainty. The chat oscillates between soliloquy and confession. There is the obvious slang of the hacker and the slang striving for coolness; there are phases of casual talk, but there is also the struggle for a moral stance that would make the action appear legitimate and justified by a higher morality and a public interest. "I've been so isolated so long", Manning writes, "I just wanted to be nice, and live a normal life... but events kept forcing me to figure out ways to survive... smart enough to know what's going on, but helpless to do anything... no-one took any notice of me." On the day the *Wired* portrait goes online he nevertheless makes contact again by way of encrypted e-mails that Lamo is, however, as he claims, unable to open due to an out-of-date PGB key. The actual chat, therefore, starts on the AOL Instant Messenger Service *AIM*, as Lamo had suggested. Manning adopts the easily decipherable identification code "bradass87", standing for Brad or Bradley and the abridged variant of the year of his birth 1987. This sort of serious carelessness of the chats displays a general pattern of action, which is clearly understandable from a human point of view but which will seal Bradley Manning's fate. Personal, often enormous, technical competence (the prerequisite for hermetically sealed and undetected operation) is counteracted by mental and social needs (that eventually lead to Manning's unmasking, his public demolition, and his criminal trial). *The desire for human exchange and the feeling of being able to speak with a like-minded person engender the loss of control. People become careless, trusting, and thus create the conditions for committing treachery as traitors that even produce their own key traces.*

The streams of information and communication between Bradley Manning and Adrian Lamo soon become public. Only two days after the beginning of the chats Lamo talks to his father, contacts acquaintances asking for advice, and as early as 25 May meets with agents of the FBI and members of Army Counterintelligence in a Californian coffee shop. He finally hands all his materials over to them—the chat transcripts, the first contact e-mails of the soldier. He had become very worried, he will say later at a conference of hackers, that Manning's masses of data could endanger "American lives". The consequence of the unmasking of the unmasker: shortly afterwards, the soldier Bradley Manning is arrested and detained in a military prison. Even at this stage, he commits another grave mistake which will further incriminate him, probably prompted by the urge to justify himself and a feeble last-ditch attempt to regain at least a minimum of control over the interpretation of his actions. He asks his aunt to place a status-notice on *Facebook*, and he tells her his password. His *Facebook* site then carries the message: "Some of you may have heard that I have been arrested for disclosure of classified information to unauthorized persons. See CollateralMurder.com."

Scandals at your fingertips

Back to the chronology of events, the decisive turns and contents of the chats. Lamo quite skilfully eggs Manning on, as *Spiegel* journalists claim to have discovered, to confess more and more. (The published chat transcripts do not contain the relevant passages at the outset.) He tells him that he is a journalist, and that their conversations are, therefore, protected by Californian press laws. He adds that he is also an ordained preacher and that everything said is, in any event, covered by the seal of the confessional.[33] Manning quite obviously trusts him, names

---

[33] Rosenbach, Marcel/Holger Stark (2011) *Staatsfeind WikiLeaks. Wie eine Gruppe von Netzaktivisten die mächtigsten Nationen der Welt herausfordert* [*Enemy of the State WikiLeaks: How a group of Net activists challenges the most powerful states of the world*], Munich: Deutsche Verlags-Anstalt, p. 145.

his approximate place of work ("Eastern Baghdad"), and even broadly describes his job. At various points in the conversation he appears somewhat surprised himself by what he is telling a total stranger whom he has never personally met in his life: "I can't", he writes, for instance, "believe what I'm confessing to you." His personal-private key experience had been, he says, the imprisonment of 15 men who had been falsely arrested by the Iraqi police — scholars who had been active in fighting the corruption of the political elite in the entourage of the Prime Minister Nuri al-Maliki. Manning was ordered to investigate the case and with the help of a translator found out that the men were not criminals but critical intellectuals. He had immediately informed his superior about the result of his investigation but this officer simply didn't want to know and instead ordered him to go out and help the Iraqi police arrest more people and catch more criminals. Experiences of this kind had increased his already existing doubts and made it clear to him that he "was actively involved in something that [he] was completely against..." Manning: "everything started slipping after that... I saw things differently."

In the chat, the American soldier with the perilous yearning for exchange and clarification reveals, for instance, that he has sent 260,000 documents from US embassies to *WikiLeaks*, documents that throw a garish light upon the backgrounds of American diplomacy. He has, furthermore, delivered Guantanamo files to the white-haired "Aussie" (the Australian Julian Assange) and his organisation. These data sets, together with the "Gharani airstrike videos" and the "Iraq war event log", the Guantanamo files, and finally that "State Department cable database", are the significant highlights. They simply must not be secreted "on some server stored in a dark room in Washington, DC", they are public data whose knowledge is vital for the people. Bradley Manning writes: "Hillary Clinton and several thousand diplomats around the world are going to have a heart attack when they wake up one morning and find an entire repository of classified foreign policy is available, in searchable format, to the public." This embarrassment and this demolition appear to him as a "world-wide anarchy in CSV format" and as a "climategate with a global scope, and breathtaking depth... it is beautiful, and horrifying". He notes that hundreds of scandals are concealed in these materials, and that he is actually astounded how easy it was for him to get hold of the materials and to remove them from the office. The safety precautions of the network environment that he went to work with in his Iraqi base, "Hammer", were rudimentary but existent. The computers for accessing information classified as secret, for instance, were not connected to the generally available Internet. Soldiers could not simply connect USB sticks to their computers — that would have made it too easy to load them with crucial data and smuggle them through the lax controls to the outside world.

Figure 5: **Bradley Manning, the *WikiLeaks* informant, in uniform. He has been sentenced to 35 years in prison.**

The crucial security gaps, however, were the CD and DVD drives that could not only play music and films but also store materials. Therefore, Manning used a rewritable music CD that he had labelled "Lady Gaga". He deleted everything and copied the data of the network onto this CD. It was extremely easy and nobody suspected anything. "[L]istened and lip-synced to Lady Gaga's Telephone while exfiltrating possibly the largest data spillage in American history", he states quite frankly. Despite the extremely critical aspects of the situation, this act demonstrates in a strangely curious and anecdotal manner some elementary facts of the digital age. *In the digital present, data sets can be rapidly copied with no loss of quality, they can be copied easily without anyone taking notice, and they can be transported without much effort. Filing cabinets for storing mountains of information and trucks to transport conspicuous tons of paper under everybody's eyes are no longer necessary. Basically just one CD is needed to store and shift enough material to put pressure on a world power.*[34] A brief reminder, for the sake of comparison: in the year 1971 Daniel Ellsberg, a high-ranking official in the American Ministry of Defence, circulated the so-called *Pentagon Papers* — secret documents unveiling the scandalous propaganda tricks of his government during the Vietnam war. The whistleblower Ellsberg, today a defender of *WikiLeaks*, needed months to copy a few thousand pages.[35] It took several months for excerpts from the *Pentagon Papers* to appear in leading American newspapers like the *New York Times* and the *Washington Post*.[36] Bradley Manning,

---

[34] Cf. here the illuminating essay on the loss of control in the digital age published by Michael Seemann on 06 April 2011 under the title "Vom Kontrollverlust zur Filtersouveränität" [From the loss of control to the sovereignty of filters]: http://carta.info/39625/vom-kontrollverlust-zur-filtersouveranitat/ (Retrieved 25 September 2013).

[35] Gellman, Barton (2010) Person of the Year 2010: Runners-Up. Julian Assange. In: *Time.com*, 15 December 2010, http://www.time.com/time/specials/packages/article/0,28804,2036683_2037118_2037146,00.html (Retrieved 25 September 2013).

[36] A reporter of the *New York Times* recently asked Daniel Ellsberg what he would have done with the *Pentagon Papers* in a media situation like the present one. His answer: "I wouldn't wait that long. I would get a scanner and put them on the Internet." Pitzke, Marc (2010) Left-wing icon Daniel Ellsberg: "Obama deceives the public". In: *Spiegel.de*, 09 June 2010. http://www.spiegel.de/international/world/left-wing-icon-

the whistleblower of the digital age, is suspected of having delivered a total of nearly half a million documents from the Afghanistan and the Iraq wars to *WikiLeaks*, plus the 260,000 reports by American diplomats. "A new phenomenon at a new front, a new asymmetric threat, which the US government was not prepared for", write Marcel Rosenbach and Holger Stark in their book *Staatsfeind WikiLeaks* [*Enemy of the State WikiLeaks*]. "The other side that wants to create greater transparency needs no more than an USB stick or a rewritable CD and access to the Internet. From the perspective of the military and the secret services this is the scenario of a nightmare."[37] The fact remains, in any case: the actual act of stealing can be executed comparatively quickly; the transfer of huge masses of data can be achieved in no time. In addition, the sheer quantity generates a different quality of disclosure: access is now possible for a since indefinable, unbounded public. *The scandal of this new type gains its momentum also by virtue of the sheer bulk of the manageable data, e.g. the publication of whole archives, which seems to entail that events can now be examined and controlled by everyone.*

The speedy recoverability of contradictions

The discovery of the helicopter video is also extensively explored in the chat transcripts from which only selections have yet been published. "[A]t first glance", Manning writes in the chat, "it was just a bunch of guys getting shot up by a helicopter... no big deal." Nevertheless, he thought it odd that a minivan should also emerge in the recording—obviously not a proper war machine, rather a family car. In addition, it was somewhat strange to find this material stuck with an army lawyer. He therefore takes a closer look, watches the video

---

daniel-ellsberg-obama-deceives-the-public-a-699677.html (Retrieved 10 July 2013).

[37] Rosenbach, Marcel/Holger Stark (2011) *Staatsfeind WikiLeaks. Wie eine Gruppe von Netzaktivisten die mächtigsten Nationen der Welt herausfordert* [*Enemy of the State WikiLeaks: How a group of Net activists challenges the most powerful states of the world*], Munich: Deutsche Verlags-Anstalt, p. 17.

recording several times, and reconstructs the date and the place of events. It is 12 July 2007. The shots, he establishes, are fired in the East of Baghdad. Bradley Manning enters the coordinates into the query slot of *Google* and hits upon an article in the *New York Times* describing the official army version of the event. The title of the article: "2 Iraqi journalists killed as U.S. forces clash with militias." In the text it says: "The American Military said in a statement last Thursday that 11 people had been killed: nine insurgents and two civilians. According to the statement, American troops were conducting a raid when they were hit by small-arms fire and rocket-propelled grenades. The American troops called in reinforcements and attack-helicopters. In the ensuing fight, the statement said, the two Reuters employees and nine insurgents were killed. 'There is no question that coalition forces were clearly engaged in combat operations against a hostile force', said Lt. Col. Scott Bleichwehl, a spokesman for the multinational forces in Baghdad."[38]

A more theoretical analysis of Manning's perceptual situation makes clear what profound cognitive effects a quick search of the Net and the resulting discovery of an increasing number of even more shocking items of information can have. For Manning is suddenly confronted with two different representations of one and the same event that contradict each other. To put it simply, what he sees does not correspond with what he reads. And these contradictions are immediately accessible to him due to the novel potential of the new medium. The strange observations and their upsetting implications are easy to diagnose. The importance of this situation lies in its consequences. *The scandal gains directly in comprehensible and persuasive evidential force through the rapid immediate realisation of discrepancies between different versions of reality. The scandal is fuelled by the obvious*

---

[38] Rubin, Alissa J. (2007) 2 Iraqi journalists killed as U.S. forces clash with militias. In: *New York Times*, 13 July 2007. http://www.nytimes.com/2007/07/13/world/middleeast/13iraq.html (Retrieved 26 September 2013).

contradiction resulting from the confrontation with, and the comparison of, contrasting visual and/or textual messages. It must be remembered that such divergent and contrastive versions of reality are the fundamental elements of effective disclosure in both the analogue and the digital world. They supply the energy needed for the whole business, which accompanies the unmasking process and drives it forward; and they are, quite independently of the media in play, the basic material of scandalisation. There are signs of the violation of a norm that is of public importance, here: signs of a potential war crime. At this point, two different interpretations of the events are available — and only one of these two can be correct. Either the soldiers have killed insurgents, attackers, and erroneously two employees of the news agency Reuters, or human beings have been killed arbitrarily and unnecessarily for no defensible reason. Such versions of reality and radically diverging interpretations can now be contrasted and compared in detail — due to the accessibility of the material on the Net (entering the coordinates in the query slot of *Google*, a click that leads to the *New York Times* article). One can, therefore, as demonstrated by the present case, quickly acquire the necessary supporting evidence for a more substantial grounding of one's suspicion, and then continue researching until one reaches the point of disclosure and individual outrage may become publicly effective.

The control of the controllers

Having discovered the video recording, Manning, as the transcripts show, does not immediately react to this experience of discrepancy; he is not yet quite sure what to do. In January 2010 he, therefore, sends a first and relatively harmless document on the banking crisis in Iceland to *WikiLeaks*. It is published on 18 February 2010 — as a sort of test run, a first still very cautious attempt at dealing with the whistleblowing platform and, in particular, with a form of whistleblowing that may possibly shake the world in a flash. In February, too, the helicopter video reaches *WikiLeaks*, camouflaged by means of an anonymising network — and is published in a shortened and edited version on 5 April 2010. After a mere two weeks, six million viewers have watched on *YouTube* the crime of the American soldiers gunning down a group of defenceless human beings. Julian Assange flies to Washington from Reykjavik and presents the scandal document at a conference of the National Press Club, speaking of "war crimes". Worldwide press coverage sets in. The scandal stirs up global outrage. As early as 7 April 2010, the blogger and media theorist Michael Seemann offers an impressive clear ad-hoc analysis of the ontology of the digital age: the potential for radical transformation, the potential for placing data in ever different, ever new contexts that may challenge the goals the data were originally intended to serve, may even frustrate them. *Contextual fidelity, in the digital age, may be revoked with the blink of an eye.* "It is ironic", Michael Seemann writes, "that the cameras, which are installed in the helicopters and painstakingly record all their missions, are essentially part of a huge machinery of control. […] Thanks to up-to-date technology, the Supreme Command is now present in the air with every single mission. And now we all are, too. For the machinery of control is turning into a machinery of control loss. As soon as data exist, their range can no longer be securely fenced in. Control loss intensifies with the increased use of media. In addition, the media will multiply from the journalists to the soldiers, their victims, and right on up to those silent witnesses of the Supreme Command that record everything in a cold and impassive manner. Then all it finally needs is the tiniest leak. The loss of control has reached its culmination point: Wikileaks."[39]

---

[39] Seemann, Michael (2010) Wikileaks und eine postbaudrillardsche Frage der Informationsethik [WikiLeaks and a post-baudrillardian question of information ethics]. In: *ctrl+verlust*, 07 April 2010, http://www.ctrl-verlust.net/wikileaks-und-eine-postbaudrillardsche-frage-der-informationsethik/ (Retrieved 25 September 2013).

The boomerang effects of disclosure

Seemann's diagnosis and interpretation, despite its hasty production, appears consistent and convincing. At a closer look, however, it points to yet another phenomenon that must claim equal interest. What we observe are ultimately failing attempts at communication and control, which involve the various informants and disclosers themselves. They suddenly appear transparent, too, but against their will and their original intentions. Touching spheres of power, they provoke research operations aimed at disclosing their very own motives, their origins, and their ideologies. *It appears that in these increasingly wide-ranging processes of control loss even the disclosers and the informants are stripped of their secrets. They are no longer subjects but have turned into objects; they can no longer be independent observers but are themselves observed; and they prove unable to control the flow of information according to their wishes.* The (short) history of *WikiLeaks* unfolds precisely in this polarised field of tension between attempted control and sudden control loss. At first, the operators of *WikiLeaks* seek to stage the loss of control as perfectly as possible for the others, the powerful, the attacked, and the embarrassed. They offer a stable ethos, maximum security for informants, promise potentially worldwide attention in cooperation with the traditional guiding media. Eventually, however, the *boomerang effects of disclosure* and the violence of an undesired and indomitable publicity take its grip on the informants and information controllers. Finally, even the internal life of the organisation *WikiLeaks* is unveiled. Defectors contact media, chat transcripts emerge, discrediting documents appear on the Net. Increasingly the central agent, *WikiLeaks* founder Julian Assange, becomes the object of undesired attention and suffers himself the kind of *loss of informational control* that he wanted to impose on everyone else, the opposite sides (the USA, Scientology, Sarah Palin, the members of a fascist party in the UK). Suspected sexual penchants and details of his intimate personal life are made public in connection with an allegation of rape.

It seems worthwhile to summarise the most important dates and publications for the purpose of a survey, a search for traces and patterns. In October 2006, the domain *wikileaks.org* is registered. The inspiring model may have been provided by the website *cryptome.org* of the New Yorker John Young, who had been publishing primarily secret documents since 1996. Young advocated a radical concept of informational freedom and transparency and initially cooperated with Julian Assange. In November 2007, the crucial scoop is landed: *WikiLeaks* publishes the internal guidelines for the treatment of the prisoners in Guantanamo. (The documented practices are partially in breach of international law and the Geneva Convention and show, furthermore, that the Red Cross has been actively barred from seeing individual prisoners.) In 2008, bizarre internal matters from the world of Scientology and the founder of this sect, the science fiction writer L. Ron Hubbard, are made public. In September of the same year, the Republican candidate for the Vice-presidency, Sarah Palin, is attacked because she has evidently been using her private e-mail account for business activities in order to circumvent the duty of documentation obligatory for holders of public office. Then the list of the members of the British National Party (BNP) is published, which confirms that quite a few members of the police force have signed up to this fascist party. In November 2009, *WikiLeaks* publishes the correspondence of leading climate researchers, which demonstrates that the debate about the dimensions and the consequences of global warming is not always carried out with decent means and methods. The Minton Report, a study commissioned by the company Trafigura, is published in the same year. It exposes dangerous and extremely health-damaging toxic waste dumping in Africa organised by Trafigura, which had already claimed several lives. (Trafigura had successfully managed to prevent the *Guardian* newspaper from publishing these findings. *WikiLeaks*, however, not being a tangible concrete opponent for the company lawyers, proved to be a much more formidable opponent.)[40] After a few other "minor"

---

[40] *WikiLeaks* can no longer be removed from the Net; copies of the materials

scandals, the crucial scoop, the video *Collateral Murder,* is published on 5 April 2010. Further stacks of documents follow, published in synchrony and in cooperation with prestigious quality media (*Der Spiegel, New York Times, Guardian*). A new form of agenda-setting is born, capable of arousing and engineering global outrage and generating potentially worldwide commotion and horror.

The mirroring of sites — why censorship is bound to fail

When the US electronic commerce company Amazon banished the *WikiLeaks* sites from its web servers at the beginning of December, the suggestion was advanced to mirror the sites of the whistleblowing platform, i.e. to make exact copies of the sites and keep them accessible on the servers of supporters. Within a very short period of time, 1500 so-called mirrors were accumulated. Censorship and information control had thus become impossible. The Internet would have to be switched off in its entirety to prevent general access to undesirable information. *WikiLeaks*, in addition, made it easy for its supporters: anyone signalling readiness to offer servers was asked to set up these servers and data banks with proper ports of access. The *WikiLeaks* team itself then performed the mirroring of the sites and updated the mirrors as soon as new content was placed on the original *WikiLeaks*-run servers. Copying websites is easy and without problems, anyway, and does not really require external assistance. A special search program, a crawler, will help to scan every site of the World Wide Web and save it page by page. The crawler follows all the links referring to the sub-pages of the website and saves the source codes of the pages. No expert knowledge is required for these copying processes; the relevant programs can be downloaded free from the Net. To make the mirrored sites accessible, some web space on a server must be supplied. The only snag: the copies are not necessarily up-to-date because they obviously represent a momentary state.

---

are available on numerous servers.

De-spatialised simultaneity

In this phase of a highly successful scandalisation, at the latest, a generally valid but nevertheless specifically effective feature of the modern media of communication is made manifest, which the sociologist and scandal investigator John B. Thompson termed *de-spatialised simultaneity*.[41] The example of the *WikiLeaks* website and the new scandal communities demonstrates one decisive fact: *countless people, wherever they are on this globe, can now occupy themselves with the same topic, millions can now simultaneously follow one and the same scandalous event without great expense*. Simultaneous reception only requires functioning Net access.

A few other examples of spectacular publications that have found their worldwide audience may be cited here. On 25 July 2010, the "Afghan War Diary" goes online. It comprises 76,911 documents that show the hidden dark side of the war in Afghanistan. Revealed are failed operations, fatal for children and innocent people, secret commando and death missions of US special units. The *New York Times*, the *Guardian* newspaper, and the leading German news magazine *Der Spiegel* report on numerous pages — and again catapult *WikiLeaks* documents to the top of a globally effective agenda. The "Iraq War Logs" published on 22 October 2010 comprise 391,832 reports documenting the death of thousands of civilians. They are the most comprehensive publication of military documents in the history of the USA. On 28 November 2010, the first secret status reports by US diplomats are published: "Cablegate" — internal assessments and personal-private judgements of various foreign politicians sent to the US State Department by US embassies.

In these months of frenzied activities of disclosure, Julian Assange is put under mounting pressure; details of a suspicion are made known. Two Swedish women accuse him of sexual harassment, of having forced them to have unprotected sex. A

---

[41] Thompson, John B. (2005) The new visibility. In: *Theory, Culture & Society*, vol. 22, no. 6, p. 37.

first arrest warrant is issued in August 2010 and scrapped shortly afterwards "due to incompleteness", but reissued in November. Conspiracy theories and cryptic hints at the "dirty tricks" of secret service agencies begin to circulate. A trap has been set for him, it is rumoured. The two Swedish women are suspected of being involved in a defamation scheme. Swedish bloggers and *WikiLeaks* sympathisers publish the name of one of the plaintiffs, then a photograph and a copy of her visiting card. Nevertheless, after some shilly-shallying, Interpol issues a warrant of arrest for Julian Assange. On 7 December 2010, he is arrested in London, released on bail for a high sum of money, has taken refuge in the Ecuadorian embassy in London. The *Guardian* newspaper quotes extensively from the police investigation files.[42] There is information on the (purported) details of the sexual encounter with the two women, on the conversations about contraception and possible diseases, on a burst condom (whose image can still be found on the Net today). The magazine *Wired* reports that the case files of ca.100 pages have been posted on some website for data exchange; the case files contain interrogation transcripts, photographs, notes of the investigators. Now, at the latest, the boomerang effects of transparency become manifest. *The activist of disclosure turns from hunter into hunted quarry, from the defender of a world without secrets into an individual whose existence is mercilessly illuminated right down to the last intimate detail.* During these months of dramatic demolition and controversy, some *WikiLeaks* activists approach the media with insider information. Former staff member Birgitta Jonsdottir talks to the American news website *The Daily Beast*

---

[42] On the case file and the reporting by the *Guardian* and *Wired* see: Davies, Nick (2010) 10 days in Sweden: The full allegations against Julian Assange. In: *Guardian.co.uk*, 17 December 2010, http://www.guardian.co.uk/media/2010/dec/17/julian-assange-sweden (Retrieved 25 September 2013); Saarinen, Juha (2011) Documents in Julian Assange rape investigation leak onto Web. In: *Wired*, 02 February 2011, http://www.wired.com/threatlevel/2011/02/wikileaks-sweden/ (Retrieved 25 September 2013).

and calls on Assange to withdraw as spokesman for *WikiLeaks* until the investigations of the allegations have been concluded. The German spokesman for the organisation, presenting himself as Daniel Schmitt (he is, in fact, Daniel Domscheit-Berg), voices his criticism in the magazine *Der Spiegel*. Having left the organisation, he and the journalist Tina Klopp publish a revelatory report with the title *Inside WikiLeaks* that becomes a bestseller. He creates the rival organisation *OpenLeaks*. In a weekly newspaper he discloses that the diplomats' dispatches of the US State Department are circulating on the Net in a wholly unedited form, due to a combination of misfortunes and slipshod operations. In addition, his associates provide first hints as to where the password can be found — a loss of control and a total disgrace for *WikiLeaks* with potentially life-threatening consequences for the informants who can now be identified by the whole world. And right at the onset of the constantly escalating quarrels, chat transcripts emerge that show how dysfunctional and poisoned the relationship between Julian Assange and his once most valued collaborator and friend must have been for a long time, how much suspicion, distrust, and pure terror must have reigned before Domscheit-Berg's final defection. Julian Assange, in an extreme situation, threatened him with death if he were to put documents at risk, Domscheit-Berg asserts. He quotes Assange: "If you fuck up, I will hunt you down and kill you."[43] It is still unclear who published the chat transcripts. It is still unclear what to make of the allegations of rape and sexual harassment, and how the whole story will end. It still cannot be assessed what the future of the organisation and its founder will be like. But this is of no real importance here. The important thing to note is, however, that the great scandals as well as the most private episodes, the possible wrongdoings and trickeries, all illustrate the fact that the

---

[43] Domscheit-Berg, Daniel (2011) *Inside WikiLeaks: My time with Julian Assange at the world's most dangerous website*, New York: Crown Publishers, p. 71.

chances to keep a collectively shared secret intact in the digital age have been significantly diminished. "Wikileaks has made us all aware", so the Net and journalism observer Jeff Jarvis says, "that no secret is safe. If something is known by one person, it can be known by the world."[44] The threshold for the effective, far-reaching treachery is radically lowered by the possibility of global publication; it has become extremely easy for a carrier of secrets to publish them. *The secret has turned into information that is waiting to be given away.*

Models for the marketing of secrets

One may ask oneself, however—independently of the actual events surrounding Julian Assange and the theoretical considerations of the new lightness of treachery—how the marketing of secrets was functioning inside the organisation. What were the procedures? What principles can be ascertained at least in retrospect? And in what ways did one (with even greater efforts for global effects) present the materials? The author and blogger Micah L. Sifry, in his book *WikiLeaks and the Age of Transparency,* distinguishes three models for the processing of material and the marketing of secrets, which provided guidelines during the years between the foundation and the establishing of the organisation. First, between 2006 and 2009, the dominant principle is to *document largely unedited information*, to strive for maximum neutrality. The obvious weakness of this principle: it creates the danger of the possibly all too careless publication of ultimately irrelevant, defamatory, or simply false data—with all the consequences and side effects for innocent and defenceless people who, all of a sudden, find themselves pilloried. Then there follows the hybrid phase of a publicist-journalistic self-empowerment in which *WikiLeaks* acts as editor.

---

[44] Jarvis, Jeff (2010) Transparency: The new source of power. In: *Huffington Post*, 05 December 2010, http://www.huffingtonpost.com/jeff-jarvis/transparency-the-new-sour_b_792213.html (Retrieved 25 September 2013).

The video entitled *Collateral Murder* is a shining example here. The edited version lasting a good 17 minutes was prepared by Julian Assange and his collaborators; the additional investigations, the visits to the places of the action, the processing of the statements of witnesses, and the hospital file, were carried out independently or contracted out, in order to verify the circumstances of the events. All these procedures are essentially not without their problems. The principal question is—also for informants—whether the collaborators of the whistleblowing platform have the required journalistic competence, whether they know how to contextualise and evaluate sources, how to plan and organise an investigation as impartially as possible, and how to edit the material in a media-adequate way.

Eventually the *model of the cooperation with quality media* is developed—presumably in order to deal adequately with the masses of available material, to avoid endangering innocent people, and to minimise failure by self-overestimation. This makes abundantly clear that good journalism is indeed indispensable; nothing else can guarantee the kind of professional research required to verify the accuracy of information, to reduce complexity prudently, and to evaluate things according to a transparent hierarchy of relevancies. The history of *WikiLeaks* undoubtedly also demonstrates that societally important truths do not simply establish themselves but need the functioning machinery of verification and stimulus enhancement of the mass media with their powers of sustainable topic setting. "The increasing accumulation of documents", Daniel Domscheit-Berg writes, for example, in an article about the weaknesses of *WikiLeaks*, "could no longer be processed."[45] In the meantime, mountains of material are screened and evaluated by well-established journalists, editorial decisions are delegated to independent professionals—and *WikiLeaks* is thus

---

[45] Domscheit-Berg, Daniel (2010) Der gute Verrat [The good betrayal]. In: *Freitag.de*, 14 October 2010, http://www.freitag.de/autoren/der-freitag/der-gute-verrat (Retrieved 29 September 2013).

downgraded to the rank of a powerful supplier and intermediary for large quantities of data. The materials therefore remain, one can read in a book by two journalists, "a valuable, in parts unique, mine for journalistic work",[46] nothing more. What is finally disclosed and judged relevant has to be worked out independently—in accord with all the standard rules of the profession. Different media enterprises that cooperate with Assange take this view and want to have him classified as only one source amongst others.

In this phase of the interaction, a classic technique of effective scandalisation is reintroduced: it consists in reapportioning the material and developing an independent dramaturgy of disclosure that operates with a melange of repetitions and revelations of more or less spectacular bits of news and details connected with the topic. In this way effects are maximised. Even this model has its drawbacks, however, because it immediately runs up against the problem of who is to be granted exclusive access to the material, who is the actual proprietor of the material, and who has the ultimate authority to take decisions. *For the marketing of scandals is – without question – a potentially extremely lucrative business in an increasingly escalating battle for attention.* Thus, Julian Assange is said to have threatened to sue the *Guardian* newspaper for acquiring the internal diplomatic dispatches through a former co-worker of his and planning to publish them without his consent. Assange, it is reported, said that he was the proprietor of the material and that it was also of economic relevance when and how it was published. Relations deteriorated, too, because Assange had allegedly supplied a television station with precarious documents without first consulting his other media partners. Assange apparently even tried to remove the *New York Times*

---

[46] Rosenbach, Marcel/Holger Stark (2011) *Staatsfeind WikiLeaks. Wie eine Gruppe von Netzaktivisten die mächtigsten Nationen der Welt herausfordert* [*Enemy of the State WikiLeaks: How a group of Net activists challenges the most powerful states of the world*], Munich: Deutsche Verlags-Anstalt, p. 9.

from the global media association of scandalisers following the paper's publication of a critical personal portrait, i.e. to punish the quality paper by an information ban. In brief: claims to property rights and insistence on exclusivity at the very moment of enormous public resonance again concentrate publicist control on a single person, i.e. invest this particular person with extraordinary powers—and thus counteract the plea for transparency and neutrality entered and advertised by *WikiLeaks. In the extreme case, the informant and information rebel turns into a censor for reasons of self-interest, who lays down what may be published where and when.* He is then—paradoxically enough—a gatekeeper in his own right who proceeds according to his own gusto and acts as a control freak for his own ends, who wants to impose the ending of control on all the others with the exception of himself. The history of *WikiLeaks* and its founder shows their rapid rise and dramatic falls, but it also demonstrates that such self-contradictions will not remain hidden and cannot be kept secret. One day they will become manifest, unavoidably, it seems.

4. Karl-Theodor zu Guttenberg and the power of a swarm

The laws of the old world

The scandal starts according to a classic pattern of the old media.[47] On 16 February 2011, the then Minister of Defence of Germany, Karl-Theodor zu Guttenberg, finds himself con-

---

[47] The following chapter draws on a previous publication by Bernhard Poerksen and Hanne Detel. See: Poerksen, Bernhard/Hanne Detel (2011) Evidenzerfahrungen für alle. Das kontraproduktive Krisenmanagement des Verteidigungsministers und die Logik der Skandalisierung im digitalen Zeitalter [Experience of evidence for everyone: The counterproductive crisis management of the Minister of Defence and the logic of scandalisation in the digital age]. In: Oliver Lepsius/Reinhart Meyer-Kalkus (eds.) *Inszenierung als Beruf. Der Fall Guttenberg* [*Staging as an Occupation: The case of Guttenberg*], Berlin: Suhrkamp Verlag, pp. 56-70.

fronted with evidence presented by Andreas Fischer-Lescano, university professor of law, which purports to show that parts of his thesis have been surreptitiously copied from other sources. The first account is published by *Süddeutsche Zeitung*, the leading liberal national daily newspaper in Germany. At first, no more than a few instances of plagiarism are revealed. And the laws of the old world still appear to be intact. Guttenberg promptly rejects everything, choosing the strategy of belligerent denial. A first written statement of the Minister of Defence issued on the same day declares that the allegations are "abstruse" and that his thesis is no plagiarism. And he also emphasises, without any recognisable anxiety, that he has produced his work unassisted by other people and without contributions by a ghostwriter. The journalists of people-magazines, in particular *Bild,* the leading popular daily tabloid, are on the alert, too, and provide support by means of independent articles accompanied by reader interviews. The ultra-brief summary of the pop daily's line is finally publicised by the author Franz Josef Wagner on 17 February 2011 in one of his notorious columns where he writes: "I have not the faintest idea of doctoral theses. I botched my final school exams. And I have never seen a university from the inside. Therefore, I can say from the outside: Do not wreck a good man. Fuck the doctorate." The obvious goal is to retain an extremely popular politician and Defence Minister in office, a man who is judged to be predestined for higher tasks (Prime Minister of Bavaria, Chancellor of the Federal Republic of Germany). There are many who consider him an exceptional specimen of the independent and abrasive politician who does not descend to the use of clever tactics—who is even prepared, in case of emergency, to put his own career at risk, to tender his resignation, if particular decisions are not to his liking. Some revere him as a "luminary" (*Bild*). Large sections of the public take the view that the man should stay, that the man is needed. However, already on 1 March 2011, the Minister of Defence declares his resignation and in a dramatic statement formulates the following sentences: "I have always been prepared to fight. But I have reached the limits of my powers."

What has happened? A first answer is that between 16 February and 1 March events start accumulating dramatically and the laws of the old world are rapidly losing their power. The affair turns out to be an exemplary demonstration of the hazardous and in the end unsuccessful management of scandal and crisis. It is instructive to see that the patterns of action and appeasement are recognisably those of a former era, a period where key media possess enormous power and can, in the extreme case, topple a politician or retain him in office. They possess the sovereignty of interpretation with reference to the decisive dimensions of what is happening. The sequence of events in that period still show a certain linearity, and they still follow well-established routines of scandal mongering as well as ingrained rituals of public conciliation. At the beginning, there are informants who have noticed a supposed or factual violation of a norm and report it to a medium (at least according to the ideal-type and naturally always somewhat artificial picture of the process delineated by the manuals of investigative journalism). The observations are then examined in relation to their factual substance. Informants then generally undergo a credibility check. They are asked for their motives, their sources, and their milieus. To what extent can their claims withstand severe scrutiny? Are there further indications pointing in the same direction? What are their interests, whom might they want to damage, and for what reasons? In other words, professionally trained journalists engage in research-intensive *gatekeeping*. In the slightly polemical words of Axel Bruns, they exercise "a regime of control over what sorts of content dealt with in the production processes of the printing and the broadcasting media will be made public".[48] They decide whether the viola-

---

[48] Bruns, Axel (2009) Vom Gatekeeping zum Gatewatching. Modelle der journalistischen Vermittlung im Internet [From gatekeeping to gatewatching: Models of journalistic communication via the Internet]. In:

tion of the norm corresponds with the facts as they see them, whether it is of relevance to their own media and their own addressees, whether it should therefore be made public. The checking of facts is necessarily carried out *before* publication. In this world, evidence and rumours are followed by investigation, then by the first revealing report, a possible denial, and finally by the debate about who is right and who is to be believed, and for what reasons. In this world, campaigns can function because particular key media may launch directed initiatives, may execute sovereignty of interpretation, and may establish valid interpretations. They determine what the people of a country ought to know—and what not. As gatekeepers, they blaze the trail towards the final determining judgement. In this world, the public is inescapably forced to trust the information and the views of the influential investigators or those of the advocates of the accused because they have no access to the whole truth or the massive amount of possible evidence and counterevidence. Whoever wants to come by that kind of knowledge would have to build up potentially contradictory sources, in order to arrive gradually at a judgement—without being able to claim the particularly robust and stable certainty that emerges only from personal perception and experience. Such attempts by individuals to arrive at sound judgements independently may involve time-intensive detours and patient, long drawn-out puzzle solving if they are to achieve final success at all. They absorb power and concentration. Therefore, someone who suddenly finds himself accused and is aware of these fundamental difficulties of assessment will play for time and use cunning tactics, will mobilise the outspoken public support of political party friends, set up frontlines, and transform questions of morality into questions of power. They may operate with denials and distractions based on the presupposition of unquestionably given prospects of

---

Christoph Neuberger/Christian Nuernbergk/Melanie Rischke (eds.) *Journalismus im Internet* [*Journalism on the Internet*], Wiesbaden: VS Verlag für Sozialwissenschaften, p. 107.

success—always in hope that the public will follow the personal interpretations, that the public may never be quite assured and convinced, anyway, and that the public will at some stage lose interest because other supposedly or actually more important topics dominate the headlines and other scandals claim the front pages. However, these laws of the old world are no longer unreservedly reliable in the digital age. The new agents, once condemned to passivity and dependent on the grace of the gatekeepers whenever they sought publicity, can now be key.

Crowdsourcing and the organisation of self-organisation

As early as the evening of 16 February 2011, diverse blogs show first warnings of further evidence of plagiarism. One day after the ad-hoc denial of the Minister, a furious doctoral student enters the scene of the scandal proceedings and performs—together with many helpers—a change of role in full view of an astounded public. He turns into an informant practising in public, albeit anonymously; his identity gives rise to all sorts of rumours. His name: PlagDoc, probably a coinage fabricated from the English concepts *plagiarism* and *documentation*. Using free software (*Google Docs*), he first creates a document—and in the early hours of the morning calls on people to collaborate through the micro-blogging service *Twitter*. However, after only six hours he has to announce relocation to another platform due to overloading, a platform called *GuttenPlag*. This is a *Wiki* whose functioning may now be studied in its entirety and with all due clarity: *participation is open to everyone; the roles keep changing in varying proportions between producers and recipients of texts*. Everyone may create their contributions, may correct the contributions of others, may simply study them, may aggregate the collectively produced results to more easily digestible diagrams, images, etc. In this case, there is an unambiguously defined common goal, namely the fast and comprehensive unmasking of the incorrigible plagiarist, and furthermore, by way of consequence, a maximum of individual research creativity with regard to the spotting of newspaper articles, essays, English-language publications, and of all manner of seminar and examination papers, all of which had been used by the Minister to create the collage of his thesis. It thus becomes clear what a swarm trained to focus on such an unmasking project is capable of achieving. It is not just the wisdom of the many floating freely about the digital universe which may be observed here. Such a view would be too sweeping and too imprecise—just a trendy cliché without any real analytical power.[49] What is at work and what increases and secures the swarm's performance is, however, a *combination of hierarchical and heterarchical principles*—a hybrid model that could be called *organised self-organisation*, inspired and directed by the anonymous PlagDoc and the small circle of directly initiated collaborators.[50] There are the administrators that delete entries, exclude users, marginalise agitators, and secure the conscientious debate amongst the participants.[51] The hybrid model mixes self-governance and governance by others, control and trust, concrete action guidance and general appeals to mobilise participation and collaboration. One can discover extremely precise analyses and swift success in detail discovery; one notices a culture of playfulness and dramatics, even feverish sleuthing, that definitely no longer resembles a harmless collective game of puzzle solving and guesswork. Continually, users register themselves because they have spotted something and now want to join the army of volunteers that tirelessly supplies ever more fresh evidence that is then collectively analysed and verified. Those who agitate and defame or play

---

[49] See for example: Surowiecki, James (2005) *The Wisdom of Crowds*, New York: Anchor Books.

[50] On the organisation of self-organisation see: Foerster, Heinz von/Bernhard Poerksen (2002) *Understanding Systems: Conversations on epistemology and ethics*, New York/Heidelberg: Kluwer Academic/Plenum Publishers/Carl-Auer-Systeme, pp. 90ff.

[51] More detailed information on PlagDoc and the dynamic initiatives of organised self-organisation is provided by Preuß, Roland/Tanjev Schultz (2011) *Guttenbergs Fall. Der Skandal und seine Folgen für Politik und Gesellschaft* [*Guttenberg's Fall: The scandal and its consequences for politics and society*], Munich: Gütersloher Verlagshaus, pp. 59ff.

the "buffoon" (PlagDoc's characterisation of this type of user) are removed for the simple reason that the activists want to present themselves with something like scientific sangfroid in their official announcements and publications. The programmatic declaration on the very first page of the *Wiki* runs: "We should like to make quite clear that this undertaking has nothing to do with political orientation, with a personal smear campaign or anything along these lines. Our goal is to safeguard the academic integrity of the title of Doctor in Germany so that one can safely expect all those who have earned this kind of title to possess the competence of correct scholarly procedure. By exposing the existing instances of plagiarism in the thesis under discussion, we want to facilitate the work of the examining committee of the University of Bayreuth. Should theses written by politicians at the other end of the political spectrum also be found to be 'distinguished' by plagiarised sections, we would have no problems whatsoever to proceed in the same way."

It becomes apparent, furthermore, that there are time and work schedules, that there is a well ordered all-inclusive service provided by PlagDoc and one of his fellow fighters who temporarily — because he is apparently at a conference abroad — takes care of the nightshifts from a position in the United States of America. Tools for identifying plagiarism (search engines, special software, and optimal search strategies) are introduced. The instruments of exposing fraudulent copying are to be made accessible to as many collaborators as possible and as speedily as possible. What emerges here is a most effective kind of *crowdsourcing*. The labour of unmasking is delegated to a swarm that may outdo the performance of established media houses.[52] Only one detail may be singled out, which is deeply symbolic, how-

---

[52] Pohlmann, Sonja (2011) Schwarm und Schwärmer [Swarms and swarmers]. In: *Tagesspiegel.de*, 22 February 2011, http://www.tagesspiegel.de/medien/schwarm-und-schwaermer/3872214.html (Retrieved 23 September 2013).

ever. The contributors to the documentary *Spiegel* issue—who are among the best investigative journalists of the Republic—can only track down a small fraction of examples during one single phase of their investigation and, what is more, they naturally cannot provide any immediate actualisation of the scandal events because they are hemmed in by editorial deadlines and printing dates for any particular issue of the journal. By contrast, the organised swarm develops an enormous speed in the exposure of examples of plagiarism; thus, they can make the ad-hoc denials of the Minister crumble to dust within seconds. *What has just been offered and circulated as an alternative reality is demolished immediately, in real time, so to speak.*

Crowdsourcing

Crowdsourcing is an example of swarm intelligence. Outsourcing means that some of the jobs (of a business enterprise) are delegated to external service firms. Crowdsourcing means that the mass of Internet users deals with the jobs. They work together as a community, share their knowledge, and through their cooperation generate a new quality of intelligence incomparably surpassing the performance levels of individuals. Web 2.0 and its potential of worldwide collaboration forms the basis of such crowdsourcing — sometimes paraphrased by the somewhat awkward concept of swarmsourcing. The concept was launched in public debates in 2006 by Jeff Howe's *Wired* article "The rise of crowdsourcing".

Experiences of evidence for the big public

Matthias Kremp, like many other journalists, currently occupies himself with reconstructing the chronology of events. He writes about the hunting successes of the first few days: "The very same evening, PlagDoc reported that content on 'more than 10 percent of all the pages in zu Guttenberg's doctoral thesis has been proved to be copied from other sources'. One day later, the number has grown to 29% and finally, on Saturday, the value has risen to two thirds. The activists have also compiled a synopsis of the plagiarised sources."[53] All the discoveries are categorised and recategorised as well as quantified ("944 lines of plagiarised translations") and documented variably in the form of interim balance sheets, diagrams, and images. Interested users—in the first five days *GuttenPlag* is visited 4,000,000 times—are offered a link to an easily comprehensible interactive presentation. Users may select the pages of the doctoral thesis they want to examine together with the corresponding original documents.

The practically infinite storage space of the Internet permits the accumulation of gigantic masses of items and sets of evidence, which are nevertheless extremely easy to access and can therefore potentially be examined and studied comfortably from every location on this earth with a Net connection. The documentation comprises, amongst others, the following results: pages of plagiarism of newspaper articles, pilfering from the written homework of a first semester student, reproduced spelling mistakes, argumentations swiped from prominent lawyers, the attempted intentional masking of plagiarised passages, examples of the more or less skilful stylistic adaptation of texts by other people to the personal writing style. Such are the *trade secrets of the plagiarist*, and they are rendered transparent for the recipients in a comprehensive and extremely detailed manner. The conclusions to be drawn are inescapable for all those who can read. In the words of the journalist Volker Zastrow: "Here fake and fraud have been performed systematically, in full awareness and with clear intent, not a single one of the known methods of plagiarism and camouflage has been

---

[53] Kremp, Matthias (2011) Im Netz der Plagiate-Jäger [In the web of the plagiarism hunters]. In: *Spiegel Online*, 19 February 2011, http://www.spiegel.de/netzwelt/web/0,1518,746582,00.html (Retrieved 23 September 2013).

left unused."[54] The scandalous material has thus been made accessible to the general public and allows for a *universalisation of the evidence experience* — a new dimension of insight on the part of the public that can now independently undertake the self-organised re-examination of the allegations and construct judgements accordingly, i.e. based on the concrete experience of the evidence and without great further cost as to time, money, or intellectual endeavour. The worlds of information and knowledge that once used to be strictly split between informants, journalists, and gatekeepers have begun to change shapes and colours. It is no longer the informant alone who discovers instances of plagiarism, who may experience the emotional shock of such a discovery. It is no longer just the journalist who is privileged to have this experience when examining sources of informants and undertaking independent investigations. It is the public itself that is now placed in a position to live through such experiences of evidence in all their facets — and that is now empowered (which is at least a possible effect) to disengage all judgement formation from the conditions and standards set by gatekeepers and key media that are intent upon imposing their own judgement or just one exclusive interpretation of events. The audiences of the different media might thus *emancipate themselves affectively,* and they might become outraged and revolt according to their own rules and ideas because they have undertaken independent examinations of the dimensions of the scandalised events, or because they have at least been put in a position to do so.

---

[54] Zastrow, Volker (2011) Guttenbergs verschleppter Rücktritt [Guttenberg's protracted resignation]. In: *Faz.net*, 07 March 2011, http://www.faz.net/aktuell/politik/inland/2.1673/wie-ken-den-kopf-verlor-guttenbergs-verschleppter-ruecktritt-14058.html (Retrieved 23 September 2013).

The principles of effective scandal management

It is a trivial fact, certainly, that a whole bundle of causes speeded up the resignation of the Minister. But it must be stated once again that network effects in the digital age just do not fit into the schema of trivial-linear causality. However, the massive evidence made available by *GuttenPlag* makes the crisis management of the Minister and the Federal Government of Germany appear exceptionally inept and feeble. *The reason is: the counterevidence is supplied with the denial.* Therefore, the example of this affair demonstrates indirectly, as it were, both the principles of effective scandal management and the ways in which they have been disregarded. The first and foremost principle is: one must react quickly in order to regain the power of controlling actions (*the principle of quick reaction*). Furthermore, one must — immediately — create maximal transparency, clear up allegations as rigourously as possible, lay the facts on the table — and then offer apologies in a serious and convincing act of contrition (*the principle of comprehensive clarification and trustworthy apology*). And finally: the chosen form of scandal and crisis management must never contradict the personal image as it has possibly been developed over many years, at least not in essence (*the principle of discrepancy reduction*). Paradoxically, even the disruption of all the self-staging by the scandal, even the moment of personal faltering, require a minimum of authenticity with regard to self-staging and image-cultivation, a minimum of internal consistency. Whoever has been taken to be the incarnation of the trustworthy albeit abrasive anti-politician must accordingly also be prepared to reveal deception and fraud in a straightforward way without frills — and draw the consequences. Because a personal image continues to exercise its effects and cannot simply be ignored. It is a sort of corset for the shaping and channelling of reactions, it functions as a kind of *medial straitjacket* that cannot simply be discarded as and when needed or desired. Guttenberg had always claimed a special value-orientation for his own person and for his politics. However, the affair makes clear that these very ethical-moral principles (decency, honesty) have been violated. Thus a discrepancy has become evident and public which has not been tempered by his headstrong crisis and scandal management. On the contrary, it has made him vulnerable, it has accelerated his downfall, encouraged critical reports exposing this very contradiction between the values proclaimed and the modes of behaviour now made manifest.[55]

Second-order transgression

For the moment, however, back to the chronology and the details of the events. A short while after the first general denial ("no plagiarism", "abstruse") there is a first relativisation. Guttenberg apologises for unspecified "mistakes" that his thesis may undoubtedly contain and declares that he will "provisionally" refrain from using the title of doctor. Furthermore, "all further communication about the topic" will from now be "exclusively with the University of Bayreuth", in particular with the special committee responsible for the examination of the allegations. However, he again shows himself unyielding and provokes his critics by denying any kind of fraudulent intention. He says: "At no time has there been intentional deception or have authors and sources intentionally been left unidentified." On 21 February, he finally requests in a letter to the University of Bayreuth to retract his doctoral title for good, a title this university once awarded him with the best possible grade (*summa cum laude*). And what is more, he even sharpens the tone of his own self-accusation by conceding in his letter that he committed "grave technical errors". Nevertheless he adds: "I am convinced that my work has its own scholarly merits." This pattern of confession and refusal, the *combination of confession of guilt and simultaneous relativisation of guilt* keeps recurring. At a Valentine meeting of the Hesse CDU in Kelkheim on 21

---

[55] Such water–wine debunkings (people are shown up to be "preaching water and drinking wine", i.e. they do not practise the moral standards they preach) belong among the debunking ploys especially favoured by tabloid media.

February, as well as during Question Time in the Federal Parliament on 23 February, Guttenberg again rejects the allegation that he has intentionally plagiarised and again admits to have made mistakes. He tries to curb the thrust of the increasingly fierce attacks and to quench the outrage of the opposition and certain media. In the Federal Parliament, he asserts that he will gratefully receive any "information about further mistakes". And he even suggests that his very open-minded handling of all these mistakes together with his apologies might possibly also "set an example" and serve as a general model of behaviour. This sort of hint at guilt minimalisation—which is not pursued further, though—has the clear intention of achieving a reinterpretation of this extremely precarious kind of personal scandal management so as to score moral benefit points. The friends within the party keep striving as best they can during those days to prop up the battered but still extremely popular Minister, again running the risk of unveiling contradictions and discrepancies between their own values and the deplorably slipshod justifications of the Minister's behaviour. Amongst them is, first of all, that the bearer of bad tidings, a professor at the University of Bremen, is accused of left-wing tendencies. According to another classic procedure, Guttenberg is then vigorously stylised as the *victim of a campaign,* which amounts to nothing less than an attempt to scandalise the allegations of the scandal mongers. Some friends within the party struggle hard to trivialise the plagiarism of their colleague as a lot of babble about footnotes and quoting conventions meaningful only to academics. They consider this pedantry as inappropriate and lacking piety at a time when soldiers are dying in Afghanistan and the reorganisation of the Federal Army is one of the most urgent projects requiring the Minister's full attention. The strategy here is *distraction by means of goal-directed agenda-setting.* New topics are launched, albeit without much success, which are deemed suitable to reorientate public attention and interest. On *Facebook,* spontaneously formed support groups emerge; however, their calls for public demonstrations in *real life* evaporate and remain practically without consequence.

Decision day finally arrives when the academic scholarly elite of the country feels increasingly provoked and worried by the threat to its reputation and its standards of practice—not least and especially through the scandal and crisis management of the Minister and government top brass. Federal Chancellor Angela Merkel's office releases the announcement that she did not appoint the "proprietor of a doctoral thesis" but a dynamic and successful politician. The implication is that she pleads for a sort of *personality splitting for the purpose of conciliation*. But it is precisely this separation of ministerial competence from scholarly morality and immorality that incites massive protests in academic and university milieus. As the affair progresses, numerous scholars voice their disapproval in interviews, printed articles, and letters of protest. An open letter written by several university professors is addressed to the Bavarian State Minister of Science. Doctoral students collect signatures for a letter of protest to be submitted to the Chancellor of the Republic. The doctoral supervisor of Karl-Theodor zu Guttenberg, the well-respected jurist Peter Häberle, in a public statement speaks of the "unimaginable defects" of the thesis. His no less respected colleague Oliver Lepsius simultaneously paves the way to be followed by his university in Bayreuth by expressing his assessment in a—multiply linked and quoted—television interview in the following words: "We have been taken in by a fraudster. Nobody could ever have imagined the scale of impudence with which this plagiarism was submitted. We find ourselves confronted with a degree of impudence that we have never seen before." Furthermore: "He has plagiarised according to plan, he has fabricated a hotchpotch of plagiarisms, hundreds of pages, and he believes not to have done so. He discerns a dissonance between what he has done objectively and what he subjectively wishes to have done. This is absurd." Finally, the forefront of supporters begins to fall apart. The then Federal Minister of Science, Annette Schavan—the question of whether she acted in agreement with the Federal Chancellor still remains unanswered—admits gently that she is not the only one that secretly feels ashamed of her colleague but that other party colleagues are also distancing themselves. The imminent resignation of Karl-Theodor zu Guttenberg on 1 March 2011 is first reported exclusively in the online edition of *Bild*. This is not only a last piece of evidence for the intensive cooperation and strategic partnership between Guttenberg and this pop daily but also an indication of the fact that the performance and winning power of a campaign together with a popular mass medium like *Bild* in such a constellation is clearly limited.[56]

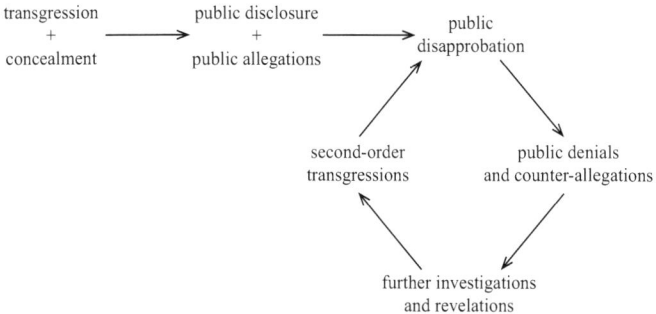

Figure 6: **The illustration shows the circular logic of scandalisation influenced by second-order transgressions.**[57]

The conclusion in the sense of a generalising summary is, therefore, that the scandal and crisis management of the Minister and the Federal Government has simply been counterproductive (irrespective of the differences between the arguments advanced). It has fuelled indignation, it has encouraged public reactions in a constantly growing number of agents of repute in

---

[56] The sovereignty of interpretation held by key media has become more fragile in the digital age, as is shown by the present case, because alternative realities have become available in a hitherto unknown multitude and variety, and because agents ready to protest may unite and form ad-hoc communities so as to derive their very own and extremely stable patterns of interpretation from the material of these realities.

[57] Thompson, John B. (2000) *Political Scandal: Power and visibility in the media age*, Cambridge: Polity Press, p. 24.

society and the media, and it has exasperated the professional academic elite because the most evident fact, the extensively documented breach of accepted scholarly norms, was so obviously held up to trivialising ridicule. Researchers of scandals have called such cases *second-order transgression.* The concept was proposed by the sociologist John B. Thompson who explains it in detail in his book *Political Scandal: Power and visibility in the media age.*

John B. Thompson shows that scandal management may itself turn into an actual scandal, in the extreme case, and that the handling of the original transgression—e.g. by means of denial or trivialisation—can possibly be interpreted as a renewed or even as the most decisive transgression. He writes: "[I]ndividuals can simply reject the allegations and deny that the transgressions took place, or deny that they were involved. But this too can be a risky strategy, since it can shift the focus of attention to the possibility of second-order transgressions which, if demonstrated, can be even more damaging for an individual's reputation than the disclosure of the original offence."[58] Things have not been quite like that in the case under discussion. Nevertheless, all the efforts to belittle the fact of plagiarism as a sort of babble about footnotes, to separate the popular Minister of Defence from the fraudulent doctoral student, i.e. to make a clean break between political competence and political morality, have so enraged the academic elite that it felt incited to hit back with forceful clarifications. The simple-minded view of the Minister, furthermore, presented with such fervent self-assuredness, that his submitted work was no plagiarism and that there had never been any intention to defraud, could only exacerbate the moral verdict and thus ignite and feed the actual scandal, constantly supplying new provoking stimuli. One conclusion may be stated in simple terms: a denial must be well founded in order to stall and diminish any

---

[58] Thompson, John B. (2000) *Political Scandal: Power and visibility in the media age*, Cambridge: Polity Press, pp. 22f.

erosion of credibility to avoid its irreversible damage. And should the denial indeed be *unjustified*, then there must at least be maximum control of the relevant communication processes, effective regulation of the access to evidence and decisive documents, if not good precautions for making such access difficult or impossible. Only in this way can a unique proprietary interpretation and view of things be preserved as the one and only reality without alternative. All this did not and could not function in the present case. PlagDoc, the furious doctoral student and conductor of an effective swarm, the publicist of a new era, kept the evidence and the counterevidence available for everyone at any time. His archive and his centre of discoveries were and are still open day and night, easy to reach, and as close as can be.

III

The New Victims & the Power of the Public

A classic definition characterises the scandal as a communicative event that reveals a "moral lapse of high-ranking persons and institutions"[1] — and whips up the moral outrage of a public whose judgement is otherwise considered more or less irrelevant. It can thus be assumed that the scandal requires a plunge from a certain height simply for dramaturgical reasons and that it owes the attention it generates particularly to the ruin of once celebrated heroes whose reputation suddenly and spectacularly implodes. According to this concept of the old mass-media dominated world, the journalists are the scandalisers, the mighty and the well-connected are the favoured objects and victims, and the members of the public form but the tail end of the communication process. They form the elements of a largely diffuse and rather passive mass whose influence is limited to honouring a bid of scandalisation with media consumption and occasional commentaries.

"No scandal breaks loose against powerless or little people" is a representative statement in an early publication on the *Phänomenologie des Scandals* [*Phenomenology of the Scandal*].[2] This kind of absolutist diagnosis is certainly no longer adequate, and

---

[1] Hondrich, Karl Otto (2002) *Enthüllung und Entrüstung. Eine Phänomenologie des politischen Scandals* [*Disclosure and Outrage: A phenomenology of the political scandal*], Frankfurt on the Main: Suhrkamp, p. 40.
[2] Gross, Johannes (1965) Phänomenologie des Scandals [Phenomenology of the scandal]. In: *Merkur*, vol. 19, no. 205, p. 400.

probably never was. The popular ("gutter", "yellow") press — tabloids and broadsheets — has always scandalised the behaviour of the powerless and the so-called little people. They have attacked purported or actual offences and produced innumerable victims by infringing their private sphere (which is, of course, part of the business strategy of this kind of popular press).[3] The reality in today's digital age is, however, that revelatory stories are directed at powerless and completely innocent people to a previously unimaginable extent. The stories and destinies of these victims are changing our conceptions of causality and proportion because they often show a seemingly strange asymmetry of cause and effect, occasion and consequence, offence and punishment. Even trivial things may now be given the scandal makeover, independently of the emotion-mongering industry of the popular press. Even completely unknown people may gain doubtful ad-hoc celebrity if the public reacts accordingly. The public may, for instance, unimpressed by the relevance prescriptions of the mass media, independently demand accountability for a self-defined grievance and thus turn from a recipient into an originator of scandals.

How should the stories of a sudden public outrage be assessed? Do they express the wisdom of the many extolled by James Surowiecki?[4] Or do individuals tangled up in a mass lose their sense of moral judgement, as Gustave Le Bon argues in his psychology, which is permeated by a pessimistic view of culture

---

[3] Media victims, according to an illuminating definition, are all those who do not push into the media and live in self-determined anonymity — and who are nevertheless exposed against their will. See: Schertz, Christian/ Dominik Höch (2011) *Privat war gestern. Wie Medien und Internet unsere Werte zerstören* [*Privacy Was Yesterday: How the media and the Internet destroy our values*], Berlin: Ullstein, pp. 58f. On the business strategies of the popular newspapers see ibid. pp. 64ff.

[4] Surowiecki, James (2005) *The Wisdom of Crowds*, New York: Anchor Books.

and a profound hatred of collectives?[5] Who is right? James Surowiecki or Gustave Le Bon? The answer: there is evidence to support both positions. Media consumer audiences in the digital age demand information and enlightenment at breakneck speed. Those seeking outrage gang together in a flurry and succumb to the storm of their cravings for revenge. In the extreme case, such clamouring for norm control leads to self-administered justice and anonymously-driven manhunts. Consequently, the morally inspired effort to perform control fails to control itself. *Scandals of a second order* arise — perhaps again registered and commented on by an attentive and morally sensitive public that now declares the means and manner of scandal mongering to be the real scandal. However, this does not always help the victims of an attack directly and immediately, even though they are unexpectedly given protection, because the stigma and the injuries will tend to linger on, albeit in altered circumstances, and all the critical commentaries and counter-commentaries may tend to fan the flames for even higher surges of outrage. The situation is only saved when the attention of all the participants begins to wane, at some later stage, and finally fades away.

1. The hounding of Gao Qianhui and the emergence of a cybermob

Careless self-demolition

On 12 May 2008, a dramatic natural disaster occurs in the province of Sichuan in southwestern China. An earthquake of magnitude 7.9 on the Richter scale kills more than 69,000 people, injures about 375,000. The Chinese nation is shocked by the catastrophe. A week later, the government decrees three days of national mourning in remembrance of the victims of this earthquake. For three days flags fly at half-mast in the entire

---

[5] Le Bon, Gustave (2002/1895) *The Crowd: A study of the popular mind*, Mineola/New York: Dover Publications, pp. 6ff.

country, for three days discotheques and karaoke bars remain closed. Even the Olympic torch relay is interrupted. In addition, big Web portals present themselves in the Chinese colours of mourning. Access to games and other entertainment sites is blocked.[6]

This reaction of the state to a catastrophe prevents 21-year-old Chinese woman Gao Qianhui from Shenyang, the capital of the province Liaoning in the northeast of China, from playing her favourite game. She is sitting in a computer room — or possibly an Internet café — and is simply furious. She is not only angry with the government that has blocked her game but with the victims of the earthquake who, to her mind, are to blame for the Net shut-down. To vent her anger she switches on the webcam of her computer and films herself while indulging in a thoughtless outburst, a so-called *rant*, an uncontrolled fury and hate speech that will ruin her reputation forever and will also soon after lead to her arrest by the Chinese police. In this soliloquy, which she herself publishes later, she vents her views on the earthquake and its victims. She is sitting there with folded arms talking to the camera with no sign of compassion: "I turn on the TV and see injured people, corpses, rotten bodies. […] I don't want to watch these things, I have no choice." She carries on talking monotonously without pause, swearing and railing. "Come on, how many of you died?", she asks. "Just a few, right? There are so many people in China anyway." And then: "You're driving everyone crazy. […] What are you doing! Do you think you're all that good-looking?" Qianhui states that the earthquake was not strong enough for her. She makes it clear that she would not have had anything against a few more victims. She also complains about the donations for the people in

---

[6] Anon. (2008) Drei Tage Staatstrauer in China [Three days of national mourning in China]. In: *NZZ Online*, 28 May 2008, http://www.nzz.ch/nachrichten/international/drei_tage_staatstrauer_in_china__1.736979.html (Retrieved 24 September 2013).

the affected region: "People are giving you cash and giving you food. And you guys are doing nothing?"

The hate diatribe of the young woman lasts for about five minutes. From time to time other people appear in the background, who watch Qianhui ranting against the earthquake victims. The resulting film is eventually published by the 21-year-old on the video platform *YouTube* on 20 May 2008.[7] The very act of publication demonstrates a peculiar *blindness towards media and situations. Her technical skills to create publicity stand in no relation to her communicative competence and her ability to anticipate the potential effects of her actions.* Obviously, Gao Qianhui does not realise that her film can now be watched the whole world over. Obviously, she completely lacks the sensitivity to appreciate the effects of her effusions in a phase of national mourning to remember the victims. She seems unaware that there are utterances that are restricted to the discrete backstage sphere and will produce harsh condemnation when presented in the front region. Her story is an exemplar of a great number of self-documented and subsequently even self-revealed norm violations that elicit processes of scandalisation on the Net, which precede the unleashed scandal and simultaneously supply the necessary material to the community of scalp hunters.

---

[7] It is unlikely that the original video can still be found online. However, numerous copies of the film are accessible. See e.g. http://www.youtube.com/watch?v=bPDhZJmRB4A (Retrieved 27 September 2013). With English subtitles: http://www.youtube.com/watch?v=IeWRTcaXYNU (Retrieved 27 September 2013).

Figure 7: **Gao Qianhui during her hate speech against victims of the earthquake.**

The search for human flesh

The wave of outrage rolling over the young woman in the days after 20 May exceeds all expectations. The event reveals, at the same time, what the conditions are that generate a vengeful cybermob.[8] The prerequisites for the emergence of such a community of outrage and fury are: a broad consensus about the repercussions of the observed norm violation; an unconditional readiness to indulge in outrage fed by moral rigorism in a collective; the belief shared by the members of this collective in being able to achieve a great common goal by using easily available means of communication — without running any risks themselves — the goal being to harm the culprit, and to redress her offence through a common act of self-administered justice. The prompter for the collective hounding of Gao Qianhui is the

---

[8] Groundbreaking on the processes of mob formation: Rheingold, Howard (2002) *Smart Mobs: The next social revolution*, Cambridge: Perseus Publishing.

epidemic spreading of her video. It is posted rapidly on all the significant Chinese discussion forums and duplicated repeatedly on *YouTube*. Several variants are produced, including different versions with English subtitles, all increasing the number of international viewings. The Chinese woman is berated in specially produced video replies; during the first night after publication, at least a dozen of such clips are uploaded onto *YouTube*.[9] Under the online article of the Chinese news agency Xinhua alone more than 29,000 commentaries accumulate.[10] It is a so-called *shitstorm* that has broken loose.

Shitstorm

In Germany the expression refers to a storm of outrage that is sparked off online and rapidly escalates on the Net. It may be directed at individuals but also at groups and enterprises.

However, the shitstorm does not stop at the mere articulation of disgust and outrage. "Now humiliate her",[11] an agitated Internet user demands — and with this appeal documents the decisive reorientation and radicalisation of the cybermob. The enraged swarm is now rooting for compensation in *real life* — but without even a moment's hesitation to consider the essential feature of the criminal justice process in Western democratic societies: the requirement that crime and punishment be placed in an adequately balanced relationship. A sentence is passed only according to a strictly regulated formal procedure by a judge who has heard evidence and arguments from prosecution

---

[9] Lin, Qiu (2008) Where angels and devils meet. In: *Xinhua General News Service*, 23 May 2008, http://news.xinhuanet.com/english/2008-05/23/content_8237906.htm (Retrieved 23 September 2013).

[10] http://comment.news.163.com/news_shehui6_bbs/4CGS78P900011229.html (Retrieved 23 May 2010).

[11] Quoted from: Fletcher, Hannah (2008) Human flesh search engines: Chinese vigilantes that hunt victims on the Web. In: *Times Online*, 25 June 2008, http://www.thetimes.co.uk/tto/technology/article 1858917.ece (Retrieved 10 July 2013).

and defence. The judicial and the executive powers operate independently. *At this stage of relentlessly rising self-righteous anger, at the latest, a peculiar paradox manifests itself: the attempt to control and sanction insubordinate behaviour by way of self-administered justice derails itself. The hounding of the scandal targets becomes scandalous in itself, and the desire to persecute the angrily commented violation of a norm changes into the violation of a norm in its own right.* "Why did so many nice and innocent people have to die. And she is still alive?" a user asks under a copy of the *YouTube* video. And another one: "You are full of shit! Every Chinese hates you now! You have no place to go to!" "If she is really serious we should simply shoot her in the head", writes someone from under the safe cloak of anonymity. And: she should suffer a slow and painful death! Qianhui's family is equally targeted by the hate of the mob, e.g. "I hope your entire family is killed by the insulted relatives of the victims". Numerous rumours about Qianhui circulate on the Net. She is at first wrongly identified as Zhang Ya.[12] Then clearly faked messages and declarations of remorse from her family appear, still using the wrong presumed name, however, and therefore identifiable as fakes even from a distance. There is this passage, for instance: "Zhang Ya is my daughter, and as parents, we have failed in educating her. […] I can only say to the people of Sichuan, the people of China: I'm sorry!"[13] Then the purported mother implores everyone not to harm her daughter. In another message a user claims to be the young woman's brother: "Hello to all netizens, I am Zhang Ya's brother. […] After watching this video, to tell you the truth, I'm also disgusted."[14] But it does not

---

[12] Lin, Qiu (2008) Where angels and devils meet. In: *Xinhua General News Service*, 23 May 2008, http://news.xinhuanet.com/english/2008-05/23/content_8237906.htm (Retrieved 23 September 2013).

[13] Quoted from: Tan, Kenneth (2008) Online lynch mobs find second post-quake target: Liaoning girl detained by the police. In: *Shanghaiist*, 22 May 2008, http://shanghaiist.com/2008/05/22/online_lynch_mo.php (Retrieved 24 September 2013).

[14] Quoted from: Tan, Kenneth (2008) Online lynch mobs find second post-quake target: Liaoning girl detained by the police. In: *Shanghaiist*, 22 May

take long to correct this because the outraged group collaborates closely in order to establish even the minutest details about the life of the 21-year-old woman and to distribute everything in numerous chats and forums.¹⁵ Soon her private and her work address are known and that her parents are divorced. Even the number of her identity card is published—and all this in hardly a day!¹⁶ *The example also allows us to observe the detective work of the cybermob, which operates according to the principle of crowdsourcing, in Chinese referred to as the search for human flesh ("Renrou Sousuo").*

Therefore, we are not dealing here with an ordinary query that just happens to be launched by many people more or less simultaneously. The intention of the outraged collective is much rather to publicise the identity of individual persons in order to render them directly vulnerable in greater measure. The aim is to transform the online hounding into a real life hunt in order to harm the incriminated persons in every conceivable way: by threatening calls to the family, by denouncing them to employers or colleagues, by exposing and humiliating them in their immediate social environment.¹⁷ On 21 May 2008, i.e. only

---

2008, http://shanghaiist.com/2008/05/22/online_lynch_mo.php (Retrieved 24 September 2013).

[15] The French magazine *Le Tigre* impressively demonstrated towards the end of 2008 how many items of information about an individual person can be spotted on the Net today, and how easily they can be put together with the help of search engines to form a comprehensive image of that individual. "Best wishes, Marc", the magazine wrote in a letter published in one of its issues. "On 5 December 2008 you turn 29." The magazine reported numerous details from Marc's life—from the name of an ex-lover to information about the last holiday in Canada with Helena and Jose. The irritating thing is: all this information could be found on the Net and was thus freely accessible. See: Meltz, Raphaël (2008) Marc L***. In: *Le Tigre,* November/December 2008, no. 28, pp. 36–37.

[16] Feng, David (2008) The Chinese Web in action: Netizens of infamy. In: *Shanghaiist,* 28 May 2008, http://shanghaiist.com/2008/05/28/netizens-of-infamy.php (Retrieved 25 September 2013).

[17] On the "search for human flesh", see also: Sondermeyer, Juliane (2011) *Clash of Cultures im Web 2.0. Der interkulturelle Scandal um Wang Qianyuan*

one day after the online publication of her video, Gao Qianhui is arrested by the police in her home town of Shengyang[18] — allegedly in an Internet café. The reason remains unclear. Some sources say that the police did not indicate what law she had broken. Other media report that the young woman was arrested on a charge of "malicious gossip"[19] or "on charges of endangering public stability".[20] She is supposed to have been held by police for three days. It is unclear what happened to her after that. She disappears abruptly and without trace from the media following the days of her arrest.

The search for human flesh

Originally, this expression — with its apparently menacing undertones — (Chinese "Renrou Sousuo") did not have any sinister ring; it simply meant an operation of research carried out collaboratively by several people. Gradually, however, the search by people turned into a search for people who had committed a purported or actual offence. Today the expression stands for an aggressive form of self-administered justice, a witch hunt according to the conditions of modern media. Its goal is to search out and publish private information and intimate details, to identify accused persons in an act of vengeful cooperation in order to harm them and possibly also their families as severely as possible. Numerous cases of this Chinese search for human flesh have since become known. And the old and harmless meaning of the expression "Renrou Sousuo" has slowly disappeared.

[*Clash of Cultures in Web 2.0: The intercultural scandal around Wang Qianyuan*], unpublished manuscript, pp. 18f.

[18] Bureau of Democracy (2009) 2008 Human Rights Report: China (includes Tibet, Hong Kong, and Macau). In: *U.S. Department of State*, 25 February 2009, http://www.state.gov/g/drl/rls/hrrpt/2008/eap/119037.htm (Retrieved 24 September 2013).

[19] Duhr, Michaela (2008) Chinesen auf Menschenjagd [Chinese on the manhunt]. In: *Netzeitung*, 29 May 2008, http://www.netzeitung.de/politik/ausland/1033617.html (Retrieved 23 September 2013).

[20] Lightman, Alex/Rachel Coleman (2009) Search (and destroy) engines. In: *H+ Magazine*, 02 June 2009, http://www.hplusmagazine.com/articles/politics/search-and-destroy-engines (Retrieved 24 September 2013).

2. The fate of the student Wang Qianyuan and the clash of cultures

Cause and effect

Amongst our conceptions of a calculable, controllable world is the notion that our intentions can be realised through actions that generate reasonably predictable effects within the field of human relations. The underlying assumption is that a cause produces an effect in a linear progression. We can refer an effect to a specific cause. Cause and effect stand in some adequate relationship with each other, following a kind of rule, as it were: weak triggering forces generally produce marginal effects; strong massive causes, by contrast, generally produce strong effects.[21] In the scandalisation processes of the digital age this common sense concept of ordered causality, relying as it does on popular views of clear sequences of steps, proportionality, and a hierarchy of forces, is not necessary applicable any more because now things tend to happen in circularly enmeshed chains of effects so that completely unexpected feedback phenomena may occur. In addition, even stimuli that may at first glance appear minimal (some spontaneous behaviour, an ad-hoc utterance, sudden flashes of insight that ultimately prove disastrous) can potentially have massive consequences. These consequences may turn out to be contrary to the original intentions of the participants, but also contrary to the intentions of persons whose autonomous activities are suddenly unhinged and whose goals are thwarted in a blatant manner. This is aptly illustrated by the story of the 20-year-old Chinese woman Wang Qianyuan, language student at Duke University, USA. On the evening of 9 April 2008, she is on her way to the library and

---

[21] On the triadic structure of the idea of causality (there is a cause, an effect, and a rule of transformation which changes the cause into the effect and the input into the output) see Foerster, Heinz von/Bernhard Poerksen (2002) *Understanding Systems: Conversations on epistemology and ethics*, New York/Heidelberg: Kluwer Academic/Plenum Publishers/Carl-Auer-Systeme, pp. 46ff.

encounters two groups, or better clusters, of demonstrators.[22] On one side, there are a few dozen supporters of the liberation of Tibet. They wave Tibetan prayer flags and banners with the inscription "Free Tibet!", distribute flyers and draw attention to the destruction of Tibetan culture and the massive infringements of human rights. On the other side are more than 100 Chinese demonstrators, who are enraged by this act of allegedly anti-Chinese propaganda because they consider Tibet to be part of the Chinese state. They thus feel provoked and humiliated by the pro-Tibet demonstrators. Lies are being spread here, they shout. Both groups face each other with increasing signs of intransigency.[23] Slogans are chanted, both sides berate each other. At times the confrontation seems on the brink of turning violent.

A balancing act between the front lines

The threatening escalation is not the result of a conflict between the Tibetan people, the followers of the 14th Dalai Lama, and the Chinese nation alone — a conflict that has been smouldering for decades. It is also the result of a concrete historical moment, the manifestation of an extremely heated atmosphere in the preparatory phase of the Olympic Games in Beijing, which is characterised by Chinese nationalism, on the one hand, and many actions of protest in non-Chinese countries, on the other.[24] The torch relay with the Olympic flame, which runs through different continents, has to be repeatedly interrupted and

---

[22] The authors would like to express their gratitude to Juliane Sondermeyer for manifold stimulating thoughts for this chapter and the exchanges concerning the case treated here.

[23] Wang herself wrote the extensive report on the events: Wang, Grace (2008) The old man who lost his horse. In: *China Digital Times*, 11 May 2008, http://chinadigitaltimes.net/2008/05/grace-wang-the-old-man-who-lost-his-horse-video-added/ (Retrieved 26 September 2013).

[24] On the worldwide protests against China's Tibet politics and the extremely nationalist reactions of Chinese politicians at the time see: Lorenz, Andreas (2008) Engel im Rollstuhl [Angel in the wheelchair]. In: *Der Spiegel*, 28 April 2008, no 18, p. 122.

redirected in the days and weeks before the events. In London, demonstrators stop the torchbearers, in Paris the torch relay is cancelled, in San Francisco the routes are varied, in New Delhi the public is for safety's sake prevented from viewing the solemn handing over of the flame in order to avoid causing unrest. Wang Qianyuan, student and ad-hoc protagonist of an inter-cultural conflict and an ultimately dramatic communication failure, is not aware of the demonstrations on the campus of her university on the evening of 9 April. She runs into them quite by accident and tries to mediate because she spots familiar faces in both camps and assumes that her knowledge of languages might help to create mutual understanding on both sides. She is filmed and photographed running back and forth between the two groups, gesticulating excitedly, trying desperately to initiate a dialogue. One of the pro-Tibet demonstrators eventually asks her to write the slogan "Free Tibet!" on his back with a felt pen—which she does, but not without wresting the promise from him to make contact with the pro-China students afterwards. In the end, however, she cannot placate him either, she is attacked as a "traitor" because she speaks English, because she uses the language of the adversaries and is therefore seen as a supporter of the causes of the Tibetan government in exile. The bystanders ask for her name and her place of origin. Unsuspecting at first but increasingly worried she provides the information and tells them about her school in Qingdao. The threats become more and more massive, however ("You should be careful, you could be killed!"), and as a result she finally has to be escorted back to her student lodgings under police protection. In the early hours of the morning, she commits a momentous mistake by trying to explain her actions, to eliminate misunderstandings and to calm emotions. In the online forum of Chinese students and lecturers at Duke University she writes an open letter to her "dear compatriots".[25]

---

[25] The letter can be read at the following Net address: Qianyuan, Wang (2008) Wang Qianyuan's open letter. In: *China Digital Times*, 10 April

It is a communicative balancing act between the hostile camps, an effort to create understanding for both sides. Wang declares that she is not at all for the secession of Tibet, she criticises the lop-sided reporting of Western media, quotes Taoist and Confucian ideas and refers to the traditions of wisdom that suggest working with the forces of the enemy in order to realise one's purposes in a quiet and considerate way and manner, not with loud screaming and by way of aggression and repression. She pleads for tolerance and for treating her Tibetan fellow country people in a more friendly and equitable way because their repression would only fuel rebellion and hamper their smooth integration. The next morning she registers, as she will say later, "a storm was raging online".[26] Most of the photographs published on the Net show her on the side of the Tibetan demonstrators. There are defamatory montages showing her half-naked. There are images similar to a "Wanted" poster with her face on them, which accuse her of betraying her people and her nation. A video of the demonstration is circulated that shows her attempts at mediation but has now turned into evidence for an anti-Chinese attitude. Wang has finally lost control over the meaning of her utterances. What she said and what she tried to do is now no longer determined by herself but by others—due to the transfer of the data and documents to another cultural space and thus to another sphere of meaning and interpretation.

The loss of inhibition in online communication and its effects

The commentaries published in popular Chinese forums are examples of the negative effects of online communication dominated by anger and hate, which the American psychologist John

---

2008, http://chinadigitaltimes.net/wp-content/uploads/2008/04/grace-wang-english-ver-3.pdf (Retrieved 25 September 2013).

[26] Wang, Grace (2008) My China, my Tibet: Caught in the middle, called a traitor. In: *Washington Post*, 20 April 2008. http://www.washingtonpost.com/wp-dyn/content/article/2008/04/18/AR2008041802635.html (Retrieved 25 September 2013).

Suler has investigated.[27] They document the comparatively risk-free discharging of the aggression of a cybermob that can at least be facilitated and enhanced by different features of that form of communication. The attackers believe that they are safe from persecution because they do not have to reveal their identity and shoulder any responsibility in *real life*. Whatever they say online is not connected with their offline existence as their own personal life remains invisible for the others and cannot be touched by potential feedback from those persons that have been labelled as enemies. They agitate from under the cloak of *anonymity* (or perhaps more precisely what may be called: *pseudonymity*),[28] they have no face-to-face contact with the accused that might lead to more discriminating and empathic communication. They have themselves no feeling for the suffering of their victims and they are not confronted in their own immediate personal world with the consequences of their actions, they cannot and are not forced to see what they have set in motion. Some of them possibly consider the digital universe as a parallel world that is governed by their personal inclinations and experimental desires and in which they do not have to feel bound by accepted conventions and authorities. A brief selection from the list of threats and insults that were published as early as 10 April 2008, the day after the demonstration, may

---

[27] Suler, John (2004) The online disinhibition effect. In: *CyberPsychology & Behaviour*, vol. 7, no. 3, pp. 321–326.

[28] In most cases, Phillip W. Brunst explains, there is no real anonymity in forums, chats, blogs, and social networks, but rather *pseudonymity*, because the contributing participants can still be identified via their IP-addresses. *Pseudonymity* is therefore a felt anonymity, although utterances can — even if with some difficulty — be connected with a person. Anonymity, strictly speaking, entails that the unmasking of identity is impossible. See: Brunst, Phillip W. (2009) *Anonymität im Internet. Rechtliche und tatsächliche Rahmenbedingungen. Zum Spannungsfeld zwischen einem Recht auf Anonymität bei der elektronischen Communication und den Möglichkeiten zur Identifizierung und Strafverfolgung* [Anonymity on the Internet: Legal and factual frameworks. On the field of tensions between the right to anonymity in electronic communication and the possibilities of identification and criminal prosecution], Berlin: Duncker & Humblot.

illustrate the dimension of the aggression: "I want to see photos!" – "I shall not let that bitch even five metres near me." – "Croak it, shameless thing." – "What? From the Qingdao Middle School? Makes us lose face in this way? Execute her on the spot." – "Inform the Ministry for State Security, the Chinese Embassy and her home district." – "Call the machine for the search of human flesh!" – "Evidence is important! We do not want to damage anyone who is innocent. But we shall never leave the wicked in peace!" – "Alarm the Customs officers to catch her, and if she has family seek them out and beat her shameless children to death, so that they can no longer harm the Chinese people." – "Traitor of our race! Traitor! Sooner or later your whole family will pay for this."[29]

However, the reactions do not remain restricted to verbal attacks; meanwhile the so-called search for human flesh has begun. The mob aims now at exposing her family and her person, seeks the existentially jeopardizing attack, the destruction of a life's career. Shortly after the first enraged attacks her telephone number, her mail address, and the numbers of her and her parents' identity cards all circulate on the Net. Wang is convinced that this kind of information can only have come from the Chinese police. Detailed navigating instructions to the house of her parents are discovered, also information on where the parents work. It is even detected without any difficulty what kind of musical instrument Wang once learnt and played. The consequences are massive. In her home country, the Qingdao Middle School revokes her final exams and vows to practice a more patriotic education in the future. It is rumoured that the authorities of the state have put her name on a sort of blacklist containing the names of people who are to be punished severely when returning to their home country. As she cannot

---

[29] See: Strittmatter, Kai (2008) Trainieren für Olympia. Die Menschenfleischsuche [Training for Olympia: The search for human flesh]. In: *Sueddeutsche.de*, 17 April 2008, http://www.sueddeutsche.de/politik/trainieren-fuer-olympia-die-menschenfleischsuche-1.204850 (Retrieved 25 September 2013).

be apprehended directly — the police controls on the grounds of Duke University are increased in the days following 9 April — various individuals attack her parents directly, forcing them to go into hiding. Their windows are smashed, their house entrance is smeared with excrement and slogans: "Kill the whole family! Kill traitors of our country!"

Figures 8 + 9: **The enraged mob acts online and offline. The first figure shows a digitally re-edited photograph of Wang Qianyuan with a sign "Traitor of the country" around her neck; in the background one can recognise the pro-Tibet demonstrators. In the second image, one can see the slogans on the wall of her parents' home: "Kill the whole family! Kill traitors of our country!"**

The scandalisation of scandalisation

What makes the case so illuminating, however, independently of its dramatic private-personal features, is the fact that the outrage on the Chinese side is contrasted by a diametrically opposed assessment on the side of the Americans. It becomes clear that the sensibility for scandal — as the sociologist John B. Thompson notes — depends on the particular historical moment in time, on the general cultural and moral climate of this historical moment, and on the value orientation and the hierarchy of the values of specific groups or even whole nations.[30] The action that is so angrily attacked by a Chinese public as the violation of a norm is glorified in the United States of America as a norm-confirming behaviour worthy of special praise. A group of Cuban American students of the University therefore takes Wang's side: "We admire Wang for standing up for her beliefs, in spite of the personal repercussions inflicted upon her by an oppressive regime. She does not stand alone." The *Washington Post* publishes an extensive reaction by her and even prints special reports on the case.[31] Other leading newspapers devote prominent space to the case; the *New York Times* even deals with the topic on its front page.[32] These reactions illustrate that the Net has provoked this ideological conflict of *weltanschauungen* and a *clash of cultures* that is enacted on a globally

---

[30] Thompson, John B. (2000) *Political Scandal: Power and visibility in the media age*, Cambridge: Polity Press, p. 15.

[31] See: Wang, Grace (2008) My China, my Tibet: Caught in the middle, called a traitor. In: *Washington Post*, 20 April 2008, http://www.washingtonpost.com/wp-dyn/content/article/2008/04/18/AR2008041802635.html (Retrieved 25 September 2013). Furthermore: Cha, Ariana Eunjung/Jill Drew (2008) New freedom, and peril, in online criticism of China. In: *Washington Post*, 17 April 2008, http://www.washingtonpost.com/wp-dyn/content/article/2008/04/16/AR2008041603579.html (Retrieved 25 September 2013).

[32] Dewan, Shaila (2008) Chinese student in U.S. is caught in confrontation. In: *New York Times*, 17 April 2008, http://www.nytimes.com/2008/04/17/world/americas/17iht-17student.12081327.html?pagewanted=all (Retrieved 20 September 2013).

visible stage. On one side are the Chinese nationalists who hound a traitor and who insist on interpreting her interviews given to US media as signs of a hostile attitude. On the other side are the representatives of Western democratic values to whose central canon of values belongs the right of free speech and the free voicing of opinions. But this is not yet the end of the story. Reconstructing this process of scandalisation makes abundantly clear that the scandalisation of the purported treacherous position of Wang's from the American side is answered by a reactive pattern of outrage that could be termed *scandal of the second order. Individuals, specific groups, or even whole nations may view a process of scandalisation as scandalous in itself and consequently perform the scandalisation of a scandalisation.* The actual scandal, it is assumed, is the way and manner in which the other side proceeds, vents its anger, and—it is thought—practises its outrage in an unjustifiable way due to the disregard of central values and norms. The implication is: *the observation of scandalisation leads to the scandalisation of the scandal that is, consequently, contextualised, evaluated, and classified anew in a totally different way.*[33] Thus, there is praise for Wang's education and her effort to argue for a compromise. Some commentators describe Wang as an icon of the right to freedom of speech and the commitment to enlightenment. Her concern for an open dialogue must be protected at all costs. The commentators on the Chinese side are called downright barbarians. The organisers of the pro-Tibet demonstration, the Duke Human Rights Coalition, published the following statement: "Duke Human Rights Coalition condemns, in the strongest possible terms, the threats made against Grace Wang and her family. As fellow Duke students, it is our responsibility to foster an atmosphere of tolerance, respect and academic freedom. The fact that a Duke student has been

---

[33] The logic of observing and the distinction between observations of the first and second order, underlying this conceptualisation, is described in the following book: Poerksen, Bernhard (2011) *The Creation of Reality: A constructivist epistemology of journalism and journalism education,* Exeter/Charlottesville: Imprint Academic, pp. 24ff.

targeted for speaking her mind at the University is an incredible violation of that same freedom. We should not be bickering, or searching for someone to blame; we should be banding together as a community to protect a fellow student."

This student Wang, who is praised in a foreign country and hated in her home country, again reacts in an extraordinary way in her letters and interviews, in her statements and analyses, and publicly declares that she has rejected her father's suggestion to apologise. She insists that she does not wish to retract anything, and she explains and promotes her perspective in a surprisingly unruffled way, anxious to stall any further escalation in the sphere of communication. Only two days after the éclat on the university grounds she publishes an extensive essay in the pro-Western *China Digital Times* which is produced by students in Californian Berkeley. This essay, a masterpiece of dialectic argumentation, is entitled *The Old Man Who Lost His Horse* and starts with the following parable:

> During the Han Dynasty—in the third century B.C.—an old man living on China's border one day lost his horse. His neighbours all said what terrible luck that was, and sympathized with the old man. But Sai Weng said: 'Maybe losing my horse is not a bad thing after all.' Lo and behold, the next day the old man's horse returned, together with a beautiful female horse alongside him. All the neighbours exclaimed: 'What great luck!' But the old man responded: 'Maybe this is not such good luck after all.' The old man had a strong young son. The boy fell in love with the new horse and rode her every day. One day the new horse got spooked by a wild animal and threw the boy from her back. He broke his leg very badly and was permanently crippled. All Sai Weng's neighbours said: 'What a tragedy, your strong son will never walk without pain again.' But the old man again said: 'Maybe this is not such a bad thing after all.' And so it went that when the New Year came, the emperor's army passed through the border region and recruited all able young men to fight in the frontier war. Because the old man's son was crippled he could not fight and was left in the village to farm with his father. Sai Weng said to his

neighbours: 'You see, it all turned out okay in the end. Being thrown from the horse and breaking his leg saved my son from fighting in the war and almost certain death. So it was in the end a lucky thing after all.' Whenever a bad thing happens in China, someone will say 'Sai Weng Shi Ma' (Remember 'The Old Man Who Lost His Horse') to remind themselves and others that apparently bad things sometimes have a silver lining.

At the end of her essay she provides her own dialectically founded justification of the norm violation. The violation of the norm, she explains, is an occasion to understand the value of the norm and to learn to appreciate it, an opportunity of directly experiencing the crossing of a frontier, of appreciating the meaning of the frontier.[34] "Like the old man who lost his horse", Wang Qianyuan writes, "I am determined to turn this apparent misfortune into a positive experience and equal opportunity for learning and growing for my fellow Han Chinese, Tibetans and Americans."[35]

3. The humiliated husband and the divorce battle of Tricia Walsh-Smith

The chameleon and the mirror

It is a strange question.[36] In the year 1974, the journalist Stewart Brand pays a visit to the cyberneticist Gregory Bateson. Stewart

---

[34] These reflections refer to the figure of thought outlined before, which hails back to Emile Durkheim. The confrontation with the outlandish, the immoral and scandalous, this father figure of modern sociology asserts, in the end allows for the re-enforcement of moral norms. It is an opportunity to make frontiers visible by crossing them.

[35] Wang, Grace (2008) The old man who lost his horse. In: *China Digital Times*, 11 May 2008, http://chinadigitaltimes.net/2008/05/grace-wang-the-old-man-who-lost-his-horse-video-added/ (Retrieved 26 September 2013).

[36] The following draws on a previous publication by Bernhard Poerksen and Wolfgang Krischke: Poerksen, Bernhard/Wolfgang Krischke (2010) Vorwort [Foreword]. In: Bernhard Poerksen/Wolfgang Krischke (eds.) *Die Casting-Gesellschaft. Die Suche nach Aufmerksamkeit und das Tribunal*

Brand, who makes the pilgrimage to this old man like many others, wants to know what colour a chameleon assumes when you put it on a mirror. Bateson has no answer. Nevertheless, he —the cyberneticist, the master of circular thinking—is fascinated by the question and circulates it amongst his students and the *scientific community*. Various researchers enter the debate. A technically gifted writer constructs a cabinet of mirrors and places a real reptile in it to find out what actually happens if you put a chameleon on a mirror. What colour will it assume? Will it retain its original colour tone? Will an iridescent and characteristically unstable kind of oscillation emerge? Will the chameleon be driven into a sort of colour madness in this world of mirrors? Will it for the sake of self-defence finally settle for a sort of basic colour, a kind of colour identity? The fascinating aspect of this question is that the chameleon and the mirror seem to fuse, that the logic of linearity is replaced by a circular network of effects.[37] Perhaps the actual outcome is not of such great importance. We prefer to imagine that we are involved in a thought experiment that throws a dazzling light on the development of the modern media, throwing into relief some of the relevant questions in connection with the current situation of the omnipresent digital media. What happens to people who live in the awareness that they are surrounded by mirrors and that the mirroring of their very personal selves may be exploited for strategic purposes? In what ways, for example, do we medialise our own history as soon as we have realised that the most visible, the most intensive mirroring, requires a specific colour code? How do we generate attention and communicative connections, and how do we scandalise for private purposes?

---

der Medien [*The Casting Society: The desire for attention and the tribunal of the media*], Cologne: Herbert von Halem Verlag, pp. 7ff.

[37] The question as to what colour the chameleon *really* assumes is unanswered. Detailed answers to this parable, which is most illuminating for theories of the media can be found in: Kelly, Kevin (1994) *Out of Control: The new biology of machines, social systems, and the economic world*, New York: Basic Books, pp. 69ff.

A reality soap for one's own ends

The actress Tricia Walsh-Smith from New York answered this archetypal question about effective self-presentation in the modern media's hall of mirrors in her own way in the year 2008. Her strategy: *self-staging according to the current rules of medial staging as practised by independent external professionals, in particular, targeted self-medialisation following the pattern of a reality soap.* Tricia Walsh-Smith tried to use the concentrated power of Web 2.0 to terrorise her husband, who was pushing for a divorce, to scandalise his behaviour, and to transform the approaching court proceedings into a tribunal in the public sphere intending to shore up points in the divorce poker and secure a television career afterwards. Her story, or all that one knows about her, is terribly banal — but nevertheless instructive. It demonstrates in what ways one can exploit the rules of the games of show business and reality television by adapting to them chameleon-style, in order to generate attention and communicative connections — at least in the short term — by polarising the public. *The medial script thus becomes the apparently authentic self-expression of her individuality and her private history.* The background story of the reality soap that she fabricates for herself is easily summarised: when her husband Philip J. Smith files for divorce after nine years of marriage, she chooses the best known of all multimedia platforms for defaming him. She underlines that he has, of course, the best contacts with the most important mass media in New York, whereas she has no access to these media and is therefore dependent on other channels. The then 52-year-old actress publishes a first video in April 2008, in which she divulges intimate details from the life of husband Philip J. Smith, millionaire Broadway impresario, who is 25 years her senior, and presents herself as a pitiable victim.[38] She had specifically engaged a professional cinematographer for making this barely six-and-a-half-minute *YouTube* video, so that

---

[38] http://www.youtube.com/watch?v=hx_WKxqQF2o (Retrieved 06 March 2010).

the result was a professionally cut film with a proper sound track. In this film Walsh-Smith accuses her husband of planning to evict her from the shared Park Avenue apartment in New York within the next 30 days. She admits that he was entitled to do that on the grounds of their marriage contract, although only for legally just causes—that, however, did not exist. "I don't know why", she sobs with tears in her eyes. The image is faded out. Then she adds abruptly: "Another thing. We never had sex." He had always used his purportedly high blood pressure as a pretext and she had naturally accepted this. However, she had discovered a year back that he must have used potency drugs, unambiguous films, and condoms. Walsh-Smith passes on these private-intimate details to her husband's secretary on the telephone. She thus chooses, quite generally speaking, a popular strategy used by obscure persons and minor celebrities, who do not really have an important story to tell or cannot offer any item of information or piece of news of public relevance, but who are terribly keen on parading themselves in public before the world, cost what it may. This kind of strategy is only too familiar from the affect-and-scream shows of afternoon television, from shows with celebrities, and from celebrity magazines. Their goal is to arouse attention and to promote the medial mirroring of the involved persons' egos. And their basis is a kind of exchange liaison in its own right: *intimacy, curiosity, and vulgarity for publicity.*[39] In accordance with this scheme and by way of the direct implementation of such an exchange Tricia Walsh-Smith on camera asks her husband's secretary, who is totally outfaced by this approach, to enquire with Smith—her husband still—what she should do with the Viagra, with the pornographic films, and the condoms.

---

[39] Poerksen, Bernhard/Wolfgang Krischke (2010) Die Casting-Gesellschaft [The casting society]. In: Bernhard Poerksen/Wolfgang Krischke (eds.) *Die Casting-Gesellschaft. Die Sucht nach Aufmerksamkeit und das Tribunal der Medien* [*The Casting Society: The desire for attention and the tribunal of the media*], Cologne: Herbert von Halem Verlag, pp. 14ff.

Figure 10: **First instalment of a reality soap for her own ends: the *YouTube* video with which everything started.**

Then the show goes on. In the living room, Walsh-Smith shows photographs from the wedding album. She pithily comments on the images of members of her husband's family: "This is Philip's oldest daughter. She is the evil one. She wants my pension. […] A bad, bad, bad person." She then leads the spectator through the luxury apartment and turns melancholy. "This is my home", she says. "Or was my home, which I am being evicted from." She does not intend to give up, however. At the end of the video she says with wide open eyes towards the camera: "I am trying to be a warrior, maybe I'll win." Her video ends with an apparently ironic-satirical cliffhanger in the form of questions, which is probably, judging by the overall context, intended to really be serious: "Will poor, vulnerable Tricia be evicted? Or will mean bad husband do the right thing? Stay tuned!" The soap is designed to go on, it will and it must go on. It appears to have found its audience, at least with this very first instalment.

Polarisation resulting from successful communication

In the first week, on *YouTube* alone about 150,000 users watch the video, one month later three million have seen it, and to this day just short of four million people have got to know Tricia Walsh-Smith's first publication.[40] About 8,500 comments have appeared, and users have multiply duplicated the revenge video and uploaded it in other places. The *YouTube* divorce can thus also be found on platforms like *MySpace*.[41] On *Break.com* the video attracts a further 550,000 viewers,[42] and in addition parodies and photo stories on the case as well as angry critical films are now in circulation. For the traditional popular press this *YouTube* divorce is an extremely attractive subject: here a minor celebrity actress voluntarily fights her war of the roses publicly in front of thousands of people — an as yet unheard-of ploy and manner of using platforms like *YouTube*. Moreover, Walsh-Smith even manages to publicise her story on international media, especially in Great Britain, her home country, and in other countries.

The reception of the divorce video shows that reactions move between extremes (approval and admiration, disgust and hatred) proving that the communication has been successful. *The resulting polarisation of the public, shaking it out of its complacency and forcing it into a debate about the right kind of evaluation, is the decisive prerequisite here for the creation of hype, the sudden excess of attention.* On one side, several commentators gather within days that support Tricia Walsh-Smith and admire her attempt to initiate an extrajudicial tribunal in the lobby of the media inferno. This group of people thinks that the alleged behaviour of her husband — the only available description of which is of her, his accuser's, making — must definitely be rated

---

[40] http://www.youtube.com/watch?v=hx_WKxqQF2o (Retrieved 03 October 2011).

[41] http://vids.myspace.com/index.cfm?fuseaction=vids.individual&videoid=32624312 (Retrieved 03 October 2011).

[42] http://www.break.com/index/tricia-walsh-smith-crazy-divorce-woman.html (Retrieved 23 September 2013).

as scandalous and as significantly more serious than her revenge campaign itself. "What a stupid bum this idiot of a husband must have been" is printed under the original video. "I love what you've done!", another user writes. And another one eggs Walsh-Smith on: "Come on girl warrior, get on with it! We all want a happy ending." Finally, there are about 2,600 positive comments vis-à-vis about 2,800 negative comments on the original video. A large number of written commentaries and video replies are frankly critical of Walsh-Smith. Someone writes: "I am very sorry about what happened in your marriage but this is absolutely not the way to solve your problem." Another one formulates very clear disapproval: "Egoistic, brainless gold diggers like her make me sick." There is a lot of abusive criticism in the commentaries, which shows a characteristic unbalanced change in the dynamics of outrage, an emotional atmosphere, and a climate of opinion that are difficult to control. *Precisely because the public now determines the timing of the processes of scandalisation in a hitherto unknown measure, the spectrum of variation of assessments can no longer be harmonised and standardised by the pronouncements stemming from merely a few select media. The consequences may consist in unexpected and sudden fluctuations in positions and images. The active scandaliser may be turned into the victim of a scandal at the drop of a hat. The subject publishing information on nuisances and grievances may all of a sudden become the object of defamation.* Moreover, the further resonance—following the sudden excess of attention—will remain comparatively incalculable and subject to enormous fluctuations—another lesson that can be learnt from Tricia Walsh-Smith's trivial mini-soap. She carries on producing *YouTube* videos of a similar kind,[43] reports on the development of her story, provides teasers for the instalments to come, organises a donation campaign, asking for money to be sent through the online service *PayPal.com*. She wants to create a

---

[43] http://www.youtube.com/user/walshsmith1 (Retrieved 23 September 2013).

foundation with the name *Women Warriors of the World United* with the amount of money remaining after the costs of the divorce case against her husband have been met. In another clip she advertises her first pop song "I'm going bonkers!" She underlines repeatedly that the song is available for purchase on *iTunes*. It is a music video that she stages in the costume and the studio of a dominatrix; and it illustrates the self-conscious and strained effort to capitalise on the achieved attention as rapidly as possible, to cash in on the still considerable public appeal. However, not one of her curious and aggressively body-centred self-advertising videos matches the success of the first one. In the final and decisive divorce court hearing – in a court of law, not on *YouTube* and not in the public arena – the judge Harold Beeler calls the videos part of a "calculated and callous campaign to embarrass and humiliate her husband".[44] The marriage contract is valid. She must vacate the apartment in Manhattan and will receive $50,000[45] – a fraction of what she had demanded and hoped for.[46]

Following this court decision, Tricia Walsh-Smith has only sporadically been heard of during the last few years. It is rumoured that she has founded an organisation which is supposed to help women in divorce suits. However, the number of clicks on the videos posted by her after the first

---

[44] Quoted from: Gammell, Caroline (2008) "Callous" YouTube rant divorcee criticises £350,000 settlement. In: *Telegraph.co.uk*, 22 July 2008, http://www.telegraph.co.uk/news/uknews/2445563/Callous-You Tube-rant-divorcee-criticises-350000-settlement.html (Retrieved 23 September 2013).

[45] Dreyer, Patricia (2008) Scheidungskrieg per YouTube. Richter kanzelt rachsüchtige Ehefrau ab [Divorce war via YouTube: Judge gives vengeful spouse a roasting]. In: *Spiegel Online*, 22 July 2008, http://www.spiegel.de/panorama/0,1518,567298,00.html (Retrieved 23 September 2013).

[46] Schaertl, Marika (2008) "Fünf Millionen Dollar!" Interview mit Tricia Walsh-Smith ["Five million dollars!" Interview with Tricia Walsh-Smith]. In: *Focus.de*, 21 July 2008, http://www.focus.de/kultur/leben/modernes-leben-fuenf-millionen-dollar_aid_319079.html (Retrieved 23 September 2013).

successful one appears to be pretty modest. Neither an admiring nor an abusively ranting public pays attention any longer. The simple reason is that she has only partially internalised the categorical imperative of a media chameleon, which is: *transform biography and personality into stories that are ever new, that are ever more dramatic*! She did not even have enough good subject matter for the second instalment of her video soap. In the first edition of her reality soap, she succeeded in generating attention in audiences of millions. Her news and narration factors were the private-intimate violation of boundaries, the public defamation of her husband, a well-known man in New York, and the weird technical and content innovation of using *YouTube* as the channel for the new genre of the divorce video. Everything that followed was, dramaturgically speaking, merely the rehash of one and the same content — an endless remix, utterly unsuitable for the wildly fluctuating demands of variation and novelty of a public that is quickly bored. Tricia Walsh-Smith eventually attempted, it was reported, to continue her reality soap with the help of professionals and to secure a show of her own on American television. She sought to change her sudden Net celebrity into a basic version of genuine traditional television celebrity so as to make money in the dominant reality of the market. According to information published in the magazine of the *New York Times*, the negotiations that initially appeared promising have long broken down. It is not known whether anyone — except the self-crowned protagonist — in any way regrets this.[47]

---

[47] Eaton, Phoebe (2008) The YouTube divorcée. In: *New York Magazine*, 01 June 2009, http://nymag.com/news/features/47389/ (Retrieved 23 September 2013).

4. The pillory website for Amir and the joys of defamation

The digital doppelgänger

In the year 2005 Thomas Sawyer is tricked by a swindler and, without being fully aware of it at the outset, avenges himself in a most brutal manner. Everything starts with an auction on *Ebay*, in the course of which the 23-year-old student from Exeter manages to purchase, under the pseudonym *spikytom*, a Hewlett-Packard office notebook from a certain *amir6626*. Sawyer pays the demanded £375 — and then has to wait, so he says, for nearly two months. After this long wait the notebook finally does arrive, but it proves to be inoperable and in essential points does not match the description given by *amir6626* on *Ebay*. "Amir's" account has meanwhile been deleted, however, and every attempt to contact him leads nowhere. About half a year later Sawyer makes a fool of the cheating trader in front of an audience of millions and administers asymmetric justice. *The appropriate proportionate relationship between cause and effect dramatically gets more and more out of kilter in the course of his attempts at scandalisation and his acts of revenge.* He first manages to reconstruct extremely private sets of data on the hard disk of the damaged notebook. Then he registers a weblog with the name *The Broken Laptop I Sold on Ebay* with a free provider and starts a cruel role-play with the following statements: "Hello. My name is Amir Massoud Tofangsazan and I live in Barnet. I'm 19 but pretend to be a lot older and like to pretend that I'm a big businessman when I'm not actually that clever."[48] The story of the laptop sale follows, allegedly written by Amir Massoud Tofangsazan himself. "Haha genius! Selling a 'working' laptop that doesn't work!", he pretends to

---

[48] Amir (2006) The very bigging of the Amir Tofangsazan story. In: *The Broken Laptop I Sold on Ebay*, 08 May 2006, http://amirtofangsazan.blogspot.com/2006/05/jump-to-amirs-leg-zone-visit.html (Retrieved 25 September 2013).

praise himself. Despite the polite requests by the buyer, he declined to return his money. Then he pretended to have moved to Dubai, hoping the buyer would forget about the case. "But he didn't forget about it. He took the hard disk out and behold! One laptop crammed with pictures that I really should have deleted before trying to sell it!" Ten images follow showing pornographic, foot-fetishist, and bisexual scenes—taken from the hard disk of the laptop, according to Sawyer. All the photos come with short ironic commentaries; some are slightly modified or pixelated. In addition, there are pictures of Tofangsazan himself, there is a scan of his passport, and there are suggestions of what else can be found on the hard disk, for instance banking details and the access specifications for Tofangsazan's e-mail account with *Hotmail*.

Here, at the latest, the reader will realise that the blog entry cannot have come from Amir Massoud Tofangsazan himself. Who would voluntarily publish photographs and data of this kind? And the following sentence reinforces the impression that somebody has hijacked another person's identity in order to wreak revenge: "What else could he do but publish this information on the Internet for the whole world to see what a sad man I really am!" In May and June 2006 updates of the blog post follow as well as a further entry with new risky data from the hard disk. Sawyer publishes private correspondence. And he adds pornographic photographs, pictures of women's legs on the underground and family pictures to the entries. In June 2006 he reveals his real identity for a moment because now Sawyer writes an entry with the title "A message to Amir"—an attempt to use public exposure for purposes of blackmail, to pronounce his judgement and to execute it.[49] "You know as well as me that you sold me faulty goods", he writes. However, he

---

[49] This blog post is obviously a letter to Tofangsazan, although it was published under the pseudonym *Amir*:
  Amir (2006): A message to Amir. In: The Broken Laptop I Sold on Ebay, 05 June 2006. http://amirtofangsazan.blogspot.com/2006/06/i-only-have-very-limited-Internet.html (Retrieved 25 September 2013).

now no longer wants Tofangsazan to return the money; he tells him to donate the £375 to a charity organisation and to apologise officially and publicly in order to protect his reputation. In return, Sawyer would remove the photos from the site and replace them with information about the donation and the letter of apology. Nothing of this kind happens, though. In February 2007 he announces — now again under the pseudonym of his antagonist Amir — that he is working on an update of the site. But all that is in fact published about a month later are three mash-ups — obviously retouched photographs that show Tofangsazan, amongst other things, as a goggle-eyed voyeur in front of dancing and sparsely clothed women.

The digital pillory

They are called *reportyourex.com*, *people2avoid.com*, *iShareGossip.com*, or *rottenneighbor.com*. They emerge and vanish, are suddenly offline one day because their providers have clashed with the laws of their country, because a group of hackers has attacked them, or simply because their producers have lost interest. Despite all their diversity they only serve one single purpose: defamation by scandalising purported or actual violations of certain norms. They are pillory websites, platforms for anonymous mobbing, disgrace on suspicion, ambush attacks. Sometimes bounties are offered, or chases are initiated. The topics to be found here comprise the whole spectrum of behaviour worthy of criticism — depending on ideology and political conviction. There have always been and still are "Wanted" posters exposing pimps and prostitutes and their clients, the opponents of homosexual marriage, drug-taking students, or that show police photographs of alleged or actual criminals (so-called mugshots). There are sites where violence against the opponents of abortion is advocated in an only flimsily disguised way and on which targeted manhunts are promoted. One can find photographs on these pages, also names and addresses, personal data or suggestions that may turn out to be handy when further investigations are required. It is, as a rule, impossible to determine what is correct and what not. There is no opportunity to reply or protest or consider a second opinion; there are only monologues of directed aggression.

Emergence of an epidemic

Sawyer sends an e-mail to all the contacts in Tofangsazan's *Hotmail* account—that is all he does to make the site known.[50] Nevertheless the blog is accessed 2.3 million times within three and a half weeks.[51] Four years later nearly 4 million visits have been registered.[52] If all the paths of information are searched out and recovered in detail, then the case illustrates a form of distribution that the publicist Malcolm Gladwell, in his book on the *tipping point*—the moment of tipping over and collapsing, the dramatic moment of the quality leap—has metaphorically described as an epidemic, without however applying the concept systematically to the sudden excesses of attention in the digital age. "To appreciate the power of epidemics", Gladwell writes, "we have to abandon this expectation about proportionality. We need to prepare ourselves for the possibility that sometimes big changes follow from small events, and that sometimes these changes can happen very quickly."[53] Information and messages that spread in this massive and disproportionate way must have specific properties. They must be *infectious*—to remain with the chosen imagery—not necessarily relevant yet interesting, and precisely for this reason of importance to many. They must definitely be comprehensible and they must permit connection with and within diverse worlds of experience. They must also encourage forwarding, retelling, and commenting, i.e. stimulate communicative processing that will again increase dissemination. However, if the new quality of the *tipping point* is finally to be reached, something more is needed. Malcolm Gladwell

---

[50] Interview by the authors with Thomas Sawyer, 19 June 2010.
[51] Corinth, Ernst (2006) Rache ist online [Revenge is online]. In: *Telepolis*, 01 June 2006, http://www.heise.de/tp/artikel/22/22797/1.html (Retrieved 23 September 2013).
[52] http://amirtofangsazan.blogspot.com/2006/05/jump-to-amirs-leg-zone-visit.html (Retrieved 02 July 2010). A hit counter lists every visit to the website even though it may come under the same IP-address.
[53] Gladwell, Malcolm (2001) *The Tipping Point: How little things can make a big difference*, New York/Boston: Little, Brown and Company/Back Bay Books, p. 11.

suggests in general terms something which is demonstrated in detail by the case of the successfully scandalised notebook vendor, namely: one or more *connectors*.[54]

> **Prominent connectors**
> They are agents on the Net and in the media, well-known and in the proper sense of the word optimally connected networkers. What they achieve by means of suggestions and recommendations, commentaries and reports, is to ennoble the topic under discussion, as it were, and to establish contacts between different groups, subcultures, and audiences in different networks due to their own multiple participation in all sorts of networks.

In the case of Amir Massoud Tofangsazan, the prominent mediators are primarily bloggers who link the site and inform other selected newsgroups, and journalists who play the role of central connectors. There is also a well-known newsletter that spreads the link to this site, and numerous forums discuss this revenge blog and refer to it.[55] A certain *toto* reports in the commentary area on Sawyer's blog that he has posted photographs from the site together with a link to the blog in the seven —according to him—most active newsgroups. "This should generate some hits", he writes. In addition, *Wikipedia* develops an extensive entry on Amir Massoud Tofangsazan. After a most instructive debate in which the principle of relevance is contrasted with the principle of interestingness, the entry is deleted

---

[54] This concept is used by reference to Malcolm Gladwell's concept of connector that denotes persons (outside the Internet). See: Gladwell, Malcolm (2001) *The Tipping Point: How little things can make a big difference*, New York/Boston: Little, Brown and Company/Back Bay Books, pp. 38ff.

[55] See e.g. http://www.technofriends.de/thema-wie-ein-englischer-student-einen-Internet-gauner-blo%C3%9Fstellt-1948.html; http://www.p45.net/boards/showthread.php?t=82727; http://forums.macnn.com/89/macnn-lounge/296887/how-not-sell-broken-laptop-ebay/ (Retrieved 08 March 2010).

by an administrator, but it may still be found on other sites.[56] If the web information service *Alexa* is to be believed, then even more than four years later links from a total of 231 websites will still lead to the blog of the *Ebay* revenger.[57] Apart from blogs, forums, and newsletters, the traditional mass media also function as prominent mediators and help to spread the information and break down barriers among the public — not without the powerful support of an interested Net community that addresses specifically selected potential multipliers. *BeatPoet* announces that the link will be sent to all national newspapers: "Wonder who'll pick it up first?" And indeed numerous national and international media pick up the story, without however carrying out further investigations of their own; they simply reproduce the case without any further and more in-depth analysis. Only the British tabloid newspaper, the *Daily Mail,* deserves credit for giving Amir Massoud Tofangsazan a voice and, in fact, his very own voice.[58] Tofangsazan is quoted there with the following words: "I am shaking all over and I fear my reputation is going to be ruined." The laptop was not damaged and he had nothing to do with the pornographic photographs or the images of women's legs. "The last few days have been a nightmare, some of my friends have seen it and my father is very angry." Tofangsazan's father, Mohammad, tells the reporter of the *Daily Mail* that this story is extremely upsetting for the family.

---

[56] http://en.wikipedia.org/wiki/Amir_Tofangsazan (Retrieved 08 March 2010).

[57] http://www.alexa.com/search?q=http%3A%2F%2Famirtofangsazan.blogspot.com%2F&r=site_screener&p=bigtop (Retrieved 08 March 2010).

[58] Anon. (2006) Revenge of the Ebay customer sold "faulty" laptop. In: *Daily Mail Online*, 30 May 2006, http://www.dailymail.co.uk/news/article-388189/Revenge-eBay-customer-sold-faulty-laptop.html (Retrieved 28 September 2013).

The loss of proportion

For Thomas Sawyer himself all this is in no way cause for getting agitated but rather more a proof of his effective work, which he registers with satisfaction. With the help of *ClustrMaps.com*, the student with an obviously extremely high competence in media technology documents not only the number of visitors to his blog but also reconstructs their origins. The maps make clear that *The Laptop I Sold on Ebay* has achieved worldwide publicity. People on all continents visit the blog, most of them from Europe and North America. He clearly had not expected such an enormous wave of attention. "Wow", he writes, visibly surprised in his blog, "this really is going swimmingly isn't it?! I never could have imagined such a response. [...] anyway, I'm off to keep staring at the hit counter; I just can't believe how popular this site is getting! Can we break the million?" In other commentaries he actively urges people to spread the link to his site, opens a *PayPal* account for donations, and places advertisements in his blog, which earn him about £900. It is illuminating, furthermore, that numerous commentators support his approach and method, although the dubious morality of this form of self-administered justice is obvious: the pilloried Amir Massoud Tofangsazan is given no opportunity to defend himself and to comment on the story from his point of view in some adequately organised procedure. *The presumption of innocence is made to appear meaningless; the suspicion nourished by one single individual replaces proper evidence of guilt, the punishment by public defamation is executed without hearing the accused.*[59]

Some of the numerous commentaries by supporters are occasionally downright euphoric as to what opportunities to cause public damage are revealed and demonstrated here. "Such sweet revenge! Laptopguy, you're one clever bloke", one can hear, for example, from *RooRoo*. Others try to heat up the

---

[59] See here also: Solove, Daniel J. (2007) *The Future of Reputation: Gossip, rumor, and privacy on the Internet*, New Haven/London: Yale University Press, p. 117.

emotional atmosphere. He has the hope, one commentator writes, who naturally wants to remain anonymous, that Amir will be deported with his family. As an alternative he wishes for the death or the suicide of the young man. "I hope the slimy bas*ard jumps in front of a bus so no one will ever have the misfortune to come into his presence again [...] Please Amir, Kill yourself", he writes under the pseudonym *Wazzer*. In another mocking reaction we read: "Good luck with the plastic surgery and name change Amir." Only very few of the intensively debating commentators on the website cautiously vote for a different view of things and pose the question whether the actual offence and the publicly executed punishment still stand in an adequate proportionate relationship.[60] So the voices do still exist, albeit only very few, that stress that here is a *characteristic asymmetry of cause and effect*. "I think that revenge should be equivalent to the offence", one can read from *qawsedrf*. Some writers advise Sawyer to engage the police and the judiciary instead of administering self-justice. "The Internet is a very powerful instrument", a contributor writes, "and it seems that many people use it for their personal interests on a global level that never existed before. What we have to learn as Internet users is that this power requires a profound awareness of responsibility on the part of the users." For a moment even Thomas Sawyer develops doubts and reflects in one of his commentaries on the experience that he might very well have lost the control over his revenge campaign, that he was able to trigger this campaign but has now to admit that he had no power or ability to control and determine its effects. "I'm starting to think that this has gone far enough", he writes and hints at stopping the revenge campaign in the digital universe. Yet nothing of this kind actually happens. The site is still online today although it has changed hands and the present proprietor uses his web presence to advertise self-brewed beer and cigar-

---

[60] Solove, Daniel J. (2007) *The Future of Reputation: Gossip, rumor, and privacy on the Internet*, New Haven/London: Yale University Press, p. 95.

ettes. However — luckily for the accused — the case has since lost in attractiveness. There are no new entries any more. The chase has ended.

IV

The New Technologies & the Opportunities of Ruthless Documentation

Anyone desiring to launch a proposal for outrage or trigger a scandal in this day and age has all the opportunities for doing so. The instruments are waiting to be used, the technologies are available. All that is needed is maybe a Smartphone, an unobtrusive digital camera, and access to the Internet for transmitting or posting the images and the audio clips, the videos, and the text files. It is not difficult to set up a blog or even a pillory site, to combine texts, photos, and videos. It is no problem to explain even more complex states of affairs and corroborate them with original documents. The available storage capacity for material data is theoretically infinite.

The instruments and the technologies for investigating norm violations, for documenting these comprehensively, and for finally publishing the resulting materials—with a possible worldwide echo—are within everybody's reach. Search machines relieve everyone of the drudgery of on-the-spot investigations and facilitate comfortable ad-hoc research. Mobile phones, digital cameras, and voicemail services make the boundaries between the private and the public fuzzy. With their help, we can document and prove what has actually happened, and we can thus prop up even the most nebulous of suspicions with evidence that cannot be easily rejected. Occasionally, just one symbolically loaded image or just one crucial minute of a mobile phone video showing everything is sufficient. *YouTube*, blogs, forums, and personal websites may be used to publish materials and to distribute them. They can, whenever needed, also be used as bypass media, making it possible to circumvent and foil the orders of relevance of the gatekeepers and to grant personal perceptions of individuals a previously unknown publicity. Whatever one has done or somebody else has done or said may someday be transformed into data, documents, and thus potential evidence of scandals. Sometimes it is difficult to ward off the impression that we are dealing with *zombie information* because the data — in permanent storage — may not only be retrieved but updated at will, posted anew, recombined and revitalised in infinitely extended and repeated cycles. They can suddenly re-emerge and in their new contexts they can abruptly turn into proofs of scandals and documents of offences.

Digitalisation itself is the decisive factor here, changing scandal cultures worldwide. The Net philosopher Peter Glaser writes in the essay already quoted that "the transition to the digital aggregate leads, first of all, to a kind of highly reactive primeval soup composed of fragments and atomised cultural goods. It resembles the free radicals of chemistry that seek to combine in an aggressive manner."[1] And as soon as there are freely circulating radicals they may possibly spread at great speed and finally be available in the form of infinitely re-combinable bits of data and items of information, as long as there is the hankering after scandalisation in at least a few people and as long as there is a public that is bent upon outrage. It must simply be acknowledged that data can now be more easily acquired, connected, transferred, reconstructed — and permanently stored — than ever before.[2] The extreme implication is

---

[1] Glaser, Peter (2009) Kulturelle Atomkraft [Cultural atomic power]. In: *Berliner Zeitung*, 25 August 2009, http://www.berliner-zeitung.de/archiv/die-digitalisierung-zersetzt-alte-medienformen---ihre-atome-suchen-hitzig-nach-neuer-synthese-kulturelle-atomkraft,10810590, 10661634.html (Retrieved 24 September 2013).

[2] Seemann, Michael (2011) Vom Kontrollverlust zur Filtersouveränität [From loss of control to the sovereignty of filters]. In: *Carta.info*, 06 April

that the distinction between past, present, and future evaporates and a new and simple plane of time emerges and remains, a strangely frozen present of enduring, eternal actuality.

1. The photographs of Abu Ghraib and modern eyewitness testimony

From simulation theory to reality shock

In January 1991 bombs were being dropped on Iraq, it was the time of the first Gulf war, a war that was advertised as a tightly focused surgical operation and a military action of extreme precision. One of the standard arguments advanced by prominent media theorists and image critics, at the time, consisted in the diagnosis of the disappearance of reality. The agony of what was conceived of as real was vociferously proclaimed, entailing the assertion that the very rush of the images, of the aseptic filmlets and the hectic twitching bombardment clips of the war, would obliterate the traditional distinction between reality and illusion. On the occasion of that war, the French philosopher and media theorist Jean Baudrillard granted an interview to two journalists of the leading German newsmagazine *Der Spiegel*. It still makes instructive reading today as a document of intellectual mischievousness and postmodern lightness of touch that would probably be fairly impossible to carry off in today's age of pitiless documentation, and that would therefore appear utterly pathetic. Jean Baudrillard's thesis in 1991 was that authentic reality representation had become impossible, that the media had replaced the indicative by the *irrealis* and that the mechanisms of appearance had installed their reign in a totalitarian way. Even the images of dead and injured people were no longer capable of unsettling the atmosphere of a great spectacle and an entertaining stage management; one could never be sure that the presented pictures of injured and dead people had

---

2011, http://carta.info/39625/vom-kontrollverlust-zur-filtersouveranitat/comment-page-1/ (Retrieved 24 September 2013).

not been manipulated by someone. Baudrillard: "In the realm of the images there are no [...] criteria for truth and falsity. We experience everything like a script. We are part of a great production."[3] Right at the beginning of the interview, Baudrillard introduces the simulation theses that he has elaborated in many of his essays in a radically overstated form. He claims that it is not the media that turn the war into a virtual event—the war is not taking place at all. At the end of the interview, the two journalists ask him to comment on the rumour that he had been invited to join the war as a reporter in order to acquire first-hand experience on the ground. Baudrillard laughs at being confronted with this idea and says that he would not be suited for this kind of job. After all, he would "nourish" himself with the "virtual"[4]—a declaration of intellectual bankruptcy from a distance, which redefines the refusal to test hypotheses by primary personal experience as a philosophical position. The author Susan Sontag has sharply attacked this kind of "[f]ancy rhetoric" in her astute book *Regarding the Pain of Others*.[5] "To speak of reality becoming a spectacle", she writes about Jean Baudrillard and related thinkers, appears to her to be "a breathtaking provincialism. It universalizes the viewing habits of a small, educated population living in the rich part of the world,

---

[3] Seidl, Claudius/Nikolaus von Festenberg (1991) "Der Feind ist verschwunden"—Spiegel-Interview mit dem Pariser Kulturphilosophen Jean Baudrillard über die Wahrnehmbarkeit des Krieges ["The enemy has disappeared"—Spiegel interview with the Paris philosopher of culture, Jean Baudrillard, on the perceptibility of war]. In: *Der Spiegel*, 04 February 1991, p. 220.

[4] Seidl, Claudius/Nikolaus von Festenberg (1991) "Der Feind ist verschwunden"—Spiegel-Interview mit dem Pariser Kulturphilosophen Jean Baudrillard über die Wahrnehmbarkeit des Krieges ["The enemy has disappeared"—Spiegel interview with the Paris philosopher of culture, Jean Baudrillard, on the perceptibility of war]. In: *Der Spiegel*, 04 February 1991, p. 221.

[5] Sontag, Susan (2003) *Regarding the Pain of Others*, New York: Farrar, Straus and Giroux, p. 97.

where news has been converted into entertainment."⁶ And further: "It [this small population] assumes that everyone is a spectator. It suggests, perversely, unseriously, that there is no real suffering in the world."⁷

It is of course questionable whether the followers of Jean Baudrillard would still be able to trade the same philosophical gags about the disappearance of reality and the non-existence of medially transmitted suffering with equal nonchalance today — and whether they would still find an audience via the newsmagazines of modern democratic states. The simulation theorists would not even have to leave the secure environment of their European universities today should they wish to check their diagnoses developed at a great distance by taking the risk of being emotionally affected by all the devastating counterexamples. According to their theory, they would not *really* have to go to war; they would not necessarily have to board a plane for Baghdad in order to stand face to face directly and personally with the cruelty practised there and to subject the news messages to the reality test. *The immediate testimony of eyewitnesses would be superfluous because the effects of such eyewitness testimony can today be produced from a distance and in medialised form.* To test their theses of simulation and stage management, Jean Baudrillard's followers can now simply open their laptops and enter an address in their browser, e.g. http://www.salon.com/2006/03/14/introduction_2. They will find a survey and a catalogue of the emblematic images of the second Gulf war that would make any rash and overhasty self-distancing impossible even at such great distance. They would be able to see the torture photographs and the torture videos from the prison of Abu Ghraib, whose authentic quality cannot reasonably be doubted. Several thousand imprisoned Iraqis were

---

[6] Sontag, Susan (2003) *Regarding the Pain of Others*, New York: Farrar, Straus and Giroux, p. 98.
[7] Sontag, Susan (2003) *Regarding the Pain of Others*, New York: Farrar, Straus and Giroux, p. 99.

interned in this prison at the end of 2003: real and alleged criminals, mentally ill individuals, men, women, and young people, people who happened to be at the wrong place at the wrong time during a raid or a spate of arrests. They were tortured pitilessly and sadistically due to the unconditional conviction that they had to be "boiled soft" — as was stated later in the investigation protocols — that they had to be destabilised by brute force so as to make them give away secrets in the ensuing interrogations.[8] It does not require prophetic gifts to see that the grand theses about deception and manipulation, the invocation of shows and spectacles, can only be rejected with horror in the light of such documents — or can only be maintained at the price of totally irresponsible dogmatism. The reality shock provoked by these images and videos is too massive; it would make any similarly sweeping talk about simulation appear as nothing but a cynical denunciation of knowledge.

Images and ciphers

The American Internet magazine *Salon* that had prepared and published the above quoted comprehensive documentation in 2006 provides its own statistic of the horror. *Salon* correspondent Mark Benjamin writes, with reference to an internal report, that there are 1,325 photographs of prisoner abuse, all taken between 18 October 2003 and 30 December 2003. Furthermore, there are 93 videos documenting the abuse, 660 pornographic pictures, 546 pictures of apparently dead prison inmates, 29 pictures of soldiers simulating or performing sexual acts, 20 pictures of a soldier with a swastika painted between his eyes. 37 pictures show military dogs used for intimidating prisoners. The photographs of slaughtered animals give a strange impression.[9] The *Salon* journalists decide on a selection of pictures that

---

[8] In court, the accused would later often justify their actions by claiming to have been officially-unofficially encouraged.

[9] Benjamin, Mark (2006) Salon exclusive: the Abu Ghraib files. Never-published photos, and an internal army report, show more Iraqi prisoner

are judged to be acceptable to the public; they present it as "The Abu Ghraib files". 279 photos and 19 videos are easily accessible by everyone. The editors have added reports to the "archive of horror" (*Spiegel Online*) that are kept in a deliberately factual tone, summarising the outcomes of the diverse court cases, diary notes by soldiers, and interrogation protocols, with a view to providing context and clear meaning to what is represented.[10]

On these pictures, taken during weeks and months — their time codes allow the precise chronological reconstruction — one can see naked or largely unclothed prisoners who are kept tied to bedposts in unnatural and painfully dislocated body positions for hours and, furthermore, wear women's pants on their heads — a method of humiliating Muslim men that was common everyday practice in the prison of Abu Ghraib. Some of the prisoners show injuries. Other prisoners are attacked by agitated dogs, worked up for the purpose, and bitten on their legs and genitals, and others again are heavily beaten up by guards with the utmost force. Some are obviously psychotic. On one of the photos, one recognises a man who has smeared his face and his body with sludge and excrement. Other pictures show an Iraqi who is beating his head bloody on the door — without being subjected to the use of force, it is said. One video documents that Iraqi prisoners are forced to masturbate in the group. Then there are, of course, also all those photographs that have entered the collective visual memory, photos that are bound to remove the last alibi for any mind that is still geared towards purposive ignorance and light-hearted escapist thought games.[11] These pictures are tangible evidence for the

---

abuse — evidence the government is fighting to hide. In: *Salon.com*, 16 February 2006, http://www.salon.com/news/feature/2006/02/16/abu_ghraib/ (Retrieved 27 September 2013).

[10] Wittrock, Philipp (2006) Abu-Ghureib-Folterskandal. Archiv des Grauens geöffnet [Abu-Ghureib torture scandal: Archive of horrors opened]. In: *Spiegel Online*, 15 March 2006, http://www.spiegel.de/politik/ausland/0,1518,406163,00.html (Retrieved 27 September 2013).

[11] See also in another context: Illies, Florian (2011) Die Macht der Bilder [The power of images]. In: *Die Zeit*, 17 March 2011, p. 49.

fact that an effective scandal is dependent on a relatively small number of rapidly retrievable images. *These very images then become the symbols and the ciphers for the totality of the norm violations in question; they can evoke the events in a compact form provoking strong emotional reaction.*[12] The photograph of the so-called "man in the hood" is possibly the best-known emblematic image of this kind from Abu Ghraib. It shows an Iraqi wearing a hood and a prison blanket like a poncho, standing on a small box and holding electric wires. Should he lose his balance and fall, the torturers threaten, he would execute himself with electric shocks. Another picture shows Private Lynndie England who has achieved dubious fame as the so-called "leash girl". Lynndie England here leads a prisoner, nicknamed "Gus", from his isolation cell with a belt slung around his neck, having him crawl on all fours across the bare floor. Another equally startling picture shows the pleasure obviously derived by the torturers from sadistic choreography and stage management. The photo, another emblem of the mercilessness of the American military, shows the entwined naked bodies of several prisoners piled upon each other to form a pyramid, with their torturers Charles Graner, Lynndie England, and Sabrina Harman posing for the camera with big smiles on their faces. The photograph of the so-called iceman that can also be found in the *Salon* collection documents a scandal that has not yet been properly redressed. It shows a still unidentified man, who was killed during an interrogation and whose dead body had to be kept for some time on a bed of ice in a shower room of the prison wing. As the melting ice water began to collect in front of the shower rooms, some of the soldiers working in this wing discovered the corpse;

---

[12] On the actual origin and development of some of the emblematic images see: Gourevitch, Philip/Errol Morris (2008) Exposure: The woman behind the camera at Abu Ghraib. In: *New Yorker*, 24 March 2008, http://www.newyorker.com/reporting/2008/03/24/080324fa_fact_gourevitch (Retrieved 26 September 2013); and Gourevitch, Philip/Errol Morris (2009) *Standard Operating Procedure: A war story*, London/Basingstoke/Oxford: Picador, pp. 135ff. and pp. 195f.

they even recalled hearing screams during the night without, however, worrying about them. They first examined his wounds and then photographed him. They removed the blindfold from the corpse in order to look at his face, which had been horribly disfigured by the heavy beatings. The crucial photograph shows the American Sabrina Harman bending over the dead body, grinning happily and triumphantly sticking her thumb up in the air. This picture, too, displays its characteristic power and dreadfully shocking impact because it short-circuits two contradictory spheres of meaning: the cruelty of torture and the mischievous cheerfulness of a young woman whose amusement is reminiscent of a holiday.

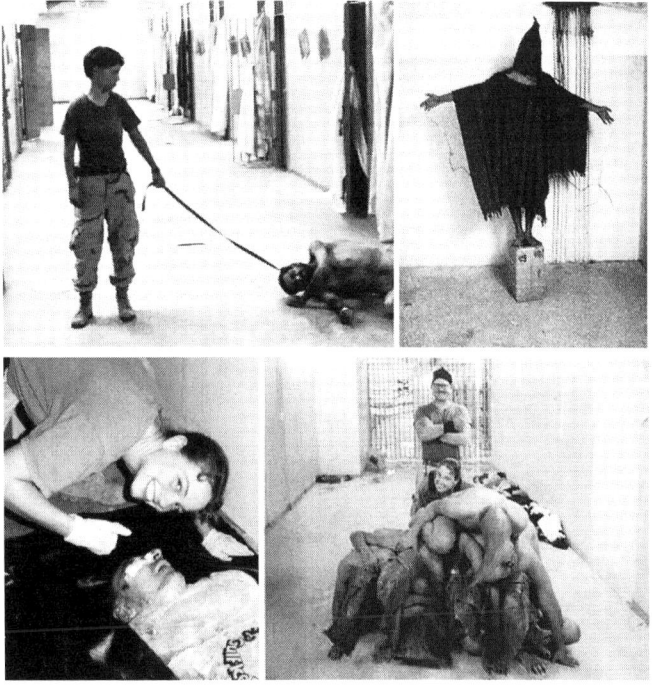

Figures 11 + 12 + 13 + 14: **Emblematic images of the torture scandal of Abu Ghraib circulating worldwide: "the man on the leash", "the human pyramid", the so-called "man with the hood", and the "iceman".**

The self-fabricated panopticon

It is one of the topoi of image-critical analysis in connection with the work of the French philosopher Michel Foucault to refer to the thought model of the panopticon of the philosopher Jeremy Bentham developed at the end of the eighteenth century.[13] Bentham's aim was to perfect the surveillance of prison inmates. He therefore conceived of a circular prison building with all the single cells arranged around its centre in the pattern of a fan. This design permitted the guards and other staff to observe every single inmate from an inspection house in the centre without being seen themselves. The inmates are aware of this state of potentially total visibility although they cannot possibly know whether they are actually observed in every moment of their imprisonment. They consequently adapt their behaviour correspondingly, so the theory implies. They internalise the idea of potential control and allow themselves to be disciplined accordingly; and they behave as if they were actually observed all the time simply because this might indeed be the case.

If the thought model by Jeremy Bentham is made the basis for an analysis of the torture pictures in the present digital age, a fundamental change becomes apparent that has to do with the relationship between guards and guarded, between observers and observed. The omnipresent digital media have become and are still becoming ever smaller and ever more powerful, cameras, mobile phones, and video cameras in particular. They make it possible (independently of the personal goals of the agents) to interchange roles and perspectives in a radical way. Observers are suddenly observed themselves, guards likewise guarded, and prison warders become prisoners by virtue of their very lust for documentation that manoeuvres them into the prison while forgetting that the pictures and film sequences they produce might one day jeopardise their very existence.

---

[13] Foucault, Michel (1991/1975) *Discipline and Punish: The birth of the prison*, London/New York: Penguin Books, pp. 200ff.

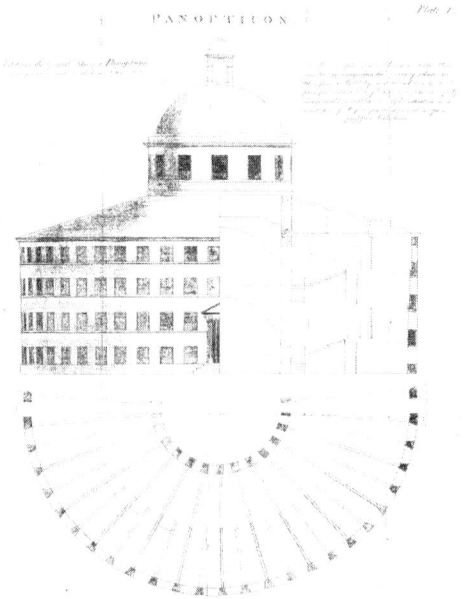

Figure 15: **The drawing of Jeremy Bentham's panopticon — from the centre of the building, every single cell may be inspected.**[14]

They observe themselves as well as others, but are unaware of the possible consequences of their being observed and without taking into account the mobility of data and documents in the digital age.[15] This

---

[14] Bentham, Jeremy (1791) *Panopticon: Or, the inspection-house*, Dublin: Thomas Byrne.

[15] In spring 2011 a crime was publicly reported that certainly matches the torture scandal of Abu Ghraib: a group of American soldiers, the magazines *Der Spiegel* and *Rolling Stone* revealed, had carried out regular hunts for civilians in Afghanistan, had executed them for fun and the lust to kill, and had staged the murders as acts of self-defence by planting enemy weapons on the victims. And again the perpetrators of the crimes supplied the evidence themselves in the form of their own pictures and videos; the investigation secured about 4,000 photos. For the details of this media-technically comparable scandal see: Goetz, John/Marc Hujer (2011) Adams Krieg [Adam's war]. In: *Der Spiegel*, 21 March 2011, pp. 64–71. Furthermore: Boal, Mark (2011) The kill team:

form of mental innocence and naïveté counteracting anticipation in a self-fabricated panopticon can be shown up compellingly by the concrete examples under discussion. The procedures and motives of those who fabricated the pictures and videos in Abu Ghraib have meanwhile been analysed in detail. A special, in parts apologetic, film about the torture photographers (*Standard Operating Procedure*) is in its entirety available on the Net. A book based on this film has been published. It reconstructs the history of the origins of these modern icons of horror without, however, reprinting a single picture. It exclusively follows the perspective of those perpetrators who were later taken to court and who make up a core group consisting of only a few of the persons shown in the pictures. Only these few are sentenced to imprisonment, by the way—an illuminating detail, again demonstrating the power of images. All the many others who must have been involved, for instance in the torturing and killing of the "iceman", who have attended to wounds, transported injured persons, and bullied other prisoners, got off scot-free. No pictures of these persons exist that could be made public. Personnel of the CIA or the Defence Intelligence Service are not prosecuted, anyway. Put succinctly, this means: each one of the torture photographs highlights one single specific moment of aggression—but the overwhelming impact of these photographs masks and conceals a hidden subsidiary world of unobserved crimes and events.

The medium of blameless participation

The reservist Jeremy Sivits, who took the picture of the human pyramid, is amongst those who are prosecuted in a court of law. His punishment consists in one year in jail and a dishonourable discharge from the army. The American private Lynndie

---

How U.S. soldiers in Afghanistan murdered innocent civilians. Plus: An exclusive look at the war crime images the Pentagon tried to censor. In: *Rolling Stone*, 27 March 2011, http://www.rollingstone.com/politics/news/the-kill-team-20110327 (Retrieved 25 September 2013).

England took several pictures — and can be seen in them. In one of them she leads a prisoner, who is forced to crawl on the ground, from his cell with a belt around his neck, thus visually documenting an archetypal scene of brutal, sexually connoted dominance.[16] In another one, she is shown laughing and pointing at the genitals of prisoners who are forced to masturbate. Then she photographs fellow soldiers without a flash so that they remain unaware of being photographed. She finally gets a prison sentence of three years and becomes, as is reported, the "face of Abu Ghraib".[17] The Rolling Stones sing about her; she is parodied in an episode of *The Simpsons*. She becomes the personification of the torture scandal. *The example of Lynndie England shows that a scandal always needs concrete persons, culpable individuals that can be held responsible for their actions, because they could have acted differently and could have chosen alternatives.*[18] Portraits and interviews in big magazines have been upsetting people because they made quite clear that Lynndie England did *not* recognise and accept her own responsibility, that she did not feel any remorse for what she did, that she shrugged off the pain and suffering of the torture victims and much rather con-

---

[16] For an analysis of this picture see: Sontag, Susan (2004) Endloser Krieg, endloser Strom von Fotos [Endless war, endless stream of photos]. In: *Sueddeutsche.de*, 24 May 2004, http://www.sueddeutsche.de/politik/folteraffaere-endloser-krieg-endloser-strom-von-fotos-1.914679 (Retrieved 24 September 2013).

[17] Streck, Michael (2008) Lynndie England. Das Gesicht von Abu Ghraib [Lynndie England: The face of Abu Ghraib]. In: *Stern.de*, 19 March 2008, http://www.stern.de/politik/ausland/lynndie-england-das-gesicht-von-abu-ghraib-614585.html (Retrieved 24 September 2013). Furthermore: Jones, David (2009) Why the hell should I feel sorry, says girl soldier who abused Iraqi prisoners at Abu Ghraib prison. In: *Mail Online*, 13 June 2009, http://www.dailymail.co.uk/news/article-1192701/Why-hell-I-feel-sorry-says-girl-soldier-abused-Iraqi-prisoners-Abu-Ghraib-prison.html (Retrieved 25 September 2013).

[18] The connection between freedom and responsibility (and, consequently, guilt) is discussed in general terms in the following book: Foerster, Heinz von/Bernhard Poerksen (2002) *Understanding Systems: Conversations on epistemology and ethics*, New York/Heidelberg: Kluwer Academic/Plenum Publishers/Carl-Auer-Systeme, especially pp. 36f.

sidered herself as a victim of unfair deception. It is a common procedure of rejecting guilt by subjects of scandalisation to redefine their actions as externally determined events and their former power as factual powerlessness due to appalling circumstances and oppressive forces.[19] Many pictures were taken by specialist Sabrina Harman, a military police woman from Maryland, with a traditional digital camera. She was also the one who laughingly bent over the disfigured face of the killed "iceman", triumphantly sticking up her thumb in her rubber glove. Her sentence: six months in prison. Staff sergeant Ivan Frederick — sentenced to eight and a half years in prison — had his picture taken sitting on an Iraqi detainee. He also admitted tying the electric cables to the hands of the so-called "man in the hood" and to having threatened him with lethal electric shocks; in addition, he admitted forcing prisoners to masturbate.[20]

He can be seen with a camera in his hands in a picture of the man in the hood, whose horribly helpless suffering reminds some observers of the image of the crucified Christ. This is most instructive because the act of taking a photograph is obviously seen as granting the persons with cameras a particular form of justification and a sort of moralising rationalisation of what they are doing. Taking up the camera thus obviously allows the perpetrators a (fictitious) change of role and an act of briefly distancing themselves — allowing them, furthermore, to suppress rising scruples. In some of their letters and statements the torturers give the impression that they understand the camera —

---

[19] See in particular the following interview: Streck, Michael/Jan Christoph Wiechmann (2008) Die Frau aus dem Folterknast [The woman from the torture nick]. In: *Stern*, 19 March 2008, pp. 30ff.

[20] The journalist Carolin Emcke has written a portrait of Ivan Frederick and an illuminating analysis of the diffuse command structures in Abu Ghraib, which laid down a direction but, at the same time, left manoeuvring space for excesses. Emcke, Carolin (2005) Anatomie der Folter. Der Befehlskörper von Abu Ghraib [Anatomy of torture: The body of command of Abu Ghraib], http://www.carolin-emcke.de/de/article/15.anatomie-der-folter-der-befehlskoerper-von-abu-ghureib.html (Retrieved 25 September 2013).

perhaps only in some semi-aware way and manner—as a *medium of blameless participation*, as an instrument of distance-creating documentation. The camera is supposed to relieve its user subjects of their role and responsibility for what is happening: its users are only *recording* what is happening, they are only agents of *transmission*, and not active aggressive perpetrators of crimes.[21] Even Charles Graner, the leading performer of crimes, who was sentenced to ten years in prison, occasionally justified his actions towards Lynndie England with the statement that somebody had after all to document the events in Abu Ghraib in as credible as possible a way. War veterans would need documentary evidence for traumatising experiences after their return home, for the purposes of free therapy and adequate treatment, without which they might perhaps be ignored and rebuffed. A large number of photographs, namely 173 of the 279 pictures published by *Salon.com*, were taken with his Sony FD Mavica. And it was he who spread the photographs showing the tortures. Graner boasted about them, copied them on CDs, passed them on to acquaintances in his unit, showed them openly to his superiors and to higher-ranking military persons who had no objections—and so actually used his camera as an instrument for the documentation of his own crimes. His brutal

---

[21] It is interesting, in this context, to read the extended excerpts from the letters by Specialist Sabrina Harman to her friend in the USA, quoted by Philip Gourevitch and Errol Morris. She is constantly struggling with her doubts and pricks of conscience that keep flaring up and legitimates the many pictures she has taken of scenes of violence and torture with an alleged duty to documentation. Nobody would otherwise ever believe, she argues, what she had seen. The example of Sabrina Harman clearly shows (quite independently of the ethical-moral assessment of her role) that the withdrawal to the position of merely a photographing observer may be used as a justification. The reflection of the use of a particular medium here serves to claim the position of an ultimately innocent agent who has done nothing the whole time but collect evidence for disclosure at some later date. Gourevitch, Philip/Errol Morris (2008) Exposure: The woman behind the camera at Abu Ghraib. In: *New Yorker*, 24 March 2008, http://www.newyorker.com/reporting/2008/03/24/080324fa_fact_gourevitch (Retrieved 25 September 2013).

treatment of the prisoners is described in an interview by the Iraqi Mohanded Juma Juma, which was first published by the *Washington Post* and is still accessible online. "They stripped me from my clothes", he said, "and all the stuff that they gave me and I spent 6 days in that situation. [...] Approximately at 2 at night, the door opened and Graner was there. He cuffed my hands behind my back and he cuffed my feet and he took me to the shower room. When they finished interrogating me, the female interrogator left. And then Graner and another man, who looked like Graner but doesn't have glasses, and has a thin moustache, and he was young and tall, came into the room. They threw pepper on my face and the beating started. This went on for a half hour. And then he started beating me with the chair until the chair was broken. After that they started choking me. At that time I thought I was going to die, but it's a miracle I lived. And then they started beating me again. They concentrated on beating me in my heart until they got tired from beating me. They took a little break and then they started kicking me very hard with their feet until I passed out. In the second scene at the night shift, I saw a new guard that wears glasses and has a red face. He charged his pistol and pointed it at a lot of the prisoners to threaten them with it. I saw things no one would see, they are amazing. They come in the morning shift with two prisoners and they were father and son. They were both naked. They put them in front of each other and they counted 1, 2, 3, and then removed the bags from their heads. When the son saw his father naked he was crying. He was crying because of seeing his father. And then at night, Graner used to throw the food into the toilet and said ,'go take it and eat it'. And I saw also in Room #5 they brought the dogs. Graner brought the dogs and they bit him in the right and left leg. He was from Iran and they started beating him up in the main hallway of the prison."[22]

---

[22] Prisoner Interview/Interrogation Team, 10th Military Police Battalion, 3rd Police Group, Abu Ghraib Prison Complex (2004) *Translation of Statement*

These are the moments and scenes that Graner records on photographs in order to save them from oblivion and to keep them for a global public to view at a later date. Paradoxically, *he evidently does not really know himself what he is photographing when he is taking his pictures*.[23] He has no idea that the pictures will forever connect him with the horrors of torture, will make him a hate figure as soon as they are placed in a different, in a new context. He is constantly at the centre of the excesses of violence and loves to present himself in the pose of a victorious conqueror. He can be watched beating prisoners, his hands protected by rubber gloves against the blood of the maltreated, he can be seen sewing up the wounds of tortured persons or holding down a prisoner on a stretcher like an animal killed in a hunt.

The uncanny clone

The pictures essentially document — apart from the substantial violence — a semantic universe in its own right, a peculiar world of meaning of its own. In this world, superiors right up to the American Minister of Defence, Donald Rumsfeld, and the President George W. Bush, promote the humiliations, possibly even recommend them, and certainly tolerate them. Thus they provide a fundamental and not totally implausible pattern of self-justification for the perpetrators on the grounds that there had been different pronouncements by the American leadership that made the prohibition of torture appear more or less obsolete.[24]

Provided by Mohanded Juma Juma, 18 January 2004, http://media.washingtonpost.com/wp-srv/world/iraq/abughraib/152307.pdf (Retrieved 25 September 2013).

[23] On these considerations see: Seemann, Michael (2010) Die Krankenakte von Tut Ench Amun [The medical record of Tutankhamun]. In: *CTRL-Verlust*, 11 January 2010, http://www.ctrl-verlust.net/die-krankenakte-von-tut-ench-amun/ (Retrieved 30 September 2013).

[24] In August 2002, George W. Bush proclaims the right to disregard the prohibition of torture in times of crisis. In December of the same year, his Defence Secretary, Donald Rumsfeld, approves in an internal memorandum the following interrogation methods, amongst others, for the prison

In this other world, torture is perhaps not completely legal but in any case legitimate, and those who are made to suffer are not accepted as human beings with equal rights but are defined as aggressors and terrorist warriors. They are a menace, and not an equal opponent that deserves a minimum of respect. In this other world, pictures of violence can be made more attractive by adding sexual humiliation carried out allegedly for the preparatory purpose of optimally effective interrogation, but perhaps also in order to furnish the pictures circulating amongst the comrade soldiers with additional stimulation and kicks. But this self-created semantic universe, this specific reality of torturers and photographers, only exists for a select public. *This peculiar reality must be sealed off in precisely determined ways in order to control information. This undertaking is, however, doomed to fail for a double reason. For one, the material has become extremely mobile, it can easily be copied and transferred, stored and archived independently of any locality. Furthermore, it is passed on in the most breathtakingly sloppy way and in no way treated with the scrupulous care it requires.* When the then Staff Sergeant Joseph Darby returns to Abu Ghraib from a family holiday, he is told that he has missed a bloody shoot-out but that it has been preserved on film.[25] He

---

camp of Guantanamo: intimidation of prisoners with dogs, refusal of warm meals, standing upright in uncomfortable positions for unlimited periods of time, undressing of prisoners for interrogation. Rumsfeld, however, retracts this extensive authorisation of bullying prisoners in January 2003 and draws up new guidelines. The original warrant practically remains in place, however. On this theme complex see also: Vorsamer, Barbara (2009) Fünf Jahre Abu Ghraib. Chronologie des Folterskandals [Five years of Abu Ghraib: Chronology of the torture scandal]. In: *Sueddeutsche.de*, 14 May 2009, http://www.sueddeutsche.de/politik/fuenf-jahre-abu-ghraib-chronologie-des-folterscandals-1.462901 (Retrieved 17 September 2013).

[25] On the following see: Gourevitch, Philip/Errol Morris (2009) *Standard Operating Procedure: A war story*, London/Basingstoke/Oxford: Picador, pp. 232ff. Furthermore: Schorn, Daniel (2007) Exposing the truth of Abu Ghraib. In: *CBS News.com*, 24 June 2007, http://www.cbsnews.com/stories/2006/12/07/60minutes/main2238188.shtml (Retrieved 25 September 2013).

asks Charles Graner for information and is given two randomly picked CDs that, however, do not contain the expected pictures of the mentioned shoot-outs but the torture photographs that will soon circulate round the world. Presumably, he was given the torture images by mistake or simply because of the characteristic negligence that illustrates how secure and safe everybody felt that the crimes committed would be understood as something normal, that the semantic universe would not really be taken to be something obscene, bizarre, or just downright criminal.[26] Darby copies both CDs and returns them to Graner. At first, he cannot classify and contextualise the images. But as soon as he recognises on a photograph his fellow servicemen behind the "human pyramid", he realises that the pictured scenes have been played out in the prison and therefore in his very own personal world. He understands that he is not looking at some perverse joke amongst American soldiers but at the humiliation and torturing of prisoners. After some hesitation — well aware of the potential consequences of such a betrayal, particularly the possible bullying — he decides to inform his superiors, who start investigations in January 2004 and, as far as one knows, immediately inform the US Minister of Defence, Donald Rumsfeld, and soon after also the American President.

In the prison itself, a hectic search for other pictures begins; questionnaires are distributed. For a short time amnesty boxes for questionable material are set up, probably not even, and possibly not even primarily, with the intention of carrying out a more thorough investigation and examination, but mainly with

---

[26] Tangentially: Charles Graner boasts before his fellow soldiers with the claim that he is involved in an affair in Abu Ghraib with the still very young Lynndie England; and he offers photographic evidence to corroborate his claim. He e-mails pictures showing him and England having sex to friends and acquaintances. Jones, David (2009) Why the hell should I feel sorry, says girl soldier who abused Iraqi prisoners at Abu Ghraib prison. In: *Mail Online*, 13 June 2009, http://www.dailymail.co.uk/news/article-1192701/Why-hell-I-feel-sorry-says-girl-soldier-abused-Iraqi-prisoners-Abu-Ghraib-prison.html (Retrieved 25 September 2013).

the purpose of securing as many pictures as possible in order to contain the damage and prevent the further spreading of discrediting material.[27] Even the relatives of soldiers who are living in the USA are contacted and asked for pictures that might have reached them via e-mail from Iraq. It is as yet not known who passed the torture documents to the media but the final collapse of the semantic universe of Charles Graner and his collaborators can be pinned to an exact date: 20 April 2004. On this day the US television station *CBS* shows the first pictures from the whistle-blower that travel around the world within days and produce an outcry of indignation. The reputation of the US is damaged immensely because the official justification of the Iraq war—consisting not only in the search for weapons of mass destruction but also in the removal from power of the dictator Saddam Hussein and the securing of human and freedom rights —is here blown to bits before the eyes of the world. High-ranking military personnel, the Minister of Defence, Donald Rumsfeld, and the Secretary of State, Condoleezza Rice, offer their apologies. The American President, George W. Bush, has himself quoted with the statement that he had never ordered torture.

At this point in time, the pictures have long become ubiquitous and have become the codes of a reality that can no longer be denied. They can be found in the marketplaces of Iraq. Enlarged to poster size, they are stuck to the walls of houses, they are passed from hand to hand in photo albums, they are spread as e-mail attachments, stored on CDs[28]—and they naturally provoke horrible forms of retaliation as well as images

---

[27] As for the criticisms of the investigation process and the potential destruction of evidence, cf. Gourevitch, Philip/Errol Morris (2009) *Standard Operating Procedure: A war story*, London/Basingstoke/Oxford: Picador, pp. 245ff.

[28] Amnesty International (2009) Abu Ghraib und kein Ende [Abu Ghraib and no end in sight]. In: *Amnesty Journal*, June 2009, http://www.amnesty.de/journal/2009/juni/abu-ghraib-und-kein-ende (Retrieved 27 September 2013).

of revenge and counter-images of immense cruelty.[29] Even caricaturists and artists take up the by now worldwide available motifs. The silhouette of the man in the hood, according to the art historian W.J.T. Mitchell, changes into an "uncanny clone", a symbol of public remembrance, which remains intelligible even in the context of a parodying advertisement.[30] Only a single example must suffice here to show this method of creative estrangement and explicit violation of context. One day anonymous activists in New York distribute the image of a silhouette placed against a monochrome background, thus reminding observers of the iPod dancer and the corresponding advertising campaign by Apple. This time, however, the dancer stands on a small black box—and he has a hood on his head, wires in his hands, a poncho draped round his body. The Apple logo has been substituted with a bomb and instead of "iPod" it now says "iRaq".

However, these forms of an aesthetic and inevitably somewhat light-hearted variant of the accusation do not succeed in establishing themselves as new emblematic images because they are simply not strong enough to approximate let alone surpass the shock effect of the original photographs. But it is still instructive that *the dramatic original images obviously produce their impact much more directly than anything that is written. And the images are, furthermore, not open to contradiction in a comparable way.*

---

[29] In May 2004 a video is circulated that documents the beheading of the kidnapped Amerian Nick Berg. His kidnappers declare the action to be a reaction to the torture in Abu Ghraib.

[30] Quoted from: Boehme, Tim Caspar (2011) Bilder des Krieges gegen den Terror. Die Gespenster der Vergangenheit [Images from the war on terror: The ghosts of the past]. In: *Taz.de*, 19 May 2011, http://www.taz.de/1/leben/kuenste/artikel/1/die-gespenster-der-vergangenheit/ (Retrieved 25 September 2013).

Figure 16: The fusion of two iconic images—the so-called "man in the hood" and the iPod dancer.

That images may outdo words and texts, that visual signs may prevail over linguistic signs and may even surpass them with instant persuasive power, is endorsed by the fact that the crimes in Abu Ghraib had already become known in December 2003 through a note smuggled out of the prison. However, Iraqi lawyers had raised questions as to the trustworthiness of what was described. In the note from the prison, a woman reported that several female prisoners had been raped by American prison warders and were now pregnant. She asked Iraqi resistance groups to bomb the prison in order to spare the inmates further shame. The correctness of her allegations was confirmed officially after an internal investigation. However, the report of the desperate woman—lacking as it did any documentary image—did not trigger equally shocked reactions amongst the public, and even amongst the essentially sympathetic lawyers scepticism prevailed. By contrast, photographs still seem to guarantee reality and truth. They are not *assertions that can easily be denied* and explained away *but pieces of evidence* that can stand on their own — although they do require linguistic explication.³¹

From the authenticity of the material to the reliability of the source

Nevertheless, the ascription of unqualified authority to photographic images may appear surprising because a long-lasting debate, not only within academic circles, has been concerned with the loss of authority of the documentary image, a debate that has in fact been aiming at the destruction of its quality as evidence and its aura of pure and immediate factuality. The central argument is the following, to put it briefly: *a photograph is a paradoxical construct of subjectivity presenting itself pseudo-objectively, pretending to be realistic appearance and authentic staging*. The reasons are simple: a photograph can be edited with little effort and faked without trace, particularly with currently available image processing software tools.³² In addition, any photograph inevitably incorporates a particular perspective. It therefore cannot claim to be a representative section of the world because it systematically obscures a huge and tremendously multi-faceted residual reality. The crucial question is then whether this undoubted fact makes it impossible to trust the torture photographs of Abu Ghraib. Do they lose their evidential force; is their authority reduced by such a general

---

31 In the year 2009, the *Daily Telegraph* newspaper reveals that there are apparently pictures showing the rape of a woman and of a man. Nothing has become known about the offenders, and the photographs have not been published. On these events, see the following newspaper reports: Harding, Luke (2004) The other prisoners. In: *Guardian.co.uk*, 20 May 2004, http://www.guardian.co.uk/world/2004/may/20/iraq.gender (Retrieved 27 September 2013); Gardham, Duncan/Paul Cruickshank (2009) Abu Ghraib abuse photos 'show rape'. In: *The Telegraph*, 27 May 2009, http://www.telegraph.co.uk/news/world news/northamerica/usa/5395830/Abu-Ghraib-abuse-photos-show-rape.html (Retrieved 27 September 2013).
32 Bolz, Norbert (1993) *Am Ende der Gutenberg-Galaxis. Die neuen Communicationsverhältnisse* [*At the End of the Gutenberg Galaxis: The new conditions of communication*], Munich: Fink, pp. 166ff.

suspicion of their having been stage-managed? This is not at all the case, as all the reactions to the visual material show. A review of the publications and reflections on the power of images with regard to the Abu Ghraib case yields the following results: there is no criticism of images and stage management. All too massive is the overwhelming impression of reality, all too shocking and obscene the content of the documents. Pure naked horror prevails. There is no comment from the simulation theorists; no disciples of the philosopher Jean Baudrillard can bring themselves to test the master's theses about the agony of what is conceived of as real in a confrontation with the freely floating material from Abu Ghraib. Only Tony Blair, the former British Prime Minister, is said to have voiced the assessment that the images could not possibly be genuine. But his view remains the exception. Why? What features of the material and its communicative context could possibly block the common ad-hoc doubts and the fundamental suspicion of stage management (a well-tested defence strategy to ward off guilt)? Or to pose the question differently: what are the reasons that make the impression of authenticity and truth irrepressible? The first and material-related answer is that the photos and videos exhibit their very own aesthetics of authenticity. *This aesthetics of authenticity, however, consists in its anti-aesthetics – this is the decisive paradox.* Each one of the pictures lacks the trappings of perfection and that is the reason why they appear so genuine, so real.

It is more than obvious that the cameras were not worked by professionals. The photographs have turned out blurry and smudgy, the persons are badly caught, their faces are frequently truncated, and the scenes are only dimly lit. The second and context-related answer is that in the digital age the photographic document no longer carries evidential force because it is too easily manipulated. *The trustworthiness of the source of images and the authority of the persons and institutions reacting to the publication of the images have since become the decisive kind of qualifying meta-information.* In the present case, the reactions of the American government and the statements by Donald Rumsfeld,

Condoleezza Rice, and George W. Bush—the public apologies, the proclamation of disgust, the insistent assertions not to have known anything about the situation in the prison of Abu Ghraib —have certified the genuineness of the material in a derivative way, as it were, and thus reinforced its evidential force. And even the finally sentenced perpetrators were and are, of course, particularly credible witnesses for the prosecution. Photographs and films have made innumerable human beings in the whole world eyewitnesses of a crime. Consequently, it is not the images themselves that still outrage and shock today; it is, quite tangibly, quite directly, the reality of what they show.

2. The camera phone film from Hong Kong and the mobile phone as an all-purpose weapon

The triumphant advance of an indiscrete technology

Hong Kong is one of the places in this world that is teeming with mobile phones. For every thousand inhabitants there are 899 mobile phone contracts; adding prepaid cards raises the number to 1712. This means that many people living in this Asian metropolis use more than one mobile phone. The majority of these mobile phones are, as is now customary with many models, fitted with a camera. Mobile phones have long ceased—universally by now—to be a status symbol or a plaything for elites; they have become integrated in everyday communication. They are used for appointments and the writing and sending of e-mails and short messages (via SMS or WhatsApp), they serve to record the normality of people's lives, to shoot photographs of things and events to remember, to make wacky videos, to manage addresses, to access *Facebook, Twitter,* or *YouTube*, and to listen to music. And they can also be used as *multipurpose weapons of scandalisation,* and can thus be understood, in the true sense of the word, as a mass medium that defies the traditional constellation of surveillance—only a few powerful people observe a large number of comparatively powerless people—with "total surveillance from below".[33] Mobile phones can be used unobtrusively to document actual or alleged norm violations committed by other people and to make these documents accessible to an interested public on suitable platforms. And this very thing happened in the case of the unemployed Hong Kong man Roger Chan Yuet-tung, who has since become known worldwide under the name *Bus Uncle*.[34] His story exemplifies a kind of communication that vacillates between genuine outrage and quirky fascination. Without the mobile phone and without the globally growing lust for mutual observation it would certainly never have taken off.[35]

Everything starts on the evening of 27 or maybe 29 April 2006—nobody really knows when exactly because the dates and references in circulation vary. At about 23.00h, 51-year-old Roger Chan Yuet-tung is travelling on the double-decker express bus 68X in Hong Kong in the direction of the Yuen Long district, where his home is—all this is held to be correct— and he keeps speaking on his phone in a very loud voice the whole time. A passenger sitting behind him, later identified as

---

[33] Kreye, Andrian (2007) Handy-Videos als Kontrollmacht. Digitale Häme [Mobile phone videos as a force of control: Digital gloating]. In: *Sueddeutsche.de*, 03 January 2007, http://www.sueddeutsche.de/politik/handy-videos-als-kontrollmacht-digitale-haeme-1.843857 (Retrieved 29 September 2013).

[34] For the reconstruction of the case see e.g.: Bray, Marianne (2006) Irate HK man unlikely Web hero. In: *CNN.com International*, 09 June 2006, http://edition.cnn.com/2006/WORLD/asiapcf/06/07/hk.uncle/ (Retrieved 29 September 2013); Lam, Agnes (2006) Bus uncle taught me a lesson. In: *South China Morning Post*, 30 May 2006, p. 3; Lam, Agnes (2006) Along for the ride. In: *South China Morning Post*, 03 June 2006, p. 16; Soong, Roland (2006) Bus uncle. In: *EastSouthWestNorth*, 24 May 2006, http://www.zonaeuropa.com/20060524_1.htm (Retrieved 28 January 2010).

[35] See in this connection the insightful essay on "surveillance practiced as a workaday activity" by Schroer, Markus (2003) Sehen und gesehen werden. Von der Angst vor der Überwachung zur Lust an der Beobachtung? [Seeing and being seen: From the fear of surveillance to the lust for observation?] In: *Merkur*, vol. 57, no. 2, pp. 169–173.

Elvis Alvin Ho, feels disturbed, taps Chan on the shoulder and asks him to lower his voice.[36] In doing so, he uses the Cantonese word for uncle, which in Hong Kong is a polite way of addressing older men. Despite this, Chan throws a tantrum and begins to berate the 23-year-old real estate agent. "Why did you tap on my shoulder?" he wants to know from Ho. "I've just been speaking on the phone." Ho reacts in a conciliatory manner, but this makes Chan even angrier. "I don't know you. And you don't know me. So why are you doing this?", he furiously questions him, turning back and bending over the seat to face Ho, his finger stopping only a few centimetres away from Ho's face. The elderly man in his white shirt repeatedly challenges him to apologise. When Ho does so, however, Chan still cannot stop. He goes on screaming that the quarrel has not been resolved. Six minutes his outburst of anger lasts, for six minutes he screams at Ho without intermission, while Ho remains sitting there in a strikingly relaxed manner, his arm lazily stretched over the back rest of his seat. This posture fuels Chan's rage even more. "I am under pressure, you are under pressure. Why are you provoking me?", he wants to know. Swear words fly, Chan reviles Ho's mother, roars vulgar insults through the speeding bus—until his mobile phone starts ringing again. He mumbles "Blast!", turns away and starts talking on the phone again.

---

[36] From this point, the incident is recorded on video, which makes the reconstruction of the case easier. See: http://www.youtube.com/watch?v=H20dhY01Xjk (Retrieved 29 September 2013).

Figure 17: **Roger Chan Yuet-tung's angry outburst in a Hong Kong night bus — recorded by a mobile phone camera.**

Chan and Ho have no idea, simply do not realise that another passenger, Jon Fong, accountant and student of psychology, is filming Chan's tantrum and his tirades from the other side of the aisle. He is using his mobile phone as an *indiscrete technology* — in the precise wording of the sociologist Geoff Cooper — as an instrument of effective scandalisation, as it is globally omnipresent nowadays.[37] 4.6 billion people own a mobile phone, a 2010 estimate says. More than a billion handsets are fitted with a camera function, a technology that lends its users the power to function as amateur reporters, spies, or evidence gathering wit-

---

[37] Cooper, Geoff (2002) The mutable mobile: Social theory in the wireless world. In: Barry Brown/Nicola Green/Richard Harper (eds.) *Wireless World: Social and interactional aspects of the mobile age*, London: Springer, pp. 19–31.

nesses.[38] It blurs the differences between once strictly separated spheres of communication, between the private and the public spheres, backstage and front region, everyday world and working world—as here illustrated by the story of the *Bus Uncle* in Hong Kong. Only two days after the encounter on the bus, the then 21-year-old Jon Fong publishes the pixelated camera phone video on *YouTube* under the pseudonym *sjfgjj*, without however naming the two performing central agents.[39] It is his hobby, he says later. And he wanted to save the material in case the two men started to fight and hit each other.

The camera phone film as evidence of a scandal: the downfall of John Galliano

It is not a question of rumours and assumptions but of certainties. Camera phone films and their own peculiar anti-aesthetics increasingly function as providers of evidence of scandals, evidence that is viewed as particularly authentic. A prominent example is the Dior designer John Galliano. He had to leave his job because in December 2010 (and shortly afterwards again), drunk in a Paris café, he had screamed anti-Semitic tirades — and was filmed by a camera phone on at least one of these occasions. On a video that is accessible on the Net a voice from behind the scene asks him: "Are you blond, with blue eyes?" He replies: "No, but I love Hitler." And he goes on: "And people like you would be dead today. Your mothers, your forefathers, would be… gassed and… dead." When the British tabloid newspaper *The Sun* published the video online, his career with the renowned fashion house was over, and everybody hastened to explain that racism and anti-Semitism would not be tolerated under any circumstances. His sudden downfall illustrates the power of an indiscreet but omnipresent technology that can destroy an image within the shortest conceivable span of time.

---

[38] Wong, May (2007) Erfindung mit Nebenwirkungen. Der Vater des Foto-Handys [Invention with side effects: The father of the camera phone] In: *Spiegel Online*, 26 May 2007, http://www.spiegel.de/netzwelt/mobil/0,1518,484976,00.html (Retrieved 25 September 2013).

[39] http://www.youtube.com/watch?v=H20dhY01Xjk (Retrieved 29 September 2013).

Hype around a marginal piece

However, the video is not only watched by a few of Fong's friends and acquaintances. It turns into a *YouTube* hit and thus becomes an example of how an essentially unimportant incident can be scandalised by a single individual and consequently, thanks to the concentrated power of Web 2.0, develop into an event and a curious Internet meme that attracts worldwide attention. The very banal and infinitely trivial content of the story throws into sharp relief the formal features that tend to shore up an excess of global attention or at least render it likely. In May 2006, the video had already become one of the favourite viewings on the platform. It continued to gain in importance because of a self-reinforcing mechanism of attention grabbing, a *ranking principle*, whose essential feature is to reward achieved attention with even greater attention. It is an all too well-known phenomenon that books ranking high on a list of bestsellers sell even better simply for that reason alone. The same applies to hit lists on their corresponding Net platforms. *YouTube* (loading an average 48 hours of video material every single minute) automatically computes rankings and recommends videos by their viewing frequency, thus obviously in turn attracting even more viewers to the high-ranked films. The reception career of *Bus Uncle* can no longer be reconstructed in precise detail. An author of the news agency Associated Press sees the film in position 2 in this month,[40] other sources claim it had made it to position 1.[41] Be that as it may, the fact is that the video—the meme—has reached millions of people within an extremely short time—and that, due to the process of permanent feedback,

---

[40] Associated Press (2006) Grumpy man on a bus becomes star of the Internet. In: *Guardian.co.uk*, 26 May 2006, http://www.guardian.co.uk/technology/2006/may/26/news.newmedia (Retrieved 29 September 2013).

[41] Bray, Marianne (2006) Irate HK man unlikely Web hero. In: *CNN.com International*, 09 June 2006, http://edition.cnn.com/2006/WORLD/asiapcf/06/07/hk.uncle/ (Retrieved 29 September 2013).

more and more people have increasingly become interested in Chan.

> **Memes**
>
> Memes are units of information that diffuse through a culture and a public, keep seeping continually, are often endlessly varied and copied, but essentially retain their identity. According to the inventor of the concept, sociobiologist Richard Dawkins, memes may consist in a single slogan or sentence, a song line or an entire song, an idea, a religious concept, a whole ideology or *weltanschauung*. Images and even distinct film sequences may become memes and populate our world of imagination, possibly ousting other concepts. This age of the Net has seen the renaissance of the doctrine of memetics, itself now a meme.

About three weeks after the upload, 1.2 million hits are registered, a week later 1.9 million. By the end of June 2011 the video lists nearly 4.1 million hits. Users rate it 3,968 times, 4,322 visitors store it amongst their favourites. As there are numerous copies on *YouTube* and other platforms, it is impossible to establish the total number of hits. The number for all the circulating copies of the film is supposed to have already reached 5.9 million on 29 May 2006, one month after the upload of the original video.[42] How many millions of viewers have clicked it since then up to the present day remains unclear. Obviously, the subtitles in English and in Mandarin have been of decisive importance for the international circulation and the global impact of that outburst of anger. Even viewers not fluent in Cantonese can thus understand the content of the dialogues and the expressions of defamation and the video can, consequently, cross the language barrier and reach its enormous audiences. The subtitled copies are also clicked several million times. By

---

[42] Soong, Roland (2006) Bus uncle. In: *EastSouthWestNorth*, 24 May 2006, http://www.zonaeuropa.com/20060524_1.htm (Retrieved 18 January 2010).

the end of September 2013 the two most popular *Bus Uncle* videos with bilingual subtitles list about 4.1 million hits.[43] The comments on *YouTube* make clear how enthusiastically the users are reacting to the video. "Hahahahahahaha, so funny!!!!!!!", *DonLi* utters, for example. There is a particularly intensive debate on who is actually to blame for Chan's angry outburst. Opinions differ widely, showing characteristic battles for opinions and interpretations in a public that articulates itself uninhibitedly but with freely discharged aggression, clamouring for the validity of its own positions without any previous tests of relevancy by gatekeepers. What has in fact happened, how should it be assessed? The majority of commentators criticises Chan and his behaviour. Some even think that the norm violation is a particularly grave one and demands the public pillory. "Oh man", we read, "this type is crazy […]. He has the worst behaviour in the world, he is ridiculous." Many of the comments are extremely aggressive. One—obviously anonymous—*hoyun* writes: "Damn it, every time I watch this video I would like to hit this old man." Some comments are directed at Ho. "In my opinion, this guy has behaved like a dirty swine. You can see how impertinent he was when the uncle threw his tantrum", writes *highcontrast*. Others call Ho a coward. He should have fought with Chan, several users demand.

The observer's blind spot

It is interesting to note that, despite the diversity of the reactions, all the comments are directed exclusively at the people performing in the film. Fong's behaviour—the secret filming and the upload of the video—is rarely questioned or made a topic of discussion. This reflects a general pattern, a

---

[43] Both videos are accessible through the following URLs: http://www.youtube.com/watch?v=RSHziqJWYcM (Retrieved 20 September 2013); http://www.youtube.com/watch?v=EsYRQkmVifg (Retrieved 20 September 2013).

normal and typical narrowing of vision that shifts the observer and the discloser of an event into a blind spot. The question is no longer what he has actually done when bringing his camera phone into position, when he took on the role of a self-created norm police and made no attempt to mediate and pacify but instead mulishly concentrated on his filming—and also whether one would like to live in a world of possible total transparency.[44] *The public takes the final video product for granted, without investigating the story of its origins and development, without analysing the way and manner of its publication and without, in the extreme case, scandalising the procedure itself.*

It is also striking (though not typical) that the hits continue to increase and the number of video viewings keeps rising. Instead of reporting massively on the mobile video and debating it for a few days or weeks, both Internet users and the traditional media deal actively with different aspects of the incident for nearly three years. Then, finally, stagnation sets in, only then the public apparently turns its attention to other topics. The questions immediately arising are now: Why? What is so captivating about such an unimportant norm violation? How is the stabilisation of such an inherently fragile kind of attention achieved? A first and rather generally formulated answer is: *the absolute prerequisite in any event is new stimuli*. Furthermore, there is a possibility of constantly updating and modifying interests and enthusiasm by transforming the original seriousness of the outburst of anger into a more or less cheerful game with public participation. In this way, the original medially fixated content might at the very least be given a new form; it could, for instance be parodied and alienated. This kind of ironical-creative processing of the material obeys a central commandment, orients itself by a fundamental requirement that must be met if the attention of the public is to

---

[44] The concept of "norm police" was created by Daniel J. Solove. See: Solove, Daniel J. (2007) *The Future of Reputation: Gossip, rumor, and privacy on the Internet*, New Haven/London: Yale University Press, p. 85.

be retained. It is first of all necessary to offer something new, something extraordinary and unconventional. Secondly, what is offered must remain comprehensible and connectible at all costs so as to avoid frightening the public away with merely warped and hermetic incomprehensibility. The special challenge is to find a schema, a recollection, on the one hand, and to break and frustrate it in a comprehensible and perhaps even exhilarating way, on the other, in order to produce a kind of stimulation surplus. This kind of communicative balancing act can be captured in a tentative formula in the following way: *vary what is known in such a way as to turn it into something unknown; but still allow the unknown to be recognised as something known.*

Remixing and resampling

In this very understanding of playful variation creating new stimuli for reception, for instance by parodying and alienating what has long been known in an inspiring way, some *YouTube* users soon generate manifold mash-ups of the video. They fabricate collages and recombinations of images and sounds, data and video sequences, which set the core event of the tantrum into ever new, ever different contexts. There is, for example, a *Star Wars* version of the key scene, in which Chan and Ho fight with lightsabers, or a *Taxi Driver* variant. A rap song combines the most popular utterances in the quarrel between Chan and Ho with a song of the Hong Kong singer Sammi Cheng, and a karaoke remix invites listeners to join in a sing along. The upshot is: according to research published in the *Asian Journal of Communication*, all in all 127 different mash-ups of the *Bus Uncle* film have appeared on *YouTube* between 29 April 2006 and 18 June 2007.[45] In this timespan alone, the video inspired 77 users to react to the original film with one or more creations of their own. The majority of the variants and vari-

---

[45] Chu, Donna (2009) Collective behavior on YouTube: A case study of "Bus Uncle" online videos. In: *Asian Journal of Communication*, vol. 19, pp. 343ff.

ations consist in remix versions with popular music (37.9%), but there are also completely novel, creative products by *YouTube* users (the study just mentioned quotes a share of 22.7%). Some of the mash-ups (9.8%) connect the original recordings with excerpts from films. Most of the video replies exhibit a joking and sarcastic undertone; there is no serious commentary at this stage.[46]

The traditional media, curiously enough, adopt a special role. Local and regional media are the first to report; they even instigate a regular chase for the central performers, going so far as to offer financial rewards for their detection. This kind of local-regional reporting carries on for weeks on end. When the quarry *Bus Uncle* is finally spotted and presented in diverse exclusive interviews, he is transformed into a public personality. For this reason, it is now obviously a subject of general interest that he is offered a job by a steakhouse chain. And it is indeed an international news agency that distributes the news message that three masked nameless persons turn up at his new workplace and beat him up so badly that he has to be taken to hospital.[47]

However, it is not just the artistic-creative mash-ups, it is not just the medially driven chase or the sudden attack on the neo-celebrity Chan that keeps the interest in place. Certain supplementary events are staged with the intention of completing the dramaturgical script and injecting a little more tension into what is happening. Therefore, a media enterprise arranges a meeting of the protagonists. A group of journalists persuades Chan (allegedly for money) to pay his former antagonist Ho a visit at his firm in Mongkok in order to apologise for his behaviour and

---

[46] Chu, Donna (2009) Collective behavior on YouTube: A case study of "Bus Uncle" online videos. In: *Asian Journal of Communication*, vol. 19, p. 346.
[47] Associated Press (2006) Three men beat up Hong Kong's "Bus Uncle". In: *The Star Online*, 08 June 2006, http://thestar.com.my/news/story.asp?file=/2006/6/8/apworld/20060608152634&sec=apworld (Retrieved 29 September 2013).

to offer him the business proposal of a "Bus Uncle Rave Party". Ho, however, throws the group out of his office and complains not to have been informed beforehand. At the end of May, the case finally creates an international stir. First of all, a message from the news agency Associated Press is published that triggers a spate of articles.[48] But this is no longer mere news reporting on the case; the incident is analysed and reinterpreted as a symptom – and it therefore again increases in value having thus been furnished with intellectually more demanding elements and interpretations. "'Bus Uncle' is cinéma vérité", the *Washington Post* columnist Eugene Robinson writes, for example. "It's amazing that in nanoseconds, a slice of Hong Kong life can be experienced in Washington, Johannesburg or Moscow."[49] Often in these reports the question is posed as to whether there may be some deeper meaning somewhere in his vulgar actions, or that his outburst of anger could perhaps be understood as a significant event in the sense of a diagnosis of the times. "Chan's phrases", writes Marianne Bray of *CNN*, for instance, "reflect the pressure that comes from living in a city where 6.9 million people are squeezed into 1,104 square kilometers […] of land."[50]

Democratisation of celebrity

Repeatedly other *YouTube* videos are compared with the *Bus Uncle* video; there is suddenly a *Police Uncle*, a *Train Uncle*, or a *Bus Auntie*. In other words: the case has set up a peculiar

---

[48] Associated Press (2006) Grumpy man on a bus becomes star of the Internet. In: *Guardian.co.uk*, 26 May 2006, http://www.guardian.co.uk/technology/2006/may/26/news.newmedia (Retrieved 29 September 2013).

[49] Robinson, Eugene (2006) When life makes you cry uncle. In: *Washington Post*, 09 June 2006, http://www.washingtonpost.com/wp-dyn/content/article/2006/06/08/AR2006060801533.html (Retrieved 29 September 2013).

[50] Bray, Marianne (2006) Irate HK man unlikely Web hero. In: *CNN.com International*, 09 June 2006, http://edition.cnn.com/2006/WORLD/asiapcf/06/07/hk.uncle/ (Retrieved 29 September 2013).

schema of observation in its own right and has made Chan a celebrity that is famous for no other reason than for being famous. His ad-hoc career provides extensive illustrating material for the generally noticeable *democratisation of celebrity*. "The control of attention and importance is no longer available to only a few professionals", the diagnosis runs, "but it is potentially and at least in the perception of many free for all."[51] Now, there are the traditional stars that have acquired their status through professional work, competence, and a carefully cultivated image. They are bathed in an "aura of inaccessibility".[52] But, as the present example shows, there is also an increasing number of people who present themselves publicly, who have acquired no competence or are not in any way singled out by an interest-arousing social position (high office, famous name).[53] They have no secrets, no special aura, no specific talent, but they generate fascination because they have more or less accidentally stumbled or been pushed into the garish light of publicity. They generally behave without social skills and therefore occasionally evoke—as representative figures of a mass public without professional qualities—sympathy, but also gloating and envy. Their central and striking commonality is simply to have somehow become medially conspicuous at the right point in time and to have aroused public interest, although it cannot easily be established what their particular skills are and how the butterfly effects of atten-

---

[51] Groebel, Jo (2002) Zwischenruf. Präsenzelite oder die Demokratisierung der Prominenz [Interjection: Elite by presence or the democratisation of celebrity]. In: Ralph Weiß/Jo Groebel (eds.) *Privatheit im öffentlichen Raum. Medienhandeln zwischen Individualisierung und Entgrenzung* [*Privacy in the Public Space: Media activity between individualisation and border loss*], Opladen: Leske + Budrich, p. 508.

[52] Meckel, Miriam (2009) Objektiv betrachtet [The objective view]. In: *Süddeutsche Zeitung Magazin*, no. 27, p. 25.

[53] Poerksen, Bernhard/Wolfgang Krischke (2010) Die Casting-Gesellschaft [The casting society]. In: Bernhard Poerksen/Wolfgang Krischke (eds.) *Die Casting-Gesellschaft. Die Sucht nach Aufmerksamkeit und das Tribunal der Medien* [*The Casting Society: The desire for attention and the tribunal of the media*], Cologne: Herbert von Halem Verlag, pp. 17ff.

tion-creation function in detail. This radical separation of prominence and competence also characterises Chan, whose real achievement is his secretly recorded tantrum — the initial spark setting off his media and celebrity career absolved in record time. As soon as he is famous and notorious, the traditional mechanisms of the celebrity business kick into action and increase his publicity according to the fundamental principle of the so-called *Matthew effect*: *unto every one that hath shall be given.*[54] Or put differently: *publicity enhances publicity.* Interviews with Chan are published that are elevated to the rank of lead stories. He is nominated by a public service radio station in Hong Kong for the election to Man of the Year 2006; and he makes it to second position just barely failing to reach the top position! Collaborators of *Wikipedia* produce entries on this incident that are since available in Cantonese, English, French, and Swedish. Fan articles have begun to circulate. An online shop in the USA sells T-shirts, teddy bears, and also handbags with an engraved Chan head. Boxer shorts and buttons with translations of *Bus Uncle* statements are also to be had, also mobile ringtones for download with the best-known quotations that have become proverbial in Hong Kong ("I am under pressure. You are under pressure."). In brief: the story of the night bus in Hong Kong, the scandal that was never a scandal at all and was nevertheless treated as such by an enthused public, lives on and has turned its protagonist into a Net celebrity, a star of the new age. Entering the expression *Bus Uncle* in *Google* in English or Cantonese, thus enacting a modern proof of existence, will still generate an enormous quantity of hits — even after several years. To be precise, the number of hits today as these lines are being written is 64,700.

---

[54] Jan Schmidt describes this principle as the "the rich get richer" phenomenon. See: Schmidt, Jan (2009) *Das neue Netz. Merkmale, Praktiken und Folgen des Web 2.0* [*The New Net: Features, practices and consequences of web 2.0*], Konstanz: UVK Verlagsgesellschaft, p. 57.

3. The calamitous e-mail and the easiness of misfortune

Change of modes of communication

Innumerable e-mails are sent every day. In most cases, the electronic mail reaches the intended addressee. From time to time, an e-mail happens to end up with the wrong recipient — which is usually of no great further consequence. Often such a message is ignored; occasionally its sender is informed. However, selecting the wrong mail address, i.e. the wrong recipients, for one's mail may cause extremely embarrassing effects. Sometimes a single mouse click proves to be a serious error because it suddenly and unexpectedly creates totally unwanted publicity, the effects of which cannot be negated despite immense effort. One moment of inattentiveness suffices. On 22 June 2006, at 09.43h, 21-year-old Susanne Klauser sends her first e-mail of the day, "Morning slice!", to her colleague Tina Braun[55] — both at work for the German Federal Labour Agency — and receives the reply "Hey Baby, everything okay?" at 09.44h. "Am just sort of tired and have earache. Fred came last night for three quarters of an hour. Had shaved specially! And then he didn't want me. No sex for practically two weeks. Well, nothing doing. How was your evening then??" An animated dialogue about most intimate affairs unfolds between the two women. Ten e-mails whizz back and forth, quickly adding up to a sizeable collection of texts. And then Susanne Klauser inadvertently mistypes her friend's e-mail address before sending message number eleven, and at 12.01h sends the whole accumulated package of e-mails to the central mailing list of her department — triggering an extremely "juicy affair" (*Bild* newspaper).

The story is illuminating not so much for the content it confers but because it provides the opportunity of a detailed

---

[55] The names of the two women and other involved persons were anonymised, as a matter of course. We have also decided not to provide detailed source references because we are primarily interested here in the illustration of a principle, not in renewed stigmatisation.

examination of the changes in modes of communication and the stepwise expansion of a communicative circuit. At the beginning, the two women obviously practise a highly private *one-to-one communication*, the status of which, however, is fragile and strangely porous due to the peculiar character of the medium. A single typing error, not spotted in time, will immediately integrate other addressees. An e-mail program will usually make ad-hoc suggestions of possible recipients, anyway, as soon as the first few letters are being typed in. Furthermore, any sent e-mail can be forwarded to other persons at lightning speed. In the case of the two women, the unfortunate sending of the e-mails to all the addressees on the department's mailing list is first followed by a *phase of some-to-some communication, still taking place within the narrowly circumscribed circle of colleagues*. E-mail publicity still remains restricted to a fairly limited kind of public whose members all know each other and work together. Eventually, however, the packet of e-mails reaches the Internet and, in a last phase of the dissemination process, the popular press and other mass media. This momentous change of the communicative circuit now lends the story potential reputation-damaging explosiveness. In this phase, different modes of communication are united. On the one hand, the mass media follow the classic *one-to-many* logic; the Net, on the other hand, functions also according to the principle of *many-to-many communication*, in practice primarily on a regional and local, but potentially also on a global, scale. The different phases of dissemination can now be precisely reconstructed. The colleagues are the first to be informed promptly and comprehensively about the sex and love lives of the two young women. Soon afterwards, the mails spread quasi-epidemically and at great speed, they are forwarded, copied, linked, commented on, and finally even translated. It is possible that one of the women's colleagues—allegedly one Andreas Schmidt, as is maintained by a blogger with the name of *Woodstock*—sends the mails to friends and acquaintances for fun and amusement, who in turn spread them further afield, and so on and so forth. In this way, the mails reach other, ever new and ever larger communicative circuits—they actually transmute into a sort of digital chain letter, multiplying according to the principle of the snowball effect. Names and e-mail addresses of people who make intimate communication accessible to an amused, gloating, and outraged public are often retained in a long list preceding the correspondence and may therefore easily be spotted. So it becomes clear once again: *the act of publication and distribution is of marginal interest to the Net community; it is not considered an action worthy of criticism nor is it considered necessary to delete its traces. The ruling idea is that the messenger is absolutely innocent.*

The spectrum of reactions

The intimate correspondence can be found on many sites of the Net, in most cases even carrying the proper names of the women. Bloggers report on it, copy the text to their sites, or offer it for downloading. On the platform *Scripd*, a German version is made available online together with a version in English, in order to increase and accelerate its further distribution. Its success is unspectacular, however, and certainly not global. In numerous forums users set links to the downloaded texts or copy them into threads, chains of consecutively arranged postings of messages and commentaries. Finally, the traditional mass media, in particular the popular gutter press, discover the story. The reporting there is largely driven and coloured by schadenfreude—and the two women are only scantily anonymised. Here is one exemplary quote from the newspaper *Berliner Kurier*: "Now there is only one thing left for the two gossip chicks: bag on the head and forward. Or emigrate. Faaaaar away…"[56] Only *Spiegel Online* manages a year later to present an analysis of the case with the necessary depth. One

---

[56] Anon. (2006) Peinlicher Verklicker. Sex-Mails an ganze Firma geschickt [Embarrassing mis-click: Sex mails sent to entire company]. In: *Berliner Kurier*, 10 August 2006, http://www.berlinonline.de/berliner-kurier/archiv/.bin/dump.fcgi/2006/0810/politiknachrichten/0033/index.html (Retrieved 29 June 2011).

can read there, for instance: "Never before could a single human being have found so much fame with a gigantic public in such a short span of time — and never before could a person have plummeted so low from such a height."[57]

What are the consequences of such massive attention? What motives may be exposed, what reaction patterns established? To clarify these questions it is worthwhile looking at the numerous comments offered by people in forums, in blog posts, or in attachments to the continually spreading mail. Here one can discover a broad spectrum of opinions and forms of reaction. One group is outraged, another gloats, and a third group shows recognisable voyeuristic interests in the contents. Some discuss the genuineness of the correspondence, others prefer an analysis, some voice sympathy, and a few prophesy the two women a media career.[58] The suggestion that the e-mails could have been composed during their working time produces indignation. "Such intimate things have no place at work. [...] the question for me now is whether they do not have enough work to do at the FLA", one of the commentators asks angrily. Numerous outraged reactions are provoked by the language of the mails. "In what kind of trash language are they talking to each other?!", one *Prusse-Liese* asks who herself does not display a quite perfect sense of style, either, and *Simon* remarks: "They surely do not need particular linguistic abilities for their jobs!" Many users think, moreover, that the incident simply confirms the bad reputation of the FLA: "Extrapolate from these dumb office clucks to the totality of the FLA employees, then one can only draw the consequence that one's application papers are better directed anywhere else than to this kind of institution!" *NoHartz* demands the dismissal of the two women: "Stupidity

---

[57] Bredow, Rafaela von/Dietmar Hipp (2009) Vergiss es! [Forget it!] In: *Der Spiegel*, 14 December 2009, no. 51, p. 123.

[58] But whatever the stance with regard to this case, whether one considers outrage or compassion as an adequate reaction or rather favours a critical-analytical debate: each of these variant reactions helps to keep the events in question communicatively alive.

must be punished, and that can only mean and will hopefully mean in this case that the two dim-witted frusties are fired right away!" A very widely shown reaction is schadenfreude. There are numerous comments like the following: "I can't contain myself ha ha ha ha!" Another user adds the following subject heading to the e-mail forwarded by him: "Guys, this is pure embarrassment… the joke of the month!" The voyeurs, no fewer in numbers, naturally react to the intimate revelations with salacious notes, for example: "I would very much like to get to know those two. They would be satisfied and relaxed in no time!" *Blood* titles his blog post on the case with the line: "Horny pussies at the FLA."

The evidence is now: *anonymity causes inhibitions to crumble*. Repeatedly, a fraction of the sceptics raises the question as to whether the dialogue can really have taken place in the documented form. "I think that this is a fake (silly season)!", writes *Goldelse* — like numerous other discussants who share the same opinion. Others reject this view; they do not believe in a hoax. "Definitively no fake. Have a friend in the FLA, and she told me last night via SMS that they are no longer allowed to go online at work", communicates one *Ciccio*. Quite apart from all these diverse outraged, obscene, and sceptical comments, one can discover a few that show a kind of analytical-reflective character. In one blog the case is said to illustrate "the far reaching influence of modern means of communication" because it shows that the Internet can destroy lives. "Barely 15 years ago such an outcome would have been unthinkable and very difficult to achieve." User *Uwe* concludes that some employees were given an e-mail crash course free of charge by the incident. He warns: "E-mails are electronic postcards! Write nothing in a mail that you would not write on a postcard!" Only very few voice their compassion with the victims and show empathy. A small number of users predict unexpected riches to come from the undesired attention, a career as talk show guests and advertising stars: "Millionaire at a stroke through TV presence, and then advertising money." Nothing of this sort actually happens. The consequences for the two women involved are largely negative. "We are constantly being goggled at, and people are whispering about us behind our backs",[59] an online medium quotes Susanne Klauser. It is alleged that the incident cost the colleague who forwarded the e-mail his job. It is also alleged that one of the women has since moved to Bavaria to take a job in a bank. It is alleged that after the publication of the éclat about the two women all the employees of the FLA have been forbidden to write private e-mails during their working hours. The truth in all this is impossible to ascertain in detail. Suggestions, assumptions, and rumours abound. One thing is, however, certain — despite all the questions about truth and factuality, the documentation of a calamitous typing error in the summer of 2006 as well as the identity of the two women can still be researched and established today without major difficulty. Communication intended for the moment is all but transitory. The digital stigma remains. There is no chance of its deletion. It will stay, unchanged.

4. The tell-tale SMS and the economy of morality

From rumour to evidence

An SMS is the medial instrument of relaxed focusing. It enforces condensation. Whoever writes SMSs comes right down to brass tacks and, as a rule, formulates in ways that do not obey the demands of standard language or written communication. An SMS is congealed purpose-driven orality, easily produced, but potentially secured for duration. The medial form itself provokes the representation of what is private; it favours the presentation of contents and intimacies which could potentially be used as evidence of norm violations in other contexts. In new contexts, SMSs could thus rise to the status of written documents thereby losing the character of trivial sensationalism or

---

[59] Völkerling, Jörg (2006) Sex-Tratsch per E-mail... und die ganze Behörde liest mit [Sex gossip via e-mail... And the entire institution can join in reading it]. In: *Bild.de*, 18 August 2006, http://www.bild.de/BTO/news/aktuell/2006/08/19/s-e-x-tratsch-email-buero/s-e-x-tratsch-arbeitsagentur.html (Retrieved 28 September 2013).

ephemeral utterances whose reality content might be subject to controversial debate. SMSs are, as a rule, directed at a defined addressee. They are ad-hoc messages stored on the mobile phones of the sender and the recipient. Due to their hybrid status, they tend to provoke a potentially risky *oblivious disregard of the medium*. This disregard of the medium—the lacking sense of the conditions of its exploitation and the actual properties of the medium used—is illustrated by the diverse scandals and affairs that owe their particular explosiveness precisely to the SMS as evidence.[60] Whoever texts in quick succession tends to overlook all too easily that the activity creates pieces of writing that may survive the moment, that the texts may not necessarily be formulated for the moment only but in fact constitute written records that will continue to exist unless they are deliberately deleted. These texts can, once torn from the original context of their intended use, become documents of defamation and demolition. They have the capacity to support flimsy rumours with definitive proof. They can, once published, endanger world stars and billion dollar industries—as is shown by the story of Tiger Woods, golfing star with a nice guy image and the first self-made billionaire in the history of sport, icon of a market ultimately dependent on his decent behaviour and the intact stage management of his public existence.

The first news item threatening the idyllic PR world, the first indication that there was something wrong with Tiger Woods, derives from an event in the early hours of 27 November 2009.[61]

---

[60] As a typical example in this context, one may quote the affair surrounding the Finnish Foreign Minister Ilkka Kanerva, who was forced to resign because he had sent a striptease dancer unambiguous SMS messages. A selection of his texts was published by a Finnish gossip magazine. See: Baker, Graeme (2008) Finnish minister quits over saucy texts. In: *The Telegraph*, 02 April 2008, http://www.telegraph.co.uk/news/worldnews/1583679/Finnish-minister-quits-over-saucy-texts.html (Retrieved 25 September 2013).

[61] On the genesis of the scandal see: Mahoney, Jill (2009) Chronology of the Tiger Woods scandal. In: *The Global Mail*, 08 December 2009 (last update: 23 August 2012), http://www.theglobeandmail.com/sports/chrono

At 02.25h the golfer crashes his Cadillac Escalade first into a fire hydrant only a few metres from his house in Florida and then into a nearby tree. His wife Elin Nordegren smashes the tail window of the car with a golf club to rescue her husband who had lost consciousness, she later tells the police. She claims to have helped in an accident, but her story fails to convince a great number of the media that favour the description of the event as an eruption of marital violence. A few days later, on 2 December 2009, the American magazine *US Weekly* publishes the confessions of the waitress Jaimee Grubbs. They provide the decisive trigger for a spate of reports running for months about a plethora of affairs. The story is now run under the title *Tigergate*. Grubbs explains that she had had a 31-month long affair with Tiger Woods. The proof: 300 SMS messages, many of which can subsequently be read on the Net and on websites of popular mass media. They are erotically allusive short dialogues quoted in many media and blogs, brief statements with the sole purpose of ascertaining mutual availability and sexual readiness.[62] They give the British columnist Alexander Chancellor cause for pessimistic laments in an essay that is of fundamental interest to media theory. In his essay dealing with love letters by the "romantic lecher" John F. Kennedy he compares and contrasts the gently courting love letters that Kennedy wrote by hand and sent by post to the Swedish woman Gunilla with the sex SMSs by Tiger Woods that are geared towards the quick satisfaction of his wants, alerting his playmates and urging them to send him nude photos. Chancellor writes: "But mobile phones must be partly to blame for the chilling nature of contemporary mating rituals. It is as

---

logy-of-the-tiger-woods-scandal/article1392768/ (Retrieved 22 September 2013).

[62] See the exemplary material in: Anon. (2009) Text messages between Tiger Woods and Jaimee Grubbs. In: *New York Post*, 10 December 2009, http://www.nypost.com/p/news/national/text_messages_between_tiger_woods_lh2ptFU8WhzJEBD8f2CCgO (Retrieved 25 September 2013).

difficult to be oafish in a handwritten letter as it is to be romantic in a text message. Letters are for keeping and rereading. Text messages are for getting to the point in the speediest and most direct way possible. Some people who have assumed that text messages are discarded as fast as they are written are now finding to their cost that this is not necessarily so."[63] Alexander Chancellor describes the shift from the invocation of nuances to the crude command, the transformation of the desired counterparts from adored subject into objects serving only one purpose. Handwritten letters and SMSs are for him metaphors for particular relationships between the personal self and the outside world.

Be that as it may. It is not just the SMS messages — disqualified as stylistically inferior — that show up and disgrace Tiger Woods. It is in particular a message from the voicemail of the mobile phone of Jaimee Grubbs that appears on the Net. Everybody who cares can listen to it. In it, Tiger Woods requests her to delete her name on her voicemail intro as quickly as possible because the contact data of his mobile phone have fallen into the hands of his wife and she might possibly ring all the numbers including hers (Grubbs'). Grubbs does indeed delete her name, she insists. However, she does not cooperate further in any way in the desperate attempts of Tiger Woods to obliterate the traces of their relationship. On the contrary, she dances through talk shows, offers interviews, poses for erotic photos, and apologises in a sentimentally staged television programme to the betrayed wife in order to stabilise the sudden peak of attention. *The declaration of remorse serves only as a scant legitimation and merely apparent moral justification of further public appearances as well as the excesses of the follow-up reporting during which new intimate details are spread out.*

---

[63] Chancellor, Alexander (2010) Compare JFK's love letters to modern sex texts. In: *Guardian*, 19 February 2010, http://www.theguardian.com/commentisfree/2010/feb/19/john-f-kennedy-charming-lecher (Retrieved 29 September 2013).

Gradually, many other affairs are made public. Other women follow the example of Jaimee Grubbs; in retrospect, one could say that she had set the standard and the style. The porn star Joslyn James publishes infinitely more crudely formulated intimate SMS messages, speaks about the details of the sexual encounters with Tiger Woods. "I can only imagine the pain she's feeling now, and I'm sorry", divulges the model Cori Rist in the US television programme *Today* — once more a staged declaration of remorse. Photographs of diverse lovers appear. Some of these lovers arrange press conferences or appear on the radio. Fantastic numbers begin to circulate, including stories and claims that elude assessment. Ever new purported or actual lovers emerge who try very hard to market their confessions by reporting alleged erotic predilections and shared parties — handing over any available material to the popular mass media and the aggressively-operating, chequebook-swinging gossip portals like *TMZ.com* — all labouring systematically to exploit the scandal as thoroughly as possible.[64]

The dramaturgy of the public confession

In his counter-offensive, Tiger Woods, striving to contain the grossly flowering rumours, chooses the *strategy of the carefully targeted reduction of sources and the safeguarding of the autonomy of his reactions*. He rejects the progressively more pressing demands for interviews but nevertheless reacts immediately himself using his website *Tigerwoods.com* as the instrument of his strictly monologically organised scandal and crisis management. Obviously, press conferences and big interviews have to be avoided because they cannot be adequately controlled. The proliferation of rumours is to be stemmed by relevance-driven focusing, public outrage is to be reduced by repeated new apologies, a self-imposed phase of withdrawal from the tourna-

---

[64] On the procedures of the editors of the gossip portal *TMZ.com* see: Bethge, Philip/Martin U. Müller (2011) Gerüchts-Reporter [Rumour reporter]. In: *Der Spiegel*, 30 May 2011, no. 22, pp. 132–134.

ment business, and by generally promoting everybody's basic right to privacy. *His website remains the only source of self-presentation – an attempt to score points through noise-free announcements undistorted by the mass media, and by cultivating direct contact with the public. The case demonstrates that celebrities create their own channel and create the desired counter-publicity themselves according to their own rules.* He comments, or got someone else to comment, on the accident in front of his house on his website *Tigerwoods.com*. His wife helped him that night, he writes. All other rumours are groundless. The whole thing is most embarrassing and painful to him, and he requests respect for his family. He reacts to the publication of US Weekly in connection with Jaimee Grubbs only a short while later on his website with the statement that he regrets "with all my heart" particular – unspecified – "transgressions". He makes a renewed effort to protect his private sphere and uses his website for criticising the excesses of celebrity journalism. "I am dealing with my behaviour and personal failings behind closed doors with my family. Those feelings should be shared by us alone", he says in a statement. "Although I am a well-known person and have made my career as a professional athlete, I have been dismayed to realize the full extent of what tabloid scrutiny really means. […] But no matter how intense curiosity about public figures can be, there is an important and deep principle at stake, which is the right to some simple, human measure of privacy. I realize there are some who do not share my view on that. But for me, the virtue of privacy is one that must be protected in matters that are intimate and within one's own family. Personal sins should not require press releases and problems within a family shouldn't have to mean public confessions."[65]

But his refusal to confess proves impossible to maintain; the pressure of his own sponsors and the power of the established

---

[65] Woods, Tiger (2010) Tiger comments on current events. In: *Tigerwoods.com*, 02 December 2009, http://web.tigerwoods.com/news/article/200912027740572/news/ (Retrieved 22 September 2013).

rituals are too strong. The whipped-up emotions of the public, according to David Rosen's diagnosis in his book about sex scandals in the US, are aiming at the humiliation and public confession of the protagonists concerned. The public clamours for the confession of personal guilt and publicly celebrated penitence. It thus changes its own moral self-ascertainment increasingly into a grand spectacle, a soap with claims to genuineness, although primarily bent upon entertainment.[66] The public wants to see and experience the sequels; it wants to participate in all the phases of the purgatory, of the medial purification. Tiger Woods finally reacts on 19 February 2010 with a precisely planned appearance in a clubhouse of the US Golf Association in Florida. Present are friends, selected supporters, employees, and business partners, and his own mother whose reactions are repeatedly caught on camera.

Figure 18: **Tiger Woods at the personally arranged press conference in a clubhouse of the US Golf Association in Florida.**

---

[66] Rosen, David (2009) *Sex Scandal in America: Politics & the ritual of public shaming*, Toronto: The Key Publishing House Inc.

Everything is televised live: the renewed confession of guilt, the troubled look at the audience, the repeated request for absolution, the announcement that he has been seeking therapeutic treatment, that he has returned to the teachings of Buddhism, the final long embrace with his mother, the soft sobbing and nose blowing. *The participants are evidently subjected to an overambitious attempt at maximally effective counter-stage management, the hollow mould of a dramaturgy aimed primarily at calming the minds, placating the sponsors, and minimising the damage to the image as well as possible.* Nothing is omitted that is required to celebrate publicly the reintegration into the established system of values. *Apology dramatics* is the name of this form of public confession designed to bring back lost credibility and perform the catharsis under the watchful eyes of the public.[67]

Advertising industry and media industry

Naturally, all this exertion is organised not only, and certainly not primarily, for the compensation of private misdeeds; it is intended simply to save and defend the fallen star's personal market and to avert the further destruction of capital. Tiger Woods had always been one of the best-paid sports persons with an annual income of more than 100 million dollars.[68]

---

[67] The dramaturgy of public declarations of remorse in different social spheres (politics, religion, sport, art) is described in the following article: Fleischhauer, Jan/Marc Hujer/Kerstin Kullmann/Dirk Kurbjuweit/ Romain Leick/Ralf Neukirch/Peter Wensierski (2010) Aufstieg einer Sünderin [Rise of a sinner]. In: *Der Spiegel*, 01 March 2010, no. 9, pp. 66–74.

See also: Serrao, Marc Felix (2011) Umgang der US-Medien mit Skandalen. Lachen und Lynchen [US media handling of scandals: Laughing and lynching]. In: *Sueddeutsche.de*, 08 June 2011, http://www.sueddeutsche.de/leben/umgang-der-us-medien-mit-skandalen-lachen-und-lynchen-1.1106654 (Retrieved 25 September 2013).

[68] Badenhausen, Kurt (2009) Forbes sports valuations: The world's highest-paid athletes. Nothing can stop the Tiger Woods money machine. In: *Forbes.com*, 17 June 2009, http://www.forbes.com/2009/06/17/top-earning-athletes-business-sports-top-earning-athletes.html (Retrieved 25 September 2013).

Already during the first few weeks after the breaking of the scandal, sponsoring contracts with the telecommunication company AT&T and the management consulting company Accenture are terminated, previously produced spots are no longer broadcast and campaigns are cancelled (e.g. the campaign for the drink Gatorade). Certain sponsors (Gillette) suspend their engagement, others at least publish a comment and declare publicly to maintain their support (Nike). The economists of an American university calculated that the sponsors had to write off between five and twelve billion dollars in stock exchange values within the first 13 trading days following the car accident and the first cautious confessions and declarations. At the same time, however, American media producers recorded an explosion in the sales of popular gossip and people magazines that uniformly flaunted the case on their front pages and dealt with the scandal in innumerable cover stories.[69] Viewed in purely economic terms, the gradual unleashing of the scandal thus led to the collision of two markets that are governed by contrary interests. Both markets need the media celebrity Tiger Woods, but in different and ultimately opposing orientations. For the advertising industry, the golfer is an indispensable "exemplary athlete without a stain" (*Stern.de*) whose long geared up career can be precisely planned and marketed in a well-targeted way. *Here every break with normality and stage management, every published misdeed, must present a threat because these businesses need morality or at least the appearance of morality of highly paid stars for their own economic calculations.* For the media industry and the global trade with emotions, on the contrary, the public demolition of the exceptional sportsperson is a top booster of ratings and sales. *Only the break with normality with its*

---

[69] On the scandalisation by the media see, for instance: Siering, Frank (2009) Das Geschäft mit "Tigergate" [The business with "Tigergate"]. In: *Stern.de*, 10 December 2009, http://www.stern.de/lifestyle/leute/tiger-woods-das-geschaeft-mit-tigergate-1528322.html (Retrieved 25 September 2013).

culmination in the sex scandal is really profitable; only the published immorality of the stars is the source of extraordinary profits.

In the meantime, this collision of interests has been resolved in favour of the advertising industry with its concept of a conflict-free and aseptic normality that is as widely and comprehensively consensual as possible. Tiger Woods and Elin Nordegren have announced their divorce and published a last common declaration on their website, the central organ of undisturbed self-presentation and private counter-publicity.[70] The sports star has returned to the golf course, accompanied by a few well-defined interviews. And the balance is right again, the matrix of pleasant staging also appears intact once more, although income losses have to be recorded. But in June 2013 Tiger Woods' annual income rose back to 78 million dollars, according to an assessment by the magazine *Forbes*; and despite everything that happened, and despite all the losses, he can still maintain his position as one of the top earners in the sports business. The scandal surrounding the treacherous SMSs is still circulating on the Net; it has not really damaged him business-wise and definitely not ruined him. All the other kinds of damage, which generated so much hot air in the moments of media outrage, inevitably remain entirely speculative.

5. The embarrassing *Twitter* message and the nature of sexuality

Definition of the loss of control

The loss of control in the digital age, according to an illuminating definition, "sets in whenever the complexity of the interaction of information outstrips the imaginative capabilities of a subject".[71] To formulate it in less abstract terms: not by any

---

[70] Anon. (2010) A statement from Elin Nordegren and Tiger Woods. In: *Tigerwoods.com*, 23 August 2010, http://web.tigerwoods.com/news/article/2010082313818490/news/ (Retrieved 25 September 2013).

[71] Seemann, Michael (2011) Vom Kontrollverlust zur Filtersouveränität [From loss of control to the sovereignty of filters]. In: *Carta.info*, 06 April

stretch of the imagination can we envision what will happen with our data, who will unpredictably get to see them, in what combinations and contexts they will one day emerge. Anthony Weiner, too, a smart Democrat high-flyer with the best contacts to the political establishment, a Congressman and former candidate for the office of Mayor of New York, could not envision the interaction of the data he had circulated. Only a few weeks before his career exploded in a cybersex scandal and he had to resign from office, he had met a reporter to talk about *Twitter* and *Facebook*.[72] Yes, he would use *Twitter* more aggressively than other politicians and Congress persons; yes, he could state with some sort of "metaphysical certitude" that he would one day commit mistakes, hurt people, and be forced to apologise. Yes, he would sometimes forget, when using the microblogging service *Twitter* in a light-hearted way, to exercise the necessary caution and consider the potential risks. He was therefore quite prepared to apologise in anticipation of any possible personal insults. One thing is now certain: Anthony Weiner was not cautious; and he had to repeat his blanket offer of apology in a dramatic-bizarre press conference only a short time afterwards.

What happened between a prophetic interview and the day of his resignation on 21 June 2011? Here are the facts. Anthony Weiner, torn between chaotic confusion and technical incompetence, informed his fans and *Twitter* followers about his sex affairs in the online universe. However, as soon as this had been made public, he instantly denied everything and offered the surprised public a conspiracy theory together with downright lies. He had to apologise as ever more of his escapades surfaced, nevertheless insisted on remaining in office, until he finally had no choice but to resign after all.

2011, http://carta.info/39625/vom-kontrollverlust-zur-filtersouveran itat/comment-page-1/ (Retrieved 30 September 2013).

[72] Parker, Ashley (2011) A candid, and prophetic, interview with Weiner. In: *City Room*, 07 June 2011, http://cityroom.blogs.nytimes.com/2011/06/07/a-candid-and-prophetic-interview-with-weiner (Retrieved 25 September 2013).

The affair begins with a stupid mistake. During the night of 27 May 2011, Weiner wants to send a self-taken camera phone picture to a college student in Seattle — and by mistake posts the photo on his official *Twitter* account. At a stroke, the image of grey underpants with the clearly visible erect penis of the politician is in evidence for thousands of followers on his *Twitter* timeline.[73] Weiner notices the mistake and in panic attempts to delete the picture, to recall the already interactive information, and to block the distribution of the attachment entitled "package.JPG". Too late. Copies of the picture have already been made, and they come to the attention of the conservative blogger Andrew Breitbart, who had once learnt his trade from Matt Drudge. When Breitbart publishes a first picture, Weiner reacts with a lie, a classic *second-order transgression*, which only further fuels the original scandal.[74] In numerous interviews, he insists that his *Twitter* account had become the prey of a hacker attack and a cruel joke; he could not really exclude that the picture did in fact show him in his underpants but he maintained that he did not send it himself. He said that he had ordered an Internet security firm to carry out an investigation as to what had happened and that he had contacted a lawyer. Then other pictures emerge and Breitbart again publishes them on his website, *BigGovernment.com*. They show the naked breast of the politician. One can see Weiner with two cats ("me and the pussys"). He is posing half-naked in front of a mirror. On another photograph, he holds up a slip of paper on which he has scribbled "me" in order to prove that it is really him, the Congressman, the Democrat hopeful. And what is more, *BigGovernment.com* carries a first discrete-indiscrete note by Andrew Breitbart saying that another clearly more obscene

---

[73] König, Michael (2011) Scandal um Anthony Weiner. Erotischer Foto-Flirt ruiniert Polit-Karriere [Scandal about Anthony Weiner: Erotic photo flirt ruins political career]. In: *Sueddeutsche.de*, 07 June 2011, http://www.sueddeutsche.de/politik/usa-scandal-um-anthony-weiner-erotischer-foto-flirt-ruiniert-polit-karriere-1.1106026 (Retrieved 25 September 2013).
[74] Cf. image after John B. Thompson on p. 96.

photograph of Weiner is available, which really left no room for imagination and speculation.[75] The 26-year-old student Meagan Broussard now outs herself in an open letter on *BigGoverment.com* as an online partner who had, however, generally refused erotic-salacious communication. "He was trying to get me to talk about myself sexually", she writes, "and I said, straight up, I'm not an open book. I was real blunt. He would ask me weird things, like 'Did you miss me?' I didn't understand that — how could I miss someone I hadn't met and didn't know? What is there to miss about me if you don't even know me?"[76] Other media now enter the fray with vigour. *Radaronline* claims to have found photos on *Facebook* and to have identified a woman called Lisa Weiss who claims to have maintained an online relationship with Weiner.[77] The never-ending and often vulgar *Facebook* correspondence with Lisa Weiss, who is working as an employee of a gambling casino, is documented at full length; the whole transcript is published for the first time — with pride![78]

The unfinished ritual

On 6 June 2011, a bizarre showdown is enacted in the ballroom of a Sheraton hotel in New York. Originally, Anthony Weiner

---

[75] Breitbart, Andrew (2011) Déjà vu: Another congressman bares naked torso (and more) for online pal. In: *BigGovernment.com*, 06 June 2011, http://biggovernment.com/abreitbart/2011/06/06/deja-vu-another-congressman-bares-naked-torso-and-more-for-online-pal/ (Retrieved 13 June 2011).

[76] Broussard, Meagan (2011) My story. In: *BigGovernment.com*, 06 June 2011, http://biggovernment.com/mbroussard/2011/06/06/my-story/ (Retrieved 14 June 2011).

[77] Pitzke, Marc (2011) Skandal-Abgeordneter. Vom Weiner zum Würstchen [Scandal Congressman: From Weiner to sausage]. In: *Spiegel Online*, 07 June 2011, http://www.spiegel.de/politik/ausland/0,1518,767015,00.html (Retrieved 13 September 2013).

[78] Anon. (2011) Rep. Weiner's cybersex chat with Las Vegas mistress — word for word. In: *Radaronline.com*, 07 June 2011, http://www.radaronline.com/exclusives/2011/06/weiner-facebook-messages-lisa-weiss-sex-chat-las-vegas-mistress (Retrieved 25 September 2013).

was due to appear at 16.00h for a press conference that was intended as a coup of liberation. But first his antagonist, the Net journalist Andrew Breitbart, makes a surprise appearance on the podium, grabs the microphone and improvises his own off-hand press conference, hastily and eagerly questioned by the journalists present. Breitbart explains that he just happened to be in the vicinity and wanted to make use of the opportunity to challenge Anthony Weiner to offer him an apology. After all, Weiner had suspected him of a crime ("hacker") in his denial, had called him a liar, despite the fact that everything that he had published was indeed the truth. In addition, he again refers to the ominous photograph in his possession that he had not yet published out of consideration for Weiner's family. However, should Weiner continue to persecute him, then he might just use that photograph as a weapon of defence. After about a quarter of an hour culminating in this public attempt at intimidation and blackmail, Breitbart finally yields the podium to the visibly shocked protagonist Anthony Weiner who now takes to the stage alone, without advocate and adviser, without his wife Huma Abedin (a close confidante and collaborator of Hillary Clinton).[79]

---

[79] Various commentators have made it quite clear after the press conference that the presence of the wife is required, that the wife is a necessary part of an effective ritual of publicly declared remorse.

Figure 19: A miscarried attempt of scandal management — Anthony Weiner's crucial press conference.

Weiner resorts to nearly all of the classic elements of a long rehearsed dramaturgy of public declarations of remorse — just about.[80] He takes full responsibility, he says. He apologises to his wife Huma, his family, his political friends and companions, to the media for his frivolous lies. Fighting the tears, he asks forgiveness for his lies; they were caused by his efforts to keep guilt and shame away from himself and to protect himself and his wife. A long and extensive round of questions follows, in which the journalists keep Anthony Weiner on the trot. Observers keep wondering for some time why he is staying for such a long time.[81] Why was his wife not present? Is she going

---

[80] On the ritual of the declaration of remorse with regard to Anthony Weiner see also: Serrao, Marc Felix (2011) Umgang der US-Medien mit Scandalen. Lachen und Lynchen [US media handling of scandals: Laughing and lynching]. In: *Sueddeutsche.de*, 08 June 2011, http://www.sueddeutsche.de/leben/umgang-der-us-medien-mit-scandalen-lachen-und-lynchen-1.1106654 (Retrieved 24 September 2013).

[81] Powell, Michael (2011) Confession and apology, long and late. In: *New York Times*, 06 June 2011, http://www.nytimes.com/2011/06/07/nyregion/from-anthony-weiner-confession-and-apology-long-and-

to divorce him? How many women did he play with online? Did he practise *sexting*, i.e. sending erotic-salacious images, during his regular office hours? Must his inclinations be classified as pathological addictions? Would he need treatment? Moreover, does he want to apologise to Andrew Breitbart? Under the pressure of the journalists in the midst of a press conference that is increasingly veering off the rails because Anthony Weiner himself keeps contributing to his own demolition with ever new disclosures and revealing answers, he first tries tactical deviation but finally does apologise to his pursuer by uttering the decisive sentence: "I apologise to Andrew Breitbart." (Breitbart will later comment on this enforced self-prostration with the following words: "Satisfaction is coursing through my veins.") However, the most important thing is: Anthony Weiner is not going to resign. He refuses to take the last step in an already carefully worked out script, in the final act of a drama that has been predetermined for a long time. *Thus the ritual of the declaration of remorse, which culminates in the personal collapse, remains unfinished and therefore ultimately without effect.* After all, he never ever met any of the six women in his life, he insists. And, the adultery was only virtual, the sexuality not genuine, not real in the sense of a direct physical encounter. And, furthermore, he did not break any law. He is determined to stay in office and refuses to hand over his mandate as a representative.

The reality of virtuality

Forgetting for a moment the horror of that situation, one may state that such reasoning is most instructive as it illustrates that *in the online universe* old questions must be posed anew and demand new answers, as the sociologist of modern media Sherry Turkle has argued. The computer and the reality it generates—so the core thesis of her books goes—work like

---

late.html?_r=1&scp=11&sq=Anthony%20Weiner&st=cse (Retrieved 25 September 2013).

evocative objects, as a provocative and stimulating mirroring of the personal self and as a cause for profound reflections of the reality of virtuality and the nature of intimacy.[82] The example of the cybersex scandal raises the fundamental question as to "what is at the heart of sex and fidelity. Is it the physical action? Is it the feeling of emotional intimacy with someone other than one's primary partner? Is infidelity in the head or in the body? Is it in the desire or in the action? What constitutes the violation of trust?"[83] The view that Weiner could survive the scandal because there was "no physical contact" and sex had only been virtual represents a minority position not really held with conviction and commitment by anyone.[84]

The argument of the comparatively marginal dramatic virtuality of the offence cannot really carry much weight, at any rate, simply because shortly after the end of the press conference events once again spectacularly come to a head, as further material reaches the public arena, raising the pressure on Weiner even further. It now becomes increasingly evident that this politician obviously had shown no real sensitivity for the very real risks he was taking with his escapades involving people who were in effect strangers to him. *He seemed to have lost his awareness of risks in the virtual hybrid sphere, acting as he was as if his behaviour were taking place in a real-irreal parallel universe not governed by the usual rules and laws.* Only a single day after his appearance in the Sheraton hotel, Andrew Breitbart is a guest on a radio show. The other people present ask him to show them the so far unpublished material. And so it happens that the Net activist, who hates the Left and has a great sense for

---

[82] Turkle, Sherry (1997) *Life on the Screen: Identity in the age of the Internet*, London: Phoenix, p. 22.
[83] Turkle, Sherry (1997) *Life on the Screen: Identity in the age of the Internet*, London: Phoenix, p. 225.
[84] Shear, Michael D. (2011) Five reasons Weiner might survive—and five he might not. In: *The Caucus. The Politics and Government Blog of The Times*, 07 June 2011, http://thecaucus.blogs.nytimes.com/2011/06/07/five-reasons-weiner-might-survive-and-five-he-might-not/?scp=18&sq=Anthony%20Weiner&st=cse (Retrieved 25 September 2013).

campaigning, allows the editors of the show to look at his Blackberry screen. As if by coincidence, some camera happens to be active, unnoticed by Breitbart, as he claims. And it is of course hardly an accident that one of the hosts of the show photographs the camera image so that the photo, which could only have been sent by Weiner himself and that presumably shows the politician's penis, reaches the Net and has been circulating there ever since.[85]

In the following days the demolition of Anthony Weiner continues, not only in the form of satirical television shows full of mockery and humorous-vulgar name games, or in a fake account on *Twitter* that opens with a photograph of his underpants. Fellow party members drop him. An ethics committee initiated by Democrats is expected to deal with the case. It is rumoured that a 17-year-old girl was among his online contacts and that diverse photos were taken in the fitness studio of Congress. But Weiner still refuses to respond to the increasingly vociferous calls for his resignation. He arranges for his spokeswoman Risa Heller to announce that he has decided to undergo therapeutic treatment in order to become a "healthier person" and a "better husband". *(Self-)admission to the clinic, medical-therapeutic treatment, is also a dramaturgically well-established element in a publicly celebrated ritual of purification.* Its goal is to reinforce the impression of the authenticity of the recognition of guilt and the sincerity of the endeavour to do penance and undergo catharsis. The "disease" is accepted, the need for action acknowledged, and the methodical-technical handling is tackled with the help of experts who will possibly one day also be prepared to confirm officially that the patient has finally been successfully and fully cured. In the case in question, however, the evasive manoeuvre (confession to the personal "disease",

---

[85] Staun, Harald (2011) Bloggen von rechts. Allein gegen die Medien [Blogging from the Right: Alone against the media]. In: *Faz.net*, 14 June 2011, http://www.faz.net/artikel/C31013/bloggen-von-rechts-allein-gegen-die-medien-30438043.html (Retrieved 25 September 2013).

withdrawal from public life, announcement of a voluntary leave of absence from professional work) comes too late. Finally, even Barack Obama advises him to resign his mandate, just in time before the former porn star Ginger Lee spills the beans in public as to how Weiner asked her to keep silent about the content of their online correspondence and to tell lies. Shortly afterwards, Anthony Weiner, the first politician to stumble over a misdirected *Twitter* message, faces the press again in an old people's home in Brooklyn — and offers his long awaited resignation, interrupted by jubilant shouts of triumphant and hate-filled hecklers ("Bye bye, pervert!"). Weiner who is fighting for his political comeback thanks his wife, his family, his voters, invokes God and the fatherland, American ideals. "I had hoped to be able to continue the work that the citizens of my district had elected me to do", he says at his last press conference as representative. "Unfortunately, the distraction I have created has made that impossible." No questions are allowed afterwards. Everything is over in the space of four minutes.

6. The social media campaign of Greenpeace and the vulnerability of power

The classic didactics of the scandal

It is evident, at first appraisal, that the action combines all the elements that is typical of a classic Greenpeace campaign; it does not rely on the Internet and it would work equally effectively with posters and hoardings, with newspaper advertisements or television films. Here we see the archetypal David versus Goliath constellation — a small and determined group of environmental activists staging a fight against a powerful global corporation with products that everybody is familiar with. Powerful, medially exploitable, images informing and representing this fight are offered, invoking depictions of the victims and the devastations they are exposed to. Everything is without doubt governed by the imperative of the clear and specifically transparent distribution of roles as well as by dramaturgical simplification. Thus everything conforms to the tried and tested and long practised textbook didactics of the scandal. It skilfully exploits the laws of human perception (orientation by the concrete and graphic, focusing on specially singled-out moments, personalisation of issues) combined with the rules of media-adequate attention control (production of inspiring images and concise messages) for the agenda of environmental protection.[86] Nevertheless, in the days following 17 March 2010, a peculiar dynamics of outrage develops. For the first time, Greenpeace uses social networks as media for campaigning with particular ardour. And the antagonist, the Nestlé corporation, the biggest producer of foodstuffs in the world, reacts in a somewhat confused and counterproductive manner.[87]

Nestlé's reaction, however, only enhances the scandalisation. The corporation tries to take charge of the scandal but in doing so only supplies fresh causes for outrage and matching new rationales. *The pattern at work here, now clearly recognisable in retrospect, is that the very attempt of control ultimately brings about the loss of control, reverses the original intention.*

To begin at the beginning. In the early hours of 17 March 2010 Greenpeace activists distribute leaflets outside numerous

---

[86] On the make-up of classic Greenpeace campaigns, see the instructive analysis by: Koch, Svenja (2009) Umweltkampagnen mit Herz und Verstand. Strategien der Greenpeace-Kommunikation [Environmental campaigns with heart and head: Strategies of Greenpeace communication]. In: Ulrike Röttger (ed.) *PR-Kampagnen. Über die Inszenierung von Öffentlichkeit* [*PR Campaigns: On the staging of publicity*], fourth revised and enlarged edition, Wiesbaden: VS Verlag für Sozialwissenschaften, pp. 109–115.

[87] On the background of the campaign see: Seibt, Sébastian (2010) How Greenpeace reduced Nestlé's Kit Kat to virtual crumbs: Interview with Daniela Montalto. In: *France24.com*, 02 April 2010, http://www.france24.com/en/20100402-environment-greenpeace-nestle-kitkat-online-campaign-palm-oil-deforestation (Retrieved 30 September 2013), and Andresen, Tino/Catrin Bialek (2010) Greenpeace attackiert Nestlé. Wenn die Empörungswelle durch das Netz schwappt [Greenpeace attacks Nestlé: When the wave of outrage sloshes through the Net]. In: *Handelsblatt.com*, 09 April 2010, http://www.handelsblatt.com/unternehmen/industrie/wenn-die-empoerungswelle-durch-das-netz-schwappt/3408080.html (Retrieved 30 September 2013).

Nestlé locations and simultaneously publish information on websites in different languages about the impact of palm oil production on the Indonesian rainforest and the orang-utans living there. Press releases and brochures present detailed factual background information — with no concern for a tendency towards hyperbolic overstatements and the unmistakable focusing on one prominent, powerful antagonist. They document the use of palm oil by Nestlé and reveal the company's business connection with the hardly known firm Sinar Mas that is involved in illegal rain forest clearances. By way of parenthesis almost, diverse products by other companies are named that also contain the palm oil won as a result of the destruction of the ancient forest. Moreover, in this earliest phase of the campaign, the crucial video is published on *YouTube* connecting the consumption of the Nestlé chocolate bar KitKat in a rather gory way with the palm oil processing of the enterprise and the fate of the great apes.[88] The film that lasts exactly one minute shows a pale and exhausted-looking office worker who — obviously after hours of shredding documents — takes a break ("Have a break, have a KitKat") and treats himself to a chocolate bar. He unpacks it, still lost in thought, sticks it between his teeth and bites into it. Only the viewers of the film and the office worker's flabbergasted colleagues can see that this chocolate bar is not a confection but the longish, slightly hairy finger of an ape. Suddenly, after the first crunchy bite, blood flows from his mouth and spurts onto the keyboard of his computer. In a brief sequence of quick and abruptly cut images a variation of the Nestlé advertising slogan follows ("Give the orang-utan a break") and then the concise accusation: "Nestlé, no palm oil through the destruction of primeval forests!"

---

[88] The video can be found, for example, at the following Net address: www.youtube.com/watch?v=IzF3UGOlVDc (Retrieved 30 September 2013).

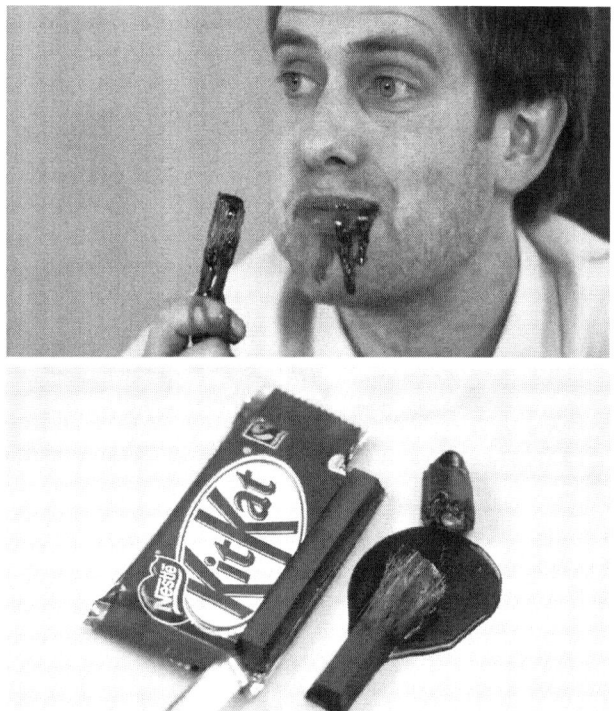

Figure 20 + 21: **Stills from the shock video by Greenpeace: the office worker chews a heavily bleeding ape finger.**

Mobilisation through censorship

It cannot come as much of a surprise that this shock video provokes Nestlé; it aggressively sledgehammers a successful brand and shifts it into a context of disgust. Moreover, the film fashions a causal chain ending with the message that the carefree consumption of the KitKat chocolate bar destroys the natural resources of the orang-utans in the Indonesian jungle, that the munching of chocolate bars ultimately kills apes. By the evening of 17 March, i.e. immediately after the launching of the campaign, the company blocks a variant of the video through the English *YouTube* channel — allegedly because of copyright infringement. The reaction is mockingly seized upon in a blog from Greenpeace as a "textbook example of the Streisand effect in social media coaching".⁸⁹ What does this mean? The so-called Streisand effect refers to the fact that the very attempt at censoring something creates precisely the kind of attention that one originally wanted to evade at all costs. It is the counterproductive attempt to control data and information, an attempt that is immediately recognised as an indicator of relevance. For this very reason, it stimulates resistance and counteractions according to the motto: *these data must be spread; they appear to be relevant and interesting for the very reason that other people want to suppress their distribution.* This is technically not only possible but feasible without great difficulty because data and information have meanwhile detached themselves from their original carrier medium, i.e. paper. The classic instruments of control have thus been rendered largely useless, e.g. counter-statements in the original publication; the blacking out of particular passages; impounding and confiscating; in the extreme case, the destruction of unwanted books and journals.⁹⁰ Therefore, the effortless act of subversive copying and dissemination appears to be necessary and an urgent requirement because the Net community believes in informational freedom as a central value ever since the days of Stewart Brand and John Perry Barlow. Censorship, on the contrary, is regarded as an archaic method of oppression and suppression that must be rejected in principle and fought unconditionally and under all circumstances.⁹¹ *On*

---

[89] Borgerding, Benjamin (2010) Nestlé in Erklärungsnot [Nestlé at a loss to explain]. In: *Greenpeace Blog*, 18 March 2010, http://blog.greenpeace.de/blog/2010/03/18/nestle-in-erklaerungsnot/ (Retrieved 30 September 2013).

[90] Kurz, Constanze (2010) Wenn die Zensur reichlich alt aussieht [When censorship looks really old and tired]. In: *Faz.net*, 20 August 2010, http://www.faz.net/artikel/C30833/aus-dem-maschinenraum-14-wenn-die-zensur-reichlich-alt-aussieht-30301237.html (Retrieved 30 September 2013).

[91] Detailed information on the publicists Stewart Brand and John Perry Barlow, their deep roots in the counterculture of the 60s, and their utopian ideas can be found in: Turner, Fred (2006) *From Counterculture to Cyberculture: Stewart Brand, the whole earth network, and the rise of digital utopianism*, Chicago/London: The University of Chicago Press.

the Net, attempts to control information, which are practised and accepted offline, are seen as norm violations in their own right, as border infringements of the second order, which are themselves subject to scandalisation. Therefore, it is not really surprising that numerous users upload the video again and respond with indignation and public protest to the attempts of eliminating an undesired clip. They intensify the efforts of copying and transferring the very material that is to be subjected to censorship. "Thank you Nestlé", writes an angry commentator on the video portal *Vimeo*, "I would never have seen this video if you hadn't had it kicked off *You Tube*. Now I'm forwarding it all my friends, though [sic] *Facebook*, and guess what they are forwarding it to all their mates. Fire your PR team. They are muppets." Greenpeace, too, reacts immediately with an ironic letter to the "dear PR division" of the corporation. Having obviously run through all the different scenarios of scandal and crisis management often enough, it can react quickly because it is familiar with the spectrum of possible reactions. Censorship—as is suggested in the best kind of blogger style—is nothing but an old fogey method from the past century that has no place in the present age. When Nestlé announces only one day after the launching of the campaign that the contracts with the supplier have been terminated and replaced by contracts with another palm oil producer, this step is immediately criticised as a "sham". The newly contracted company would acquire the necessary quantities of palm oil from intermediary traders that were still connected with Sinar Mas. The termination of the contracts could therefore not be considered extensive enough. Therefore, the scandal management by Nestlé had followed the *principle of quick reaction*, but had violated the *commandment of comprehensive transparency*. The company is forced to continue operating from the defensive. The outraged activists and the critically probing consumers are still not satisfied because they cannot record real credible changes in the corporation's actions. And so they continue to attack its defence strategies by qualifying them as superficial image cosmetics and *Greenwashing*.[92]

The Streisand effect

The Streisand effect denotes a communicative paradox: the texts and pictures that one dearly wishes to suppress — for whatever reason — gain more prominence by this very intervention and thus attain a degree of attention that they would never have achieved without the abortive attempt of control and censorship. The term goes back to the singer and actor Barbara Streisand. She went to court with the intention of removing an aerial photograph of her Californian beach house from the Internet. However, the photographer Kenneth Adelman, who had taken this picture and numerous other beach pictures in order to document the erosion of the beach, refused. Barbara Streisand not only lost the legal struggle but managed to make the image of her house even more widespread and now openly linked to her name. Only comparatively few people had previously shown any interest in the house.

Scandal and reputation management in the digital age

PR advisers help to present their clients' companies on the Net with the construction of an attractive digital identity. Victim initiatives offer similar advice. Websites like *ICorrect.com* advertise their services with online available protest speeches and pertinent statements by celebrities. Commercial firms like *Reputation Defender* or *Integrity Defenders* watch out for undesirable content, undertake to have it deleted or substituted by specially launched more positive content. Independently of the chances of success, these efforts make one thing clear: more or less effective scandal and reputation management has become a professional advice and business field in its own right in the digital age — and the promise of effective control has become especially attractive in these times of loss of control.

---

[92] Euler, Thomas (2010) 2:0—Greenpeace vs. Nestlé. In: *PR-Blogger. Neue Wege in der Communication* [*New ways in communication*], http://pr-blogger.de/2010/03/19/was-konnte-nestle-tun-und-was-tut-es/ (Retrieved 30 September 2013).

Occupation of a virtual platform

In the meantime, the protests on social networks expand. For the first time, Greenpeace offices in about 26 countries are working together in a campaign on a social web. Interested parties are informed by a regular *Twitter* feed; pre-formulated online petitions are offered online. In addition, properly instructed activists as well as an obscure number of spontaneously outraged but uninvited persons have begun to invade the *Facebook* fan sites of Nestlé and KitKat, i.e. to enter and occupy a virtual platform.[93] The comments on *Facebook* share one specific intention: changing fans into opponents. Some refer to the recently censored video, demand a long break for the endangered orangutans, and substitute their own profile images for the killer logo, a variant of the KitKat logo, which Greenpeace has made available for the users of social networks. What is actually being demanded is ultimately the ethical-moral reorientation of the business corporation as well as a specific style of communication which takes the accusations seriously and shows tangible readiness to react properly. "Hallo Nestlé", one female commentator writes, "we find this discussion here exactly right. This is after all a social media appearance. And social media means dialogical communication." However, the community manager of Nestlé still fails to accept this norm purportedly inscribed or attributed to the medium itself. He criticises the commentators, thanks them ironically for their coaching, then insists quite harshly that the rules are set by the company, and finally threatens to delete the profiles with the alienated KitKat logos. This again is a reaction leading to dire consequences and only fuelling the general outrage with new energy and stimuli. The KitKat site on *Facebook* completely disappears for a short time—another counterproductive attempt to control communi-

---

[93] Hillenbrand, Tom (2010) Unternehmen im sozialen Netz. Die Facebook-Falle [Businesses in the social web: The Facebook trap]. In: *Spiegel Online*, 16 April 2010, http://www.spiegel.de/netzwelt/web/0,1518,688975, 00.html (Retrieved 30 September 2013).

cation, resulting in even more undesired attention. Meanwhile the protests continue online and offline. Greenpeace activists protest outside the Indonesian centre of the firm in Jakarta. They inform consumers in more than 20 countries, visit supermarkets in Great Britain, Switzerland, Australia, and Denmark. In Germany alone they apply stickers to the KitKat chocolate bar in 46 locations, which show an orang-utan screaming for help. Greenpeace Germany launches another video presenting the chocolate bar as a giant machine racing through the primeval forests, destroying and killing, and leaving behind ape babies clutching each other, with hacked-off limbs and cut-off heads. The concentration on *one* product only, on only *one* causal chain and *one* animal species that is condemned to death—all this reduces complexity effectively and creates "hot patterns, emotionally and normatively loaded views"[94] consisting of compassion and disgust.

The results of a critical review of events and debates can now be characterised in the following terms. The whole operation clearly demonstrates how alarmed consumers can become activists with the support of social networks, how these networks lend them their own specific public presence and visibility in the processes of protest. One can unmistakably observe here in what ways online and offline activities may be combined and integrated for the purpose of total mobilisation. During the months following the start of the campaign, both old *and* new media, old *and* new forms of protest, are employed. On the one hand, procedures are quite traditional; instructive brochures, leaflets, flyers, also posters and protest postcards are used, dis-

---

[94] This formulation is used by Gerhard Vowe with reference to the Brent Spar campaign of Greenpeace. See: Vowe, Gerhard (2009) Feldzüge um die öffentliche Meinung. Politische Kommunikation in Kampagnen am Beispiel von Brent Spar und Mururoa [Campaigns for public opinion: Political communication in campaigns with regard to the examples of Brent Spar and Mururoa]. In: Ulrike Röttger (ed.) *PR-Kampagnen. Über die Inszenierung von Öffentlichkeit* [*PR Campaigns: On the staging of publicity*], fourth revised and enlarged edition, Wiesbaden: VS Verlag für Sozialwissenschaften, p. 81.

tributed, for example, to people frequenting pedestrian zones. In addition, there are spectacular disruptive actions in shareholder meetings, face-to-face confrontations, and public demonstrations with Greenpeace activists appearing in ape costumes. On the other hand, there is the recognisable effort to use new forms of publicity for personal and institutional purposes. *The central objective is to create self-reinforcing circuits of effects in the most diverse spheres of communication.* Whatever is happening offline will be registered and commented online in unambiguous terms, in order to trigger ever fresh cascades of reaction on the Net together with follow-up reports in the established mass media. Only one detail will be presented here to illustrate this inherent ability of a strategically skilful combination. On the morning of 15 April 2010, Greenpeace activists tie a huge protest transparency to the facade of the Frankfurt company headquarters of Nestlé. Simultaneously they display on an enormous screen erected in front of the company building the clearly visible *Twitter* messages from outraged consumers together with running online and offline comments which urge the company to part with palm oil quantities won by destroying primeval forests. Suddenly, every individual reacting to the invitation for outrage by the environmental activists becomes an activist joining the stream of the manifold expressions of indignation directed against the politics of the global company.

This concerted multimedia presentation exhibits the contours of a *participative scandal didactics,* called into existence by Greenpeace with this campaign. A public that appears to be sympathetic to one's own goals and intentions is animated to participate in a protest and is, at the same time, provided with appropriate helpful tools and ideas. It is no longer necessary to operate effectively using exciting images and actions, which might be perfect for medial exploitation, or by imparting knowledge and enlightenment according to a linear sender-recipient logic. It is more important to induce and discreetly inspire processes of self-organisation on the part of the public and eventually to realise self-organisation with respect to the great goal. What is essential and new is that the inventors of this kind of participative scandal didactics offer a—barrier-free—medial frame for individual protest communication, which makes it possible for a large number of people to join in at lightning speed, to articulate themselves without great effort and to make their own indignation visible in real time.[95]

Figure 22: **Critical consumers become activists: the *Twitter Wall* in front of the Frankfurt company building of Nestlé.**

It is a strategy of comprehensive mobilisation which proves effective. Two months after the start of the campaign, the corporation that had been pushed into the defensive finally capitulates. On 17 May 2010, Nestlé announces that it will from now on only buy natural resources from sustainable production and that it will, in particular, when purchasing palm oil, observe the most rigorous standards. The corporation further announces an alliance with the non-governmental organisation The Forest Trust and presents a detailed plan of action in order to meet a set of self-defined goals. This is recorded by Greenpeace on its own website as a resounding success. In the first few weeks of

---

[95] See also: Heuer, Steffan (2009) Scandal in Echtzeit [Scandal in real time]. In: *Brand Eins*, no. 2, pp. 76–79.

the campaign alone the shock video had been clicked one and a half million times. Innumerable comments were collected on the *Facebook* fan site of KitKat, an endless stream of protest messages and calls for boycott was tweeted and distributed via mail. "Let's celebrate our sweet success", we can read in a euphoric essay on the campaign. "You deserve a huge round of applause for helping us get that well-deserved break for the orang-utan and for Indonesian rainforests! Do some online boasting: Share it on Facebook. Share it on Twitter!"[96]

---

[96] Anon. (2010) Sweet success for Kit Kat campaign: You asked, Nestlé has answered. In: *Greenpeace.org*, 17 May 2010, http://www.greenpeace.org/international/en/news/features/Sweet-success-for-Kit-Kat-campaign/ (Retrieved 29 September 2013).

V

The End of Control in the Digital Age: A Programmatic Résumé

The pattern that connects

In 1979, a year before he died, the cyberneticist Gregory Bateson published his last book, which he had wrested from himself even though suffering from a serious illness. In the final phases of writing, he states on the first page with a certain irony, he had to cope with "severe medical adventures".[1] Among these are extensive stays in hospital, a complicated operation, and the visit of an Indonesian ghost healer who contradicts the pessimistic prognosis of the doctors who had diagnosed an essentially inoperable lung tumour. When the disease kicks in and he suspects that he must do everything to complete his work, Bateson has long been an academic superstar and an icon of counterculture. He is revered and courted, this strange man who investigates humour, observes the play of otters and the language of dolphins, researches the origins of schizophrenia and the contours of a new ecological consciousness. He calls his last book *Mind and Nature* and starts off with an introductory chapter that is as puzzling as it is fascinating. He writes this crucial text as part of a quest for a synthesis. However, he faces

---

[1] Bateson, Gregory (1979) *Mind and Nature: A necessary unity*, New York: Dutton, p. xii.

noticeable difficulties in trying to bring his equally rigorous and wild thoughts into line. On the one hand, he wants to present the central formula that explains everything; on the other hand, he wants to maintain an essentially open mind at all costs, a sort of fundamental immunity to dogmas of any kind. Moreover, he does not want to provide easy access to his work by means of didactic tricks and ruses even for his enthusiastic followers. Gregory Bateson obviously argues in a *systematically unsystematic way*. Sometimes, however, one cannot really be sure what is intentional and method in the moment of writing and what is purely uncoordinated association taking even him by surprise. In this introduction, he becomes worked up about the principles of occidental education and stresses that stories and metaphors are scientifically respectable forms of expression. He redefines the key concepts of evolutionary theory, and then somewhat randomly moves on to talk about Hinduism and problems of logic. Finally, he proposes another title for his book and another formula for balancing ideas and things. How about, he abruptly declares, calling his work *"the pattern which connects"*? And "what pattern", he asks, "connects the crab to the lobster and the orchid to the primrose and all the four of them to me? And me to you? And all the six of us to the amoeba in one direction and to the back-ward schizophrenic in another?" He continues: "I want to tell you why I have been a biologist all my life, what it is that I have been trying to study. What thoughts can I share regarding the total biological world in which we live and have our beings? How is it put together?"[2] In his last dramatic effort of reflection, Bateson wants to describe a matrix of everything alive. Having been trained in the philosophy of distinctions of the cyberneticists and information theorists, he finally sketches his understanding of the mind and of life: the operation of distinction and the perception of differences appear to him to be the common fundamental patterns

---

[2] Bateson, Gregory (1979) *Mind and Nature: A necessary unity*, New York: Dutton, p. 8 [author's emphasis].

which are characteristic of everything that lives and which constitute the essence of the mind.

Causes of the loss of control

In the search for a summarising formula at the end of a book, the approach and the method of the genius of irritation and integration, Gregory Bateson may be of decisive help. We can consequently ask ourselves now: what is the pattern that connects the stories that have been presented here in detail? What connects the defamation of a Chinese student with the story of the golfer Tiger Woods? What experience is shared by the Australian Julian Assange and the American ex-soldier Charles Graner, principal perpetrator in the torture scandal of Abu Ghraib? What has the unmasking of a Secretary of Defence by German Net activists to do with the scandals triggered by the office employee and blogger Jessica Cutler several years ago in Washington? What common pattern connects the resignation of a Federal President with the fate of the alleged *WikiLeaks* informant Bradley Manning or the events surrounding Roger Chan Yuet-tung throwing a tantrum in a night bus in Hong Kong and filmed with a camera phone? What have the experiences of the Nestlé Corporation in the confrontation with a Greenpeace campaign in common with the hapless behaviour of the politician Anthony Weiner? And how is all this connected with the destiny of two FLA employees, whose e-mail exchanges landed on the Net? *The answer is that it is the experience of an elementary loss of control that can be seen as a connecting metapattern.* The cases presented show that messages landing in the wrong channels may terminate careers and seal destinies, whether they are e-mails, photographs, interview sequences, passwords and camera phone videos, or SMS messages and *Twitter* messages. They become globally circulating proofs of offences that can no longer be removed from this world. It is now becoming easier by the day to search, connect, reconstruct, and permanently store constantly growing quantities of data — and one day transform them into public documents of disgrace. And this concerns not only the high and the mighty and celebrities but also the powerless and the totally unknown.[3] Whatever is available in digital form may one day possibly begin to circulate in an uncontrolled way, may be received by an uncontrollable number of people, may be commented on and combined, may undergo changes of its meaning, may be placed in totally new contexts, re-actualised and redistributed any time. And whoever still thinks it worthwhile to try to handle the loss of control by means of personal attempts at control or with the help of more or less qualified experts may possibly achieve the diametric opposite of what he intended to achieve—and make a personal position that may already have become somewhat unpleasant even worse. In brief: the end of control—this kind of meta-pattern, already deciphered in its infancy by the co-founder of *Wired*, Kevin Kelly, is so fundamental that even the attempts at scandal and reputation management appear to be comparatively beggarly, at worst totally counterproductive, attempts at a defence.[4]

The categorical imperative of the digital age
Always act in such a way as to make the public effects of your actions appear defensible at all times. However, do not expect that it will be of any use.

Forms of context damage

The question is now: what causes the loss of control? The first and very concrete answer is: it is simply negligence plus a lack

---

[3] See: Kurz, Constanze/Frank Rieger (2011) *Die Datenfresser. Wie Internetfirmen und Staat sich unsere persönlichen Daten einverleiben und wie wir die Kontrolle darüber zurückerlangen* [*The Data Gobblers: How Internet firms and states swallow our data and how we can get the control of our data back again*], Frankfurt on the Main: S. Fischer Verlag.

[4] See: Kelly, Kevin (1994) *Out of Control: The new biology of machines, social systems, and the economic world*, New York: Basic Books. Here the work of the blogger and media-theorist Michael Seemann must also be quoted again, presented in his blog on the topic. See: www.ctrl-verlust.net/ (Retrieved 25 September 2013).

of imagination, and – as many stories show – the oblivious unawareness of media properties and situational conditions, a kind of *blindness to possibilities*. People simply cannot imagine what can happen to and with their data, in what strange or even critical combinations they may surface in the medium of publicity, one day perhaps even ruining personal images. Sometimes the required minimum of media competence is lacking – and the situation slips out of hand. Uploading a video following a momentary whim may suddenly and unexpectedly trigger a hype that can in no way be stopped or eliminated. Sometimes the problem concerns data theft and intentional betrayal of secrets; in such cases the loss of control is the direct goal, not just an undesired effect. Sometimes an individual's craving for fame is all too conspicuous. Then there is also the burning desire for revenge and the lust for disgracing and punishing a figure in the public eye. And so on and so forth.

However, looking at the concrete cases, the multifaceted motives and the direct occasions and causes may obscure the apprehension of general underlying schemes, may not be helpful in revealing the fundamental preconditions and the variants of the loss of control with sufficient clarity. Among these preconditions is first of all and primarily the digitalisation of documents and materials, the possibility to store and copy, quickly search, connect, transfer, and publish enormous masses of data. But it does not stop there. *There is another basic mechanism, another meta-pattern of the loss of control, which will be called context damage.* The pattern of context damage connects all these cases and case histories in a hidden way, as Gregory Bateson's diagnoses of similarities have taught us to recognise.[5] What does this concept mean? Context means here quite simply the sum of the expected and the expectable conditions of communication.

---

[5] On the concept of context as the basis of the analysis of stage management in the digital age, see also: Wesch, Michael (2009) YouTube and you: Experiences of self-awareness in the context collapse of the recording webcam. In: *Explorations in Media Ecology*, vol. 8, no. 2, pp. 19–34.

Context damage means that the original contexts of the utterances and actions in all the stories and case analyses presented earlier have been blown apart, shifted, and altered. This kind of damage to the originally intended contexts that were mistakenly regarded as given and stable, and the break with the hitherto existing framework of conditions of communication and action, generate the new meaning; only these shifts and changes create the basis for effective defamation and the conditions of the possibility of unleashing scandals. What are these different variants and forms of context damage? Here they are, in a nutshell.

- The context damage provoking the loss of control is always and necessarily of a *spatial nature*. Anything said or done in one place suddenly becomes known at many other places around the world — and is, in the extreme case, registered globally and received simultaneously. The original protected and shielded informational space is blown open. *Data and documents are despatialised.*

- Context damage is, furthermore, always and without exception of a *temporal nature*. Something in the past is suddenly hauled into the present again and remains there potentially forever with no chance of being mercifully forgotten — not even with the passage of time. *Data and documents become detemporalised.*

- Such context damage is, finally, under all circumstances of a *public- and publicity-specific nature*. It is the small and select public or group dealing with personal utterances and actions which is suddenly replaced by a potentially global public. At once secrets are aired in public. Intimate and private things that have up to that point in time been confined to a small private circle are suddenly out in the open — and are commented on publicly, in the extreme case by a grinning mob. *Under certain circumstances, data and documents become globally known.*

- This kind of context damage as a basic mechanism in the loss of control in the digital age is not necessarily but often of a cultural nature. What may appear legitimate or very normal within the context of a particular culture and in the sphere of meaning of a small group or a whole continent will appear indecent, disgusting, or scandalous after the transfer into other enclaves of meaning and spheres of interpretation. The transfer into another, a new cultural context is cause for agitation and outrage. *Data and documents are interpreted anew – and may consequently give rise to scandals.*

- In the view of all those who talk and telephone, leave ad-hoc messages behind, send e-mails and SMS messages, make snapshots, shoot short films, context damage is of a *modal nature*. Human agents frequently believe in the transience of what they utter in a concrete situation and formulate and act accordingly. Quite obviously, they do not reckon with the permanent storage of what they have presented strictly for the moment. Ad-hoc comments are not stylistically perfected, their choice of words is unreflected, their mode of expression is insecure. Everything is dialogical, processual, and agitated, generally colloquial. It is *conceptual orality*, which is, however, cemented by writing and bound to cause a stir when unexpectedly published in this medium.[6] The (wrongly assumed) context of ephemeral, spontaneous, usually private communication in the personal lifeworld is thus damaged. In the view of those concerned, this may be calamitous. *Data and documents are preserved for duration; what is supposedly transitory remains permanent – and becomes an easily renewable cause for scandalisation for a big public receiving it at a distance.*

---

[6] On the distinction between conceptional and medial orality and literacy which inform these considerations, see: Koch, Peter/Wulf Oesterreicher (1995) Sprache der Nähe – Sprache der Distanz. Mündlichkeit und Schriftlichkeit im Spannungsfeld von Sprachtheorie und Sprachgeschichte [Language of proximity – language of distance: Orality and literacy in the field of tension between linguistic theory and linguistic history]. In: *Romanistisches Jahrbuch*, vol. 36, pp. 15–43.

Table 1: **Causes of the loss of control**

Preconditions of the loss of control	Digitalisation of documents/materials, data storage, data copies/data transfer, data combination, easy ways of publishing
Mechanisms of the loss of control	The original context of utterance is blasted apart, shifted, changed — the consequence of such context damage: utterances and actions become scandalisable
Concrete causes of the loss of control	Lack of media competence, craving for status, negligence, betrayal of secrets, data theft, public shaming etc.

Table 2: **Loss of control due to context damage**

Space	Protected informational spaces are blasted apart, data globally available
Time	Temporal boundaries erode, past becomes enduring present
Public	Public of personal presence becomes potential world public
Publicity	Intimate and private matters become public, secrets are revealed
Culture	Cultural contexts may be shifted rapidly. What is considered normal in one culture may — after transfer into another sphere of interpretation — appear indecent, disgusting, scandalous
Mode	Supposedly transitory orality is made permanent; ad-hoc utterances and situation-bound slips remain present

The possibility of being different

What follows from all this? Should the loss of control, in a frenzy of rhetoric, now be declared a signature of the digital age? Is it really apposite to further extend the multitude of proclamations of historic caesuras and the dawning of new ages? Are we living in an era of context damage? How can these patterns of experience of a higher order be properly assessed? Are we as careful observers witnessing the realisation of a utopia? Why such a negative attitude? Ought we not just free ourselves from the fear of the loss of control in order "to build a possibly more honest and more open society out of the new conditions"?[7] Is it necessary to see the loss of control as the harbinger of a world in which there will be no room for dictators? Are we on the road to a society of total transparency in which privacy will appear a relic of the past? Might a new kind of tolerance emerge because soon everyone will know everything about everyone else so that the radical variety of personal life designs will not only become fully apparent but consequently also fully acceptable? Will the diagnosis of deviations from norms and notions of normality (the basis of all discrimination) lose its power immediately because the "wide-ranging extent of not-being-normal is recognisable for everyone"?[8] Should one perhaps see the loss of control, to follow Kevin Kelly's magnificently suggestive prose, from the perspective of a techno-mystic and simply celebrate it? Does the eigendynamics of technology incorporate a higher will; does the complexity of a Smartphone reflect the essence of the divine, as the Net philosopher seriously would like us to believe?[9] Or is it the other way round; is the eigenpower of technology a cause for complaint, an indication of deterioration and destruction? Are the correct interpretations the prerogative of the culture pessimists? Whose history counts? The history of the victim ruined by a cybermob or the history of the Arab Spring that owes decisive inspiration to *Twitter* and *Facebook* and the possibilities of effective swarm formation?[10]

---

[7] Seemann, Michael (2010) Die Krankenakte von Tut Ench Amun [The medical record of Tutankhamun]. In: *CTRL-Verlust*, 11 January 2010, http://www.ctrl-verlust.net/die-krankenakte-von-tut-ench-amun/ (Retrieved 30 September 2013).

[8] On this variety of the digital utopia see the criticism in: Kurz, Constanze/Frank Rieger (2011) *Die Datenfresser. Wie Internetfirmen und Staat sich unsere persönlichen Daten einverleiben und wie wir die Kontrolle darüber zurückerlangen* [*The Data Gobblers: How Internet firms and states swallow our data and how we can get the control of our data back again*], Frankfurt on the Main: S. Fischer Verlag, p. 251.

[9] Kelly, Kevin (2010) *What Technology Wants*, New York: Viking, pp. 358f.

[10] On this topic cf. the following—controversial—comments and analyses: Morozov, Evgeny (2011) Facebook and Twitter are just places revolutionaries go: Cyber-utopians who believe the Arab spring has been

Any claim, however, to have found the definitive or the only possible answer endangers openness of thinking, promotes personal positions as dogmas, and furthers the creation of agitating hostile camps as they now characterise so many Net debates. For this reason alone it may be worthwhile to recall Gregory Bateson's attitude when writing the introductory chapter to his last book in the existential situation of imminent death, summing up the ways of his thinking with admirable serenity. Bateson is obviously striving for the all-embracing perspective, the grand picture. And he is at the end of his life undoubtedly on the quest for the ur-formula for life. Still, he is aware of the perils of reductionism and dashing trivialisation inherent to such an enterprise and tries to evade them by rejecting any kind of final pronouncement. Relying on stories and parables, twisting and turning his own certainties until they develop fuzzy edges, he suddenly makes us see more and better than before. He wants to maintain, for himself and for his readers, the capability of being surprised under any circumstances, a sensitivity for the possibilities of being different as it results from his attitude towards his own elementary insights. To put it differently: Gregory Bateson demonstrates that genuine thinking means playing.

---

driven by social networks ignore the real-world activism underpinning them. In: *Guardian.co.uk*, 07 March 2011, http://www.guardian.co.uk/commentisfree/2011/mar/07/facebook-twitter-revolutionaries-cyber-utopians?commentpage=all#start-of-comments (Retrieved 17 September 2013); Howard, Philip N./Aiden Duffy/Deen Freelon/Muzammil Hussain/Will Mari/Marwa Mazaid (2011) Opening closed regimes: What was the role of social media during the Arab spring? Project on information technology & political Islam, *working paper 2011.1, University of Washington*, http://pitpi.org/index.php/2011/09/11/ opening-closed-regimes-what-was-the-role-of-social-media-during-the-arab-spring/ (Retrieved 10 September 2013).

List of Figures

Figure		Source
1	German President Horst Koehler announces his resignation	© picture alliance/dpa, Photo: Wolfgang Kumm
2	Cover *Drudge Manifesto*	Drudge, Matt (1998) *Drudge Manifesto*, New York: New American Library
3	Barack Obama with a turban	http://web.archive.org/web/20080226185608/http://www.drudgereport.com/flashoa.htm (Retrieved 07 October 2013)
4	Stills from *Wikileaks* video *Collateral Murder*	http://www.youtube.com/watch?v=5rXPrfnU3G0 (Retrieved 07 October 2013)
5	The *Wikileaks* informant Bradley Manning	United States Army, https://docs.google.com/file/d/0B_zC44SBaZPoM1BOSnVNNXRyM1E/edit?pli=1 (Retrieved 07 October 2013)
6	Illustration of the circular logic of scandalisation influenced by second-order transgressions	Thompson, John B. (2000) *Political Scandal: Power and Visibility in the Media Age*, Cambridge: Polity Press, p. 24.
7	Gao Qianhui during her hate speech	http://www.youtube.com/watch?v=PmISXtnRKrM (Retrieved 05 November 2013
8	Re-edited photograph of Wang Qianyuan	http://www.99sui.com.cn/article/sort013/info-6440.html (Retrieved 20 December 2011)
9	Slogans on the wall of the home of Wang's parents	© AFP/Getty Images, Photo: Mark Ralston
10	Tricia Walsh-Smith's first video	http://www.youtube.com/watch?v=hx_WKxqQF2o (Retrieved 07 October 2011)
11 + 12 +13 + 14	Emblematic images of the torture scandal of Abu Ghraib: the "man on the leash", "man with the hood", "ice man", and "the human pyramid"	US Military
15	Drawing of Jeremy Bentham's Panopticon	Bentham, Jeremy (1791) *Panopticon: Or, the Inspection-House*, Dublin: Thomas Byrne

Figure		Source
16	Fusion of two iconic images: iRaq dancer	Forkscrew Graphics / http://web.Archive.org/web/20040628085638/http://www.forkscrew.com/iraq yellow.html (Retrieved 07 October 2013)
17	Roger Chan Yuet-tung's angry outburst	http://www.youtube.com/watch?v=RSHziqJWYcM (Retrieved 05 November 2013)
18	Tiger Woods' personally arranged press conference	© picture-alliance/epa, Photo: Lori Moffett
19	Anthony Weiner's press conference	Picture-alliance/epa, Photo: Andrew Gombert
20 + 21	Shock video by Greenpeace	http://www.youtube.com/watch?v=IzF3UGO1VDc (Retrieved 07 October 2013)
22	Twitterwall	© Andreas Varnhorn/Greenpeace

The Authors

Bernhard Poerksen, *1969, is professor of media studies at the University of Tübingen, Germany. His research projects analyse the styles of impression and image management in politics and the media, he regularly contributes comments on current affairs and debates to newspapers, radio, and television. The book he wrote in 1998 with the physicist Heinz von Foerster about the truth in perception (*Truth is the Invention of a Liar*) became a bestseller and is now considered a classic of systemic thought. In 2008 Bernhard Poerksen was honoured for the quality of his teaching and chosen "Professor of the Year".

Hanne Detel, *1983, is research associate at the Department of Media Studies, University of Tübingen, Germany. Her primary research concerns are media theories, mediatisation, the Social Web, scandalisation, and (unwanted) celebrity in the digital age. She studied journalism and communication as well as public law in Hamburg and Stellenbosch/South Africa — on a scholarship awarded by the German National Academic Foundation. In parallel, she completed her practical journalism training and worked with the German Press Agency (dpa).

Index

A

Abu Ghraib 30, 139, 141–5, 147–52, 154–61, 212
Afghan War Diary 76
Anonymity 48, 50, 100, 106, 113, 179
Apology dramatics 187
Assange, Julian 60, 66, 68, 72–4, 76–81, 212
Attention 2–4, 10, 12, 13, 15, 25, 26, 33, 42, 45, 47, 53, 54, 56–8, 73, 81, 94, 97, 99, 101, 110, 120–2, 124–7, 131, 134, 166, 169, 173, 178, 179, 183, 191, 199, 202, 204, 206

B

Back region/backstage 24, 50–2, 103, 165
Barlow, John Perry 202
Bateson, Gregory 119, 120, 210–2, 214, 219
Baudrillard, Jean 139–41, 160
Bentham, Jeremy 146, 147
Berg, Nick 157
Big Brother 4, 47
Blair, Tony 160
Blumenthal, Sidney 43
Bon, Gustave Le 100, 101
Brand, Stewart 119, 202
Breitbart, Andrew 191–3, 195–7
Brolsma, Gary 2

Bush, George W. 49, 153, 156, 161

C

Cablegate 76
Celebrity 54, 58, 100, 122, 124, 127, 171–4, 185, 188
China 101, 102, 106, 108, 110, 111, 112, 116, 118, 119, 162
Clash of cultures 107–9, 116
Clinton, Bill 35, 36, 38, 39, 43, 54
Clinton, Hillary 44, 66, 193
Collapse of context 17, 214
Collateral Murder 60, 62, 65, 75, 80
Context damage 213–7
Cooper, Geoff 164
Crowdsourcing 86, 89, 107
Cybermob 101, 104, 105, 107, 113, 218

D

Darby, Joseph 154, 155
Disinhibition/loss of inhibition 112, 113, 179
Domscheit-Berg, Daniel 78, 80
Drudge, Matt 33–7, 42–7, 191
Drudge Report 33, 36, 43–6
Durkheim, Emile 12, 119

E

Ellsberg, Daniel 68
Emcke, Carolin 150

England, Lynndie 144, 149, 151, 155
Epidemic 8, 105, 131, 176
Evidence 14, 22–7, 37, 38, 43, 44, 52, 71, 82, 83, 85–7, 89, 91, 92, 96, 98, 101, 105, 112, 114, 134, 137, 138, 143, 147, 151, 155, 156, 159, 164, 165, 179–81, 191
Eyewitness testimony 139, 141

F
Facebook 65, 94, 161, 190, 192, 203, 205, 209, 218, 219
Foucault, Michel 146
Frederick, Ivan 150
Front region 50–2, 103, 165

G
Galliano, John 165
Gatekeeper/gatekeeping 13, 30, 32, 33, 37, 46, 82, 84–6, 91, 138, 168
Gladwell, Malcolm 131, 132
Glaser, Peter 16, 17, 138
Goffman, Erving 50–2
Google 10, 48, 70, 71, 86, 174
Graner, Charles 144, 151–3, 155, 156, 212
Grubbs, Jaimee 182–5
Guttenberg, Karl-Theodor zu 82, 83, 87, 89, 91–6
GuttenPlag 86, 90, 92

H
Harding, Matt 3
Harman, Sabrina 144, 145, 150, 151

Hondrich, Karl Otto 11, 99

I
Indiscrete technology 161, 164
Iraq War Logs 66, 76
Isikoff, Michael 33, 35, 36, 38–41

J
Jarvis, Jeff 79
Juma, Mohanded Juma 152

K
Kelly, Kevin 120, 213, 218
Kennedy, John F. 182
Kerry, John 44
Köhler, Horst 18–20, 22, 23

L
Lamo, Adrian 63–5
Lee, Ginger 198
Lewinsky, Monica 35–41, 54
Loss of control/control loss/end of control 15, 30, 64, 68, 72, 73, 78, 138, 189, 199, 204, 210, 212–5, 217, 218
Luhmann, Niklas 32

M
Manning, Bradley 59, 60, 63–71, 212
Mass media 11–4, 18, 20, 24, 25, 30, 32, 34, 45, 54, 80, 99, 100, 121, 133, 176, 177, 182, 184, 185, 207
Matthew effect 174
McCain, John 44
Meme/memetics 166, 167
Merkel, Angela 95

Minton Report 74
Mitchell, W.J.T. 157

N
Noor-Elden, Namir 61

O
Obama, Barack 44, 45, 68, 198
OpenLeaks 78

P
Palin, Sarah 73, 74
Panopticon 146–8
Pentagon Papers 68
Prominent connectors 132
Proof 10, 24, 63, 134, 138, 174, 181, 182, 212
Pseudonymity 113

R
Ranking principle 166
Remix/remixing 16, 127, 170, 171
Rice, Condoleezza 156, 161
Rumsfeld, Donald 153–6, 160

S
Scandal management 15, 23, 92–4, 97, 194, 203
Scandal surfing 56, 57
Scandal of the second order 117
Search for human flesh 104, 107, 108, 114
Second-order transgression 93, 96, 97, 191
Secret 56, 64, 66–9, 73, 74, 76, 77, 79, 82, 90, 95, 142, 168, 173, 174, 214, 215, 217

Sensibility for scandal 116
Shitstorm 105
Sifry, Micah L. 60, 79
Simulation 139–42, 160
Sloterdijk, Peter 10, 13
Social web 13, 14, 205
Sontag, Susan 140, 141, 149
Stage management 28, 31, 139, 141, 144, 160, 181, 187, 188
Streisand, Barbra 204
Streisand effect 201, 202, 204
Surowiecki, James 87, 100, 101

T
Thompson, John B. 76, 96, 97, 116, 191
Tipping point 131, 132
Turkle, Sherry 195, 196
Twitter 14, 18, 20, 22, 23, 30, 86, 161, 189, 190, 191, 197, 198, 205, 207–9, 212, 218

V
Voyeurism 7–9

W
WikiLeaks 59, 60, 62, 63, 65–9, 71–82, 212
Wikipedia 3, 132, 174
Wittgenstein, Ludwig 29

Y
YouTube 14, 17, 72, 103, 105, 106, 121, 123–7, 137, 161, 165–8, 170–2, 200, 201, 214